IMPORTANT! DO NOT DISCARD!

M060278337

Included with Purchase of
The Essential Listening to Music **by Craig Wright**

Sony Music
Commercial Music Group

CENGAGE Learning®

Music Download Card

℗ 2012 Sony Music Entertainment

■ **Includes all of the music covered within the text.**

■ **Download music directly to your music library.**

Tear at Perf and Open to Learn More

←

Music

The Essential
Listening to Music

Craig Wright
Yale University

SCHIRMER
CENGAGE Learning·

Australia • Brazil • Japan • Korea • Mexico • Singapore • Spain • United Kingdom • United States

The Essential Listening to Music,
Sixth Edition

Craig Wright

Senior Publisher: Lyn Uhl

Publisher: Clark Baxter

Senior Development Editor: Sue Gleason
Wade

Assistant Editor: Elizabeth Newell

Editorial Assistant: Marsha Kaplan

Managing Media Editor: Kathryn Schooling

Senior Marketing Manager: Jeanne Heston

Marketing Coordinator: Klaira Markenzon

Senior Marketing Communications
Manager: Heather Baxley

Senior Content Project Manager:
Michael Lepera

Art Director: Faith Brosnan

Senior Print Buyer: Mary Beth Hennebury

Rights Acquisition Specialist: Mandy Groszko

Production Service/Compositor:
MPS Ltd., a Macmillan Company

Text and Cover Designer: Jeanne Calabrese

Cover Image: Kaitlyn McLachlan/
Shutterstock.com

For product information and technology assistance, contact us at
Cengage Learning Customer & Sales Support, 1-800-354-9706

For permission to use material from this text or product,
submit all requests online at **www.cengage.com/permissions.**
Further permissions questions can be emailed to
permissionrequest@cengage.com.

Library of Congress Control Number: 2011943691

ISBN-13: 978-1-111-34202-9

ISBN-10: 1-111-34202-4

Schirmer
20 Channel Center Street
Boston, MA 02210
USA

Cengage Learning is a leading provider of customized learning solutions
with office locations around the globe, including Singapore, the United
Kingdom, Australia, Mexico, Brazil, and Japan. Locate your local office at:
international.cengage.com/region

Cengage Learning products are represented in Canada by
Nelson Education, Ltd.

For your course and learning solutions, visit **www.cengage.com**

Purchase any of our products at your local college store or at our
preferred online store **www.cengagebrain.com.**

Instructors: Please visit **login.cengage.com** and log in to access
instructor-specific resources.

Printed in Canada
2 3 4 5 15 14 13

For Clark Baxter—innovator, publisher, and valued friend

Brief Contents

Contents

A custom edition of *The Essential Listening to Music* can be created to include any of the following enrichment chapters from *Listening to Music, 6th Edition*, bound into the back of the book:

Contact your local Cengage Learning representative for ordering information.

About the Author

Craig M. Wright received his Bachelor of Music degree at the Eastman School of Music in 1966 and his Ph.D. in musicology from Harvard University in 1972. He began his teaching career at the University of Kentucky and for the past forty years has been teaching at Yale University, where he is currently the Henry L. and Lucy G. Moses Professor of Music. At Yale, Wright's courses include his perennially popular introductory course "Listening to Music," also part of the offerings of Open Yale Courses, and his selective seminar "Exploring the Nature of Genius." He is the author of numerous scholarly books and articles on composers ranging from Leoninus to Bach. Wright has also been the recipient of many awards, including a Guggenheim Fellowship, the Einstein and Kinkeldey Awards of the American Musicological Society, and the Dent Medal of the International Musicological Society. In 2004, he was awarded the honorary degree Doctor of Humane Letters from the University of Chicago. And in 2010 he was elected as a member of the American Academy of Arts and Sciences, joining fellow inductee banjo player Steve Martin. In addition to *The Essential Listening to Music,* Wright has also published *Listening to Music* and *Listening to Western Music, Sixth Editions* (Schirmer Cengage Learning, 2011), and *Music in Western Civilization, Media Update* (Schirmer Cengage Learning, 2010), with coauthor Bryan Simms. He is presently at work on a volume entitled *Mozart's Brain: Exploring the Nature of Genius.*

Preface

 The Need

People lucky enough to teach music appreciation have a number of textbooks from which to choose. So why do we need another?

The Essential Listening to Music is for the instructor who wants to spend a bit more time teaching somewhat fewer major pieces. A book that discusses, say, seventy to one hundred pieces may seem at least twice as valuable as a book that covers thirty-five. But some instructors do not have the time, and some students have not acquired the ability, to devote careful attention to more than five masterworks per week over a fourteen-week semester.

Some instructors therefore prefer to take the time to help students learn to *listen to*, not just *hear*, their course music. Others assign outside readings and handouts to embed course music more firmly in its cultural context. Others want to add to the repertoire in the textbook other "teachable" pieces or pieces that the school symphony or choir may perform over the course of the semester. Others teach online—or teach at schools that reward online teaching. Many instructors want to do all these things. I do, too. And it is for these fellow instructors that I wrote *Essential Listening to Music*.

Likewise, many students wear earbuds 24/7, but need help learning to listen critically. Many prefer to listen to music more than to read long passages about music. Many will readily buy a textbook if all or most of it is assigned in class and helps them prepare for exams. And all of my appreciation students want a book packaged with music downloads and study help at an affordable price. It is for students like these that I wrote *The Essential Listening to Music*

A Core Repertoire

What pieces of music are essential for students studying Western music? While we may all debate what should comprise the "canon" of Western music, *The Essential Listening to Music* presents a cohort of pieces that many instructors would eagerly adopt. In fact, it is built on the opinions of many appreciation instructors and on what is now my own nearly forty-five years of teaching music appreciation at the college level. Thus, the compositions presented and discussed here are not only the staples of the concert hall today, but also pieces that work in the classroom. Through them the instructor can present virtually all of the elements, forms, processes, and historical changes that have appeared in Western art music during the last millennium.

For instructors who also wish to cover popular or world music, relevant text material from *Listening to Music, 6th Edition*—and the audio that accompanies it—is available online or through the Cengage custom publishing group at a small additional cost.

Writing Style

A briefer book would seem to require a more basic mode of presentation. With *The Essential Listening to Music,* I have simplified my prose and chosen a vocabulary that speaks directly to the college student of today. The book is still challenging, but it is accessible.

Technology

One fact often unrecognized is that the force driving the continual appearance of new editions of textbooks is technology. When *Listening to Music* was first under development some twenty-five years ago, the publisher considered issuing the recordings on vinyl, but instead dared move to a revolutionary new advancement: magnetic tape. Thereafter came CDs, then streaming music, and, now, downloads.

In addition, a website—now entitled CourseMate—has become a necessary companion to the book. More and more, the student turns to the website to engage content, to learn to listen and study, and to generate a work product for the course. Ever-new technology makes possible new learning tools on the web: embedded links, video, podcasts, interactive listening guides, educational games, quizzes, and the like. Many of these are directly linked in the eBook and cued in the textbook, which continues to provide the essential content "narrative" of each and every course.

 # Text Pedagogical Aids

Listening Exercises

The Essential Listening to Music, like *Listening to Music,* is the only music appreciation text on the market to include detailed Listening Exercises, some within the book and many others online, where they may be graded electronically. By means of these, students will embrace hundreds of specific passages of music and make critical decisions about them. The exercises begin by developing basic listening skills—recognizing rhythmic patterns, distinguishing major keys from minor, and differentiating various kinds of textures. The exercises then move on to entire pieces in which students are required to become participants in an artistic exchange, the composer communicating with the listener, and the listener reacting over a long span of time. Ultimately, equipped with these newly developed listening skills, students will move comfortably to the concert hall, listening to classical and popular music with greater confidence and enjoyment. To be sure, this book is for the present course, but its aim is to prepare students for a lifetime of musical listening and enjoyment. Text cues, which are "live" in the eBook, highlight the availability of online Listening Exercises.

Listening Guides

In order to keep this edition as brief as possible, the larger text's Listening Guides have been replaced with Listening Cues, containing such key information as genre and form, a concise suggestion of "What to Listen For," a cue to interactive Active Listening Guides on CourseMate, and disc symbols indicating the piece's tracks on the CD set. Brown discs containing the word "Intro" represent the Introduction to Listening CD bound into the textbook, and gold discs containing "1" or "2" represent CDs in the 2-CD set accompanying the text. Track numbers appear beneath the discs.

Print Listening Guides are available within the Active Listening Guides application and may be customized with the book. In the interactive eBook, each Listening Cue's brown or gold disc links to a live stream of the piece, and each loudspeaker icon at the base of the Listening Cue links to its Active Listening Guide.

In addition, Supplementary Listening Guides for many additional works not covered in the text are included in CourseMate and on the instructor's PowerLecture CD-ROM.

Ancillaries for Students

Introduction to Listening CD

Packaged with each new copy of the book, and not sold separately, this CD contains all of the music discussed in Chapters 1–3 on the elements of music, as well as a guide to instruments of the orchestra, which presents the instruments and then tests students' ability to recognize the instruments by themselves and in various combinations.

2-CD Set

This includes the core repertoire of thirty-five musical selections discussed in the book. On CourseMate, each selection may also be streamed by itself or in the context of an Active Listening Guide that demonstrates visually what students hear.

Streaming and Downloads

The content of all three CDs is also available streaming and as free album downloads.

Active Listening Guides

The Active Listening Guides at CourseMate feature full-color interactive and streaming listening guides for every selection on the CD sets, along with listening quizzes, background information, and printable pdf Listening Guides.

CourseMate

The text website, CourseMate, offers several challenging and interesting features. First, it allows for chapter-by-chapter self-study in which students may take a quiz to explore their knowledge of the topics presented in the chapter, as well as study appropriate flashcards, topic summaries, and demonstrations.

In addition, CourseMate contains links to the eBook; interactive versions of the text's Listening Exercises; a video of a performance of Britten's *Young Person's Guide to the Orchestra,* in whole and by instrument families; video demonstrations of keyboard instruments; links to the Active Listening Guides; eighteen iAudio podcasts on difficult musical concepts; an interactive music timeline; a checklist of musical styles with integrated musical style comparisons; musical elements, genres, and forms tutorials; Supplementary Listening Guide pdfs for music beyond that provided with the text; classroom management for instructors; and a free link to a complete online course taught at Yale by the author and featuring in-class performances and demonstrations. In addition, marginal cues in the text direct readers to related online playlists from iTunes and YouTube—all housed at CourseMate.

Students may access CourseMate using the passcode on the card bound into each new copy of the text, or purchase access online at www.cengagebrain.com.

eBook

Also available is a multimedia-enabled eBook, featuring page design identical to the print book and links to all premium media content, including streaming music and Active Listening Guides.

 # For Instructors

CourseMate's Engagement Tracker

With CourseMate, instructors can use the included gradebook, Engagement Tracker, to assess student performance, preparation, and engagement. Engagement Tracker's tracking tools allow the instructor to:

- Automatically record quiz scores.
- Export all grades to an instructor's own Excel spreadsheet.
- See progress for individuals or the class as a whole.
- Identify students at risk early in the course.
- Uncover which concepts are most difficult for the class and monitor time on task.

PowerLecture with ExamView® and JoinIn on TurningPoint®

Includes the Instructor's Manual, Supplementary Listening Guides, ExamView® computerized testing (including musical clips), JoinIn on TurningPoint®, and Microsoft® PowerPoint® slides with lecture outlines, music clips, and images, which can be used as offered, or customized by importing personal lecture slides or other material. ExamView allows instructors to create, deliver, and customize tests and study guides (both print and online) in minutes with its easy-to-use assessment and tutorial system. It offers both a Quick Test Wizard and an Online Test Wizard that guide instructors step by step through the process of creating tests (up to 250 questions using up to twelve question types), while its "what you see is what you get" capability allows users to see the test they are creating on the screen exactly as it will print or display online. ExamView's complete word-processing capabilities allow users to enter an unlimited number of new questions or edit existing questions. JoinIn content (for use with most "clicker" systems) delivers instant classroom assessment and active learning opportunities such as in-class polling, attendance taking, and quizzing.

WebTutor™ for Blackboard and WebCT

This web-based teaching and learning tool is rich with study and mastery tools, communication tools, and course content. Use WebTutor™ to provide virtual office hours, post syllabi, set up threaded discussions, track student progress with the quizzing material, and more. For students, WebTutor™ offers real-time access to a full array of study tools, including flashcards (with audio), practice quizzes, online tutorials, and web links. Instructors can customize the content by uploading images and other resources, adding web links, or creating their own practice materials. WebTutor™ also provides rich communication tools, including a course calendar, asynchronous discussion, "real-time" chat, and an integrated email system—in effect, a complete online course. For information, contact your Cengage sales representative.

CengageCompose

Instructors can easily create their own personalized text, selecting the elements that meet their specific learning objectives.

CengageCompose puts the power of the vast Cengage Learning library of content at instructors' fingertips to create exactly the text they need. The all-new, web-based CengageCompose site lets them quickly scan contents and review materials to pick what they need for their text. Site tools let them easily assemble modular learning units into the order they want and immediately provide them with an online copy for review. Instructors may add their own material, as well as enrichment content, such as the popular and global music chapters from *Listening to Music, 6th Edition*, to build ideal learning materials, even choosing from hundreds of customizable full-color covers.

The following enrichment chapters from *Listening to Music* are available for customization:

Ch. 37   American Popular Music, 1850–World War II
Ch. 38   Postwar Jazz
Ch. 39   Broadway, Film, and Video Game Music
Ch. 40   Rock: Music of Rebellion
Ch. 41   The Far East
Ch. 42   The Near East and Africa
Ch. 43   The Caribbean and Latin America

Acknowledgments

In addition to the hundreds of instructors who responded to surveys during the development of this book, I am especially indebted to the following reviewers, who provided invaluable in-depth feedback:

Gail Allen, Averett University
Dan Beller-McKenna, University of New Hampshire
Amy Black, Clayton State University
James Boldin, University of Louisiana at Monroe
Daphne Carr, Columbia University
Henrietta Carter, Golden West College
Ross Hagen, Utah Valley University

Luke Howard, Brigham Young University
Ed Jacobs, Southwestern Illinois College
Mark Jelinek, Bloomsburg University
Jennifer Mann, University of Alabama
Julie Ponce, College of Lake County, College of DuPage, and Harper College
Stacy Rodgers, University of Mississippi
Vanessa Sheldon, Norco College
Anne Swartz, Baruch College, City University of New York

I have also benefited from the help and good will of the staff of the Yale Music Library: Kendall Crilly, librarian, and Suzanne Lovejoy, Richard Boursy, and Evan Heater. Karl Schrom, record librarian at Yale, has been a source of good advice regarding the availability and quality of recordings for over twenty years. The engineering of the audio was accomplished at the Yale Recording Studio by the capable hands of Eugene Kimball. And Benjamin Thorburn generated the new musical orthography for this book.

Julia Doe, also at Yale, proofread the manuscript, contributed ideas for improved content, and developed many of the ancillary materials that appear in CourseMate.

Finally, Prof. Timothy Roden (Ohio Wesleyan University), the author of much of the web material, Instructor's Manual, and Test Bank, has corrected errors and saved me from myself on numerous occasions.

As always, it has been a privilege to work with publisher Clark Baxter and his experienced team at Schirmer Cengage Learning—Sue Gleason, Jeanne Heston, Katie Schooling, Liz Newell, Michael Lepera, and Bill Clark—as well as Tom and Lisa Smialek, original developers of the Active Listening Tools, and especially Tom Laskey, Director of A&R, Custom Marketing Group, at SONY, who has helped usher this book into the era of downloads. My heartiest thanks to all of you!

Finally, I thank my wife (Sherry Dominick) and four children (Evan, Andrew, Stephanie, and Chris), who did their best to keep the paterfamilias aware of popular culture, musical and otherwise.

Craig Wright
Yale University

The Essential
Listening to Music

The Appeal of Music

Watch a video of Craig Wright's Open Yale Course class sessions 1 and 2, "Introduction" and "Introduction to Instruments and Musical Genres," at CourseMate for this text.

Why do we listen to music? Does it keep us in touch with the latest musical trends, help get us through our morning exercise, or relax us in the evening? Each day almost everyone in the industrialized world listens to music, whether intentionally or not. The global expenditure for commercial music is somewhere between $30 and $40 billion annually, more than the gross domestic product of 100 of the 181 countries identified by the World Bank. Take the iPhone as just one example. Do most people have an "app" for ballet or for painting? Likely not. But they do have several for music. Turn on the radio and what do we hear: drama or poetry? No, usually just music; the radio is basically a transmission tool for music.

But why is music so appealing? What is its attraction? Does it perpetuate the human species? Does it shelter us from the elements? No. Does it keep us warm? Not unless we dance. Is music some sort of drug or aphrodisiac?

Oddly, yes. Neuroscientists at Harvard University have done studies that show that when we listen to music we engage processes in the brain that are "active in other euphoria inducing stimuli such as food, sex, and drugs of abuse."[1] These same researchers have explained the neural processes through which listening to particular pieces of music can give us goose bumps. There is a chemical change in the human brain, as blood flow increases in some parts and decreases in others. Although listening to music today may or may not be necessary for survival, it does alter our chemical composition and our mental state. In short, it is pleasurable and rewarding.

Music is also powerful. "To control the people, control the music," Plato said, in essence, in his *Republic*. Thus governments, religions, and, more recently, corporations have done just that. Think of the stirring band music used to get soldiers to march to war. Think of the refined sounds of Mozart played in advertisements for luxurious products. Think of the four-note "rally" motive played at professional sports events to get the crowd energized. Sound perception is the most powerful sense we possess, likely because it *was* once essential to our survival—who is coming from where? Friend or foe? Flight or fight? We get frightened at horror films, not when the images on the screen become vivid, but when the music starts to turn ominous. In short, sounds rationally organized in a pleasing or frightening way—music—profoundly affect how we feel and behave.

Music and Your Brain

Briefly defined, **music** is the rational organization of sounds and silences passing through time. Tones must be arranged in some consistent, logical, and (usually) pleasing way before we can call these sounds "music" instead of just noise. A singer or an instrumentalist generates music by creating **sound waves,** vibrations that reflect slight differences in air pressure. Sound waves radiate out

To learn more about music and the brain, see a video of "Music and the Mind" in the YouTube playlist at CourseMate for this text.

---

[1] Anne Blood and Robert Zatorre, "Intensely Pleasurable Responses to Music Correlate with Activity in Brain Regions Implicated in Reward and Emotion," *Proceedings of the National Academy of Sciences,* Vol. 98, No. 20 (Sept. 25, 2001), pp. 11818–11823

in a circle from the source, carrying with them two types of essential information: pitch and volume. The speed of vibration within the sound wave determines what we perceive as high and low pitches; and the width (or amplitude) of the wave reflects its volume. When the music reaches the brain, that organ tells us how we should feel and respond to the sound. We tend to hear low, soft tones as relaxing and high, loud ones as tension filled.

Given all the love songs in the world, we might think that music is an affair of the heart. But both love and music are domains of a far more complex vital organ: the brain (Fig. 1-1). When sound waves reach us, our inner ear transforms them into electrical signals that go to various parts of the brain, each analyzing a particular component of the sound: pitch, color, loudness, duration, direction of source, relation to familiar music, and so on. Most processing of sound (music as well as language) takes place in the temporal lobe. If we are imagining how the next line of a song will go, that decision is usually reached in the frontal lobe. If we are playing an instrument, we engage the motor cortex (parietal lobe) to move our fingers, and the visual center (occipital lobe) to read the notes. As the music proceeds, our brain constantly updates the information it receives, hundreds of times per second. At a speed of 250 miles per hour, associative neurons

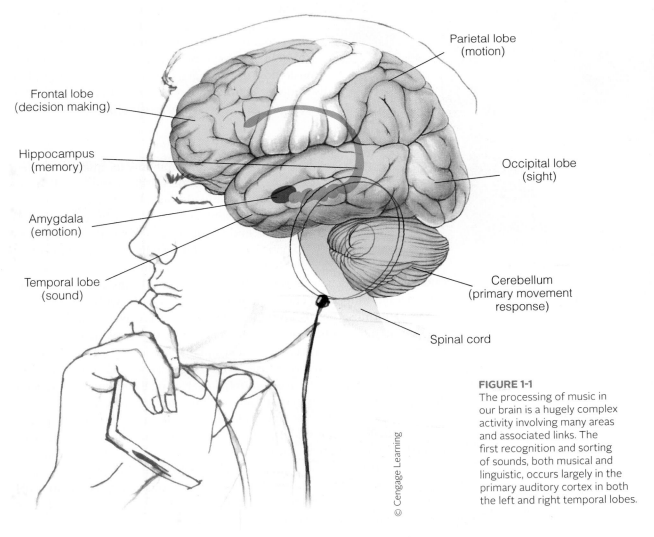

Frontal lobe
(decision making)

Hippocampus
(memory)

Amygdala
(emotion)

Temporal lobe
(sound)

Parietal lobe
(motion)

Occipital lobe
(sight)

Cerebellum
(primary movement
response)

Spinal cord

© Cengage Learning

FIGURE 1-1
The processing of music in our brain is a hugely complex activity involving many areas and associated links. The first recognition and sorting of sounds, both musical and linguistic, occurs largely in the primary auditory cortex in both the left and right temporal lobes.

integrate all the data into a single perception of sound. To sum up: Sound waves enter the brain as electrochemical impulses that cause chemical changes in the body; the human response can be to relax or, if the impulses come strongly at regular intervals, to get up and dance—to entrain with the rhythm.

Listening to Whose Music?

Tune in to a podcast about learning how to listen at CourseMate for this text.

Today most of the music that we hear isn't "live" music but recorded sound. Sound recording began in the 1870s with Thomas Edison's phonograph machine, which first played metal cylinders and then vinyl disks, or "records." During the 1930s, magnetic tape recorders appeared and grew in popularity until the early 1990s, when they were superseded by a new technology, digital recording. In digital recording all the components of musical sound—pitch, tone color, duration, volume, and more—are analyzed thousands of times per second, and that information is stored on compact discs as sequences of binary numbers. When it's time to play the music, these digital data are reconverted to electrical impulses that are then changed back into sound waves that are intensified and pushed through speakers or headphones Most recorded music now is no longer stored and sold on CDs, but distributed electronically as MP3 or M4A files. This holds true for popular and classical music alike.

Popular or Classical?

Most people prefer **popular music,** music designed to please a large portion of the general public. Pop CDs and downloads outsell classical recordings by about twenty to one. But why are so many people, and young people in particular, attracted to popular music? Likely it has to do with beat and rhythm (both discussed in Chapter 2). A regular beat or periodic pulse elicits a synchronized motor response in the central nervous system; people almost can't help but move in time to music with a good beat.

Most of the music discussed in this book, however, is what we call "classical" music, and it, too, can be a powerful force. Hearing the huge, majestic sound of a mass of acoustical instruments—a symphony orchestra—can be an overwhelming experience. Classical music is often regarded as "old" music, written by "dead white men." But this isn't entirely true: No small amount of it has been written by women, and many composers, of both sexes, are very much alive and well today. In truth, however, much of the classical music that we hear—the music of Bach, Beethoven, and Brahms, for example—*is* old. That is why, in part, it is called "classical." In the same vein, we refer to clothes, furniture, and cars as "classics" because they have timeless qualities of expression, proportion, and balance. Broadly defined, **classical music** is the traditional music of any culture, usually requiring long years of training; it is "high art" or "learned," timeless music that is enjoyed generation after generation.

Popular and Classical Music Compared

Today Western classical music is taught in conservatories around the world, from Paris to Beijing to Singapore. Western pop music enjoys even greater favor, having drowned out local popular music in many places. But what are the essential differences between the music we call popular and the music we call classical? Cutting to the quick, here are five ways in which they differ:

- Popular music often uses electric enhancements (via electric guitars, synthesizers, and so on) to amplify and transform vocal and instrumental sounds. Much of classical music uses **acoustic instruments** that produce sounds naturally.
- Popular music is primarily vocal, involving **lyrics** (accompanying text that tells listeners what the music is about and thus implies what they are supposed to feel). Classical music is more often purely instrumental, performed on a piano or by a symphony orchestra, for example, which grants the listener more interpretive freedom.
- Popular music has a strong beat that makes us want to move in sync with it. Classical music often subordinates the beat in favor of melody and harmony.
- Popular tunes tend to be short and involve exact repetition. Classical compositions can be long, sometimes thirty to forty minutes in duration, and most repetitions are somehow varied.
- Popular music is performed by memory, not from a written score (have you ever seen music stands at a rock concert?), and each performer can interpret the work as he or she sees fit (hence the proliferation of "cover songs"). Classical music, even if played by memory, is usually generated from a written score, and there is usually one commonly accepted mode of interpretation—the piece exists, almost frozen in place, as a work of art.

Classical music requires years of technical training on an instrument and knowledge of often-complicated music theory. Some musicians are equally at home in the worlds of classical and popular music. Juilliard School of Music–trained Wynton Marsalis can record a Baroque trumpet concerto one week and an album of New Orleans–style jazz the next. He has won nine Grammy awards—seven for various jazz categories and two for classical albums.

How Does Classical Music Work?

Explaining how classical music works requires an entire book—this one. But some preliminary observations are in order.

Genres of Classical Music

Genre in musical language is simply a word for "type of music." Needless to say, there are almost endless types of popular music: rap, hip-hop, blues, R&B, country, grunge, and Broadway show tunes among them. *Genre* implies not only where you might hear it performed (a bar, a jazz club, an arena, or a stadium, for example), but also how you might be expected to dress and act when you do so. A fan goes to hear Kanye West at the River Rock Casino in Las Vegas dressed casually, ready to dance and make a lot of noise. But that same person would likely attend a concert of the Boston Symphony Orchestra in Symphony Hall

> Some concerts require a large hall seating two to three thousand listeners (such as the Schermerhorn Symphony Center, Nashville, Tennessee; see p. 9). For other performances a smaller venue with two to six hundred seats is more appropriate, as we see here at the chamber music hall of the Royal Conservatory of Music in Brussels, Belgium.

WU WEI/Xinhua /Landov

attired in suit and tie, and prepared to sit quietly. Among the most prominent genres of classical music are dramatic works mounted in opera houses and large theaters. Many classical genres, however, are purely instrumental. Some are performed in large concert halls accommodating two to three thousand listeners, whereas others are heard in smaller (chamber) halls seating perhaps two to six hundred. Again, genre dictates where one goes to hear the music, what one hears, what one wears, and how to behave.

Opera Houses & Theaters	Concert Halls	Chamber Halls
Opera	Symphony	Art song
Ballet	Concerto	String quartet
	Oratorio	Piano sonata

Styles of Classical Music

Style in music is generally the distinctive sound created by an artist, composer, or performing group. Historians label as "eras" lengthy periods possessing common attributes and give them names such as "the Renaissance" or "the Enlightenment." Similarly, music historians identify eight style periods, extending from the Middle Ages to the Postmodern era.

Middle Ages: 476–1450	Romantic: 1820–1900
Renaissance: 1450–1600	Impressionist: 1880–1920
Baroque: 1600–1750	Modern: 1900–1985
Classical: 1750–1820	Postmodern: 1945–present

Sometimes the structure of the music alerts us to its style period. The music of the Classical period, for example, usually has melodies that are short and symmetrical. But most often we recognize the style period of a piece by surface details, such as the "color" of the sound or the swings in the volume—more specifically, by the type and number of instruments that we hear. The music of the Romantic era in particular enjoys striking popularity. A boxed set of "50 favorite classical melodies as sold on TV," turns out to be mostly extracts from the Romantic period. When a hundred Yale undergrads were recently asked to choose their favorite piece of "classical" music, 85 percent of their selections were from this era. The huge sound and lush, sweeping strings of the large Romantic orchestra likely account for much of the popular appeal of the Romantic style. But though we all know what we like, we don't always know *why* we like it. The aim of this book, in part, is to explain the "why."

The Language of Classical Music

If a friend told you, "My house burned down last night," you'd probably react with shock and profound sadness. In this case, verbal language conveys meaning and elicits an emotional reaction.

But music, too, is a means of communication, one older than spoken language; spoken language, many biologists tell us, is simply a specialized subset of music. Over the centuries, composers of classical music have created a language that can convey shock and sadness as effectively as do the words of poetry or prose. This language of music is a collection of audible gestures that express meaning through sound. We need not take lessons to learn how to understand the language of music at a basic level, for we intuit much of it already. The reason is simple: we have been listening to the language of Western music every day since infancy. We intuit, for example, that music that gets faster and rises in pitch communicates growing excitement because we have heard these gestures frequently, as in chase scenes in films and on TV. Still another piece might sound like a funeral march. But why? Because the composer is communicating this to us by using a slow *tempo,* regular *beat,* and *minor key*. Understanding terms such as these will allow us to discuss the language of music accurately and thereby appreciate it more fully, which is another aim of this book.

Where and How to Listen

CDs for Your Book

The Introduction to Listening (Intro) CD bound into your book and the 2-CD set that is available for purchase contain the highest-quality recordings commercially available, in terms of both musical artistry and engineering excellence. You can play them on your computer or your car stereo, of course. But if you have access to quality audio equipment (a separate player, amplifier, and speakers), that will help produce the best home audio experience.

Streaming Music

All of the music on the Intro CD and the 2-CD set is also available streaming on the text's CourseMate website and in its interactive eBook.

Downloads

By now, most of the people you know have a digital media player containing hundreds, perhaps thousands, of pieces of music. The difficulty isn't in getting the music, but in organizing the countless downloads that are there.

This textbook offers downloads for all of the music on the Intro CD and 2-CD set, which makes this as good a time as any for you to start a classical playlist. Devote a section on your listening device exclusively to classical music and arrange the pieces within it by composer. Most of the classical pieces that you will buy, despite what iTunes says, will not be "songs." Songs have lyrics, and a great deal of classical music, as mentioned, is purely instrumental: instrumental symphonies, sonatas, concertos, and the like. If you wish to do more than just listen, however, go to YouTube, which will allow you to see the performers, thereby humanizing the listening experience. There is much music available on YouTube, but a lot of it is poor quality. For the classical repertoire, search out big-name artists (Luciano Pavarotti and Renée Fleming among them) and top-of-the-line orchestras (the New York Philharmonic or the Chicago Symphony Orchestra, for example).

Live in Concert

Pop megastars now make more money from live concerts than they do from recording royalties, and so, too, with classical musicians. Indeed, for classical musicians and listeners alike there is nothing better than a live performance. First, there is the joy of witnessing an artist at work, delivering his or her craft with stunning precision. Second and more importantly, the sound will be magnificent because it is pure, often acoustical music.

Compared to pop or rock concerts, however, performances of classical music can be rather staid affairs. For one thing, people dress "up," not "down." For another, throughout the event the classical audience sits quietly, saying nothing to friends or to the performers on stage. No one sways, dances, or sings along to the music. Only at the end of each composition does the audience express itself, clapping respectfully.

But classical concerts weren't always so formal. In fact, they were once more like professional wrestling matches. In the eighteenth century, for example, the audience talked during performances and yelled words of encouragement to the players. People clapped at the end of each movement of a symphony and often in the middle of the movement as well. After an exceptionally pleasing performance, listeners would demand that the piece be repeated immediately in an **encore.** If, on the other hand, the audience didn't like what it heard, it might express its displeasure by throwing fruit and other debris at the stage. Our modern, more dignified classical concert was a creation of the nineteenth century, when musical compositions came to be considered works of high art worthy of reverential silence.

Attending a classical concert requires familiarizing yourself with the music in advance. These days, this is easy. Go to YouTube and type in the titles of the pieces on the program. Enter "Beethoven Symphony 5," for example. Several recorded versions will appear, and you can quickly compare different interpretations of the same piece. Should you need information about the history of the work and its composer, try to avoid Wikipedia, which is often unreliable. Instead, go to the more authoritative Oxford Music Online's Grove Music Online

◄ Schermerhorn Symphony Center, Nashville, Tennessee. Constructed between 2003 and 2006, the 2,000-seat auditorium is home to the Nashville Symphony as well as concerts of pop, cabaret, choral, jazz, and blues music. If that isn't enough for music lovers visiting Nashville, right across the street is the Country Music Hall of Fame.

(most colleges and universities have an online subscription) and search under the name of the composer.

But regardless of how you listen—with CDs, downloads, online, or live—be sure to focus solely on the music. This text is here to help you do exactly that, more effectively.

Getting Started: No Previous Experience Required

"I'm tone deaf, I can't sing, and I'm no good at dancing." Most likely this isn't true of you. What *is* true is that some people have remarkable memories for sounds, whether musical or linguistic. Mozart, who had perfect pitch, could hear a piece just once and reconstruct several minutes of it verbatim. But you don't need to be a Mozart to enjoy classical music. In fact, you likely know and enjoy a great deal of classical music already. A Puccini aria ("O, mio babbino caro") sounds prominently in the best-selling video game Grand Theft Auto, no doubt for ironic effect. The seductive "Habanera" from Bizet's opera *Carmen* (see Chapter 13) underscores the characters' secret intentions in an early episode of *Gossip Girl*. And Mozart is used to promote Nike basketball shoes, just as Bach is used to advertise Grey Poupon mustard. Resting beneath the surface, classical music quietly plays on our psyche.

Take the Classical Music Challenge

To test the capacity of classical music to move you, try a simple comparison. Go to YouTube and watch a video of Taylor Swift singing "Love Story," then select a recent clip of soprano Renée Fleming singing the Puccini aria "O, mio babbino caro." Whose artistry impresses you the most? Or listen to Coldplay's latest hit

Listen to Taylor Swift singing "Love Story" in the YouTube playlist at CourseMate for this text.

Compare with Renée Fleming singing "O, mio babbino caro" in the YouTube playlist.

> Taylor Swift arrives at the 46th Annual Academy of Country Music Awards RAM Red Carpet held at the MGM Grand Garden Arena on April 3, 2011, in Las Vegas, Nevada.

Fred Duval/FilmMagic/Getty Images

Hear an example of the power of Beethoven's music—his Piano Concerto No. 5—in the iTunes playlist at CourseMate for this text.

> Renée Fleming arrives for opening night at The Metropolitan Opera House at Lincoln Center in New York on September 21, 2009.

Landov

next to a rendition of Richard Wagner's "Ride of the Valkyries," comparing the sound of a rock band with that of a symphony orchestra. Which pieces gave you chills, and which ones just left you cold? Were you moved by the classical clips?

If you weren't moved, try listening to two other famous moments in the history of classical music. The first is the beginning of Ludwig van Beethoven's Symphony No. 5, perhaps the best-known moment in all of classical music. Its "short-short-short-long" (SSSL) gesture (duh-duh-duh-DUHHH) is as much an icon of Western culture as is the "To be, or no t to be" soliloquy in Shakespeare's *Hamlet*. Beethoven (see Chapter 10 for his biography) wrote this symphony in 1808 when he was thirty-seven and had become almost totally deaf. (Like most great musicians, the nearly deaf Beethoven could hear with an "inner ear"—he could create and rework melodies in his head without relying on external sound.) Beethoven's **symphony**—an instrumental genre for orchestra—is actually a composite of four separate instrumental pieces, each called a **movement.** He began the first with a musical **motive,** a short, distinctive musical figure that can stand by itself. Indeed, his now-famous SSSL motive is the musical equivalent of a sucker punch. It comes out of nowhere and hits hard. Thereafter we regain our equilibrium, as Beethoven takes us on an emotionally wrenching, thirty-minute, four-movement symphonic journey dominated by this four-note motive.

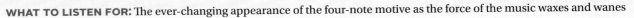

Listening Cue

Ludwig van Beethoven, Symphony No. 5 in C minor (1808)

Intro
1

First movement, *Allegro con brio* (fast with gusto)

WHAT TO LISTEN FOR: The ever-changing appearance of the four-note motive as the force of the music waxes and wanes

 Listen to streaming music in an Active Listening Guide, at CourseMate or in the eBook.

Finally, for the grandest of all sounds, popular or classical, we turn to the beginning of an orchestral work by Richard Strauss, *Also sprach Zarathustra* (*Thus Spoke Zarathustra*). Here Strauss attempts to replicate in music the enormous power of the rising sun by using all the instruments of the large, Romantic orchestra of the late nineteenth century. So impressive is this passage that it has been borrowed for use in countless radio and TV commercials (to sell digital TV and phone delivery services, insurance, and storm windows, among other things) where the aim is to astound you, the consumer, with the power, durability, and brilliance of the product. In contrast to Beethoven's composition, Strauss's piece isn't a symphony in four movements, but rather a one-movement work for orchestra called a **tone poem** (see Chapter 12). If you think classical music is for wimps, think again!

Listening Cue

Richard Strauss, *Also sprach Zarathustra* (1896)

Intro
2

One-movement tone poem

WHAT TO LISTEN FOR: A gradual transition from the nothingness of murky darkness, to shafts of light (trumpets), and finally to the incandescent power of the full symphony orchestra

 Listen to streaming music in an Active Listening Guide, at CourseMate or in the eBook.

Listening Exercise 1

To take this Listening Exercise online and receive feedback, go to CourseMate or the eBook.

Musical Beginnings

This first Listening Exercise asks you to review two of the most famous "beginnings" in all of classical music.

Beethoven, Symphony No. 5 (1808)—Opening

1. (Track 1, 0:00–0:05) Beethoven opens his Symphony No. 5 with the famous "SSSL" motive and then immediately repeats it. Does the repetition present the motive at a higher or a lower pitch level?
   a. higher
   b. lower

2. (Track 1, 0:22–0:44) In this passage Beethoven constructs a musical transition that moves us from the opening motive to a more lyrical second theme. Which is true about this transition?
   a. The music seems to get faster and builds in volume.
   b. The music seems to get slower.

3. (Track 1, 0:38–0:42) How does Beethoven add intensity to the conclusion of the transition?
   a. A pounding drum (timpani) is added to the orchestra, and then a French horn plays a solo.
   b. A French horn plays a solo, and then a pounding drum (timpani) is added to the orchestra.

4. (Track 1, 0:46–1:00) Now a more lyrical new theme begins in the violin section and is echoed by the winds. But has the opening motive (SSSL) really disappeared?
   a. Yes, it is no longer present.
   b. No, it can be heard above the new melody.
   c. No, it lurks below the new melody.

5. (Track 1, 1:17–1:26) *Student choice* (no "correct" answer): How do you feel about the end of the opening section, compared to the beginning?
   a. less anxious and more self-confident
   b. less self-confident and more anxious

Strauss, *Also sprach Zarathustra* (1896)—Opening

6. (Track 2, 0:00–0:13) Which is true about the opening sounds?
   a. The instruments are playing several different sounds in succession.
   b. The instruments are holding one and the same note.

7. (Track 2, 0:14–0:20) When the trumpets enter and ascend, does the low, rumbling sound disappear?
   a. yes
   b. no

8. (Track 2, 0:14–0:22 and again at 0:30–0:40 and 0:49–0:57) When the trumpets rise, how many different notes do they play?
   a. one
   b. two
   c. three

9. (Track 2, 1:18) At the very last chord, a new sound is added for emphasis—to signal that this is indeed the last chord of the climax. What instrument is making that sound?
   a. a piano
   b. an electric bass
   c. a cymbal

10. *Student choice:* You've now heard two very different musical openings, by Beethoven and Strauss. Which do you prefer? Which grabbed your attention more? Think about why.
    a. Beethoven
    b. Strauss

Rhythm, Melody, and Harmony

Watch a video of Craig Wright's Open Yale Course class session 3, "Rhythm: Fundamentals," at CourseMate for this text.

See Michael Jackson respond to and redefine the beat in the YouTube playlist at CourseMate for this text.

To see the power of rhythm to take control of the body, watch Christopher Walken in action in the YouTube playlist at CourseMate for this text.

M usic is an unusual art. You can't see it or touch it. But it has matter—compressed air yielding sounding pitches—and these pitches are organized in three ways: as rhythms, as melodies, and as harmonies. Rhythm, melody, and harmony, then, are the three primary elements—the *what*—of music.

 ## Rhythm

Rhythm is arguably the most fundamental element of music. Its primacy may be caused by our experience *in utero*; we heard the beat of our mother's heart before we were aware of any sort of melody or tune. Similarly, our brain reacts powerfully and intuitively to a regularly recurring, strongly articulated "beat" and a catchy, repeating rhythmic pattern. We have a direct, even physical, response to rhythm, especially when listening to pop music. We move, exercise, and dance to its pulse.

The basic pulse of music is the **beat,** a regularly recurring sound that divides the passing of time into equal units. **Tempo** is the speed at which the beat sounds. Some tempos are fast (*allegro*) or very fast (*presto*) and some slow (*lento*) or very slow (*grave*). Sometimes the tempo speeds up, producing an *accelerando,* and sometimes it slows down, creating a **ritard.** But oddly, whether they proceed rapidly or slowly, undifferentiated streams of anything aren't appealing to us humans. We organize passing time into seconds, minutes, hours, days, years, and centuries. We subconsciously group the clicking of a seatbelt warning chime into units of two or three "dings." So, too, with the undifferentiated stream of musical beats: our psyche demands that we organize them into groups, each containing two, three, four, or more pulses. The first beat in each unit is called the **downbeat,** and it gets the greatest **accent,** or stress. Organizing beats into groups produces **meter** in music, just as arranging words in a consistent pattern of emphasis produces meter in poetry. In music each group of beats is called a **measure** (or bar). Although there are several different kinds of meter in music, about 90 percent of the music we hear falls into either a duple or a triple pattern. We mentally count "ONE-two" or "ONE-two-three." There's a quadruple pattern as well, but in most ways our ear perceives this as simply a double duple.

© Phil Dent/Redferns/Getty Images

> The fluid dance patterns of Michael Jackson show how rhythm can animate the body.

Rhythmic Notation

About eight hundred years ago—in thirteenth-century Paris to be precise—musicians began to devise a system to notate the beats, meters, and rhythms of their music. They created symbols that stood for long or longer, and short or shorter, durations. Over the centuries these signs developed into the notational symbols that we use today, as seen here.

Example 2-1 ➤

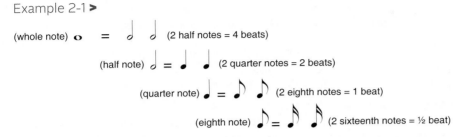

To help the performer keep the beat when playing, the smaller note values—specifically, those with flags on the vertical stem—are beamed, or joined together, in groups of two or four.

Example 2-2 ➤

Today the symbol that usually represents, or "carries," one beat in music is the quarter note (♩). Normally, it moves along roughly at the rate of the average person's heartbeat. As you might suspect from its name, the quarter note is shorter in length than the half and the whole notes, but longer than the eighth and the sixteenth notes. There are also signs, called **rests,** to indicate the absence of sound for different lengths of time.

If music proceeded only with beats organized into meter, it would be dull indeed—like the endless sound of a bass drum (ONE-two, ONE-two, or ONE-two-three, ONE-two-three). In fact, what we hear in music by way of duration is **rhythm,** the division of time into compelling patterns of long and short sounds. Rhythm emerges from, and rests upon, the durational grid set by the beat and the meter. In fact, no one actually plays just the beat, except perhaps a drummer; rather, we hear a mass of musical rhythms, and our brain extracts the beat and the meter from them. To see how this works, let's look at a patriotic song from the time of the American Revolution in duple ($\frac{2}{4}$) meter.

Example 2-3 ➤

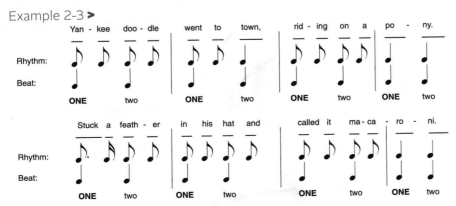

Listen to an example of Beethoven's use of rhythm in his Symphony No. 7, in the iTunes playlist at CourseMate for this text.

Listen to a podcast about the basics of hearing meters at CourseMate for this text.

Listen to a podcast about tempo at CourseMate for this text.

Here's another patriotic song, "America" (first known in England and Canada as "God Save the King"—or "Queen") arranged the same way. It is in triple ($\frac{3}{4}$) meter.

Example 2-4 ➤

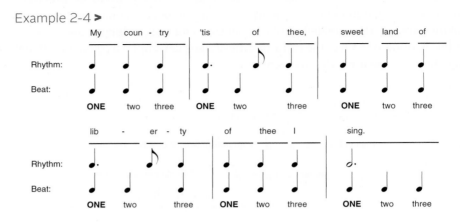

The numbers $\frac{2}{4}$ and $\frac{3}{4}$ aren't fractions, but rather **meter signatures** (also called **time signatures**). A meter signature tells the performer how the beats of the music are grouped to form a meter. The bottom number of the signature (usually a 4 representing the quarter note) indicates what note value receives the beat, and the top number tells how many beats there are in each measure. The small vertical lines in the preceding examples are called **bar lines**; they help performers keep the music of one measure, or bar, separate from the next and thus how to keep the beat. Although all this terminology of music theory might seem intimidating, the important question is this: Can you hear the downbeat and then recognize a duple meter (as in a ONE-two, ONE-two march) contrasted with a triple meter (as in a ONE-two-three, ONE-two-three waltz)? If so, you're well on your way to grasping the rhythmic element of music.

Surprisingly, much Western classical music *doesn't* have a strong rhythmic component; rather, the beauty of the music rests in the melody and harmony. Popular music, on the other hand, is often irresistible, not only because of a strong beat, but also because of a catchy rhythm, one created by syncopation. In most music, the accent, or musical emphasis, falls directly on the beat, with the downbeat getting the greatest emphasis of all. **Syncopation,** however, places the accent either on a weak beat or between beats—literally, it's "off beat." This unexpected, offbeat moment in the music creates the catchy "hook" of the tune, the part that pops up when you least expect it and sticks in your head.

A short example of syncopation can be heard in bar 2 of the chorus of The Beatles' song "Lucy in the Sky with Diamonds." The arrows show the moments of syncopation.

Example 2-5 ➤

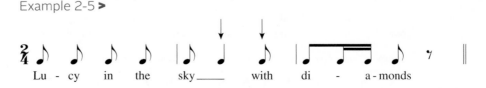

A far more complex example of syncopation can be found in the popular theme song to *The Simpsons.*

Watch a video of Craig Wright's Open Yale Course class session 4, "Rhythm: Jazz, Pop, and Classical," at CourseMate for this text.

Example 2-6 >

ONE two   ONE two   ONE two   ONE two   ONE two

If you're a fan of jazz, Afro-Cuban music, or Latin music, you may be responding to the syncopation that gives these styles their bounce or lift.

Listening Cue

The Basics of Rhythm

Intro 3

WHAT TO LISTEN FOR: Practice recognizing different levels of rhythmic activity in different pieces of music

 Listen to streaming music in an Active Listening Guide at CourseMate for this text.

Listening Exercise 2

Intro 4

To take this Listening Exercise online and receive feedback, go to CourseMate or the eBook.

Hearing Meters

On your Intro CD, track 4, you have ten short musical excerpts, each played once. (You can replay them as many times as you wish.) Identify the meter of each excerpt. To do this, you should listen for the beat and count 1–2 or 1–2–3. All pieces are in duple ($\frac{2}{4}$) or triple ($\frac{3}{4}$) meter. Enter "duple" or "triple" in the blanks. There are five examples in duple meter and five in triple.

1. (0:00) Meter: _____ Mouret, Rondeau, from *Suite de symphonies*

2. (0:26) Meter: _____ Chopin, Waltz in E♭ major

3. (0:45) Meter: _____ Beethoven, Variations on "God Save the King"

4. (1:00) Meter: _____ Prokofiev, *Romeo and Juliet*

5. (1:20) Meter: _____ Prokofiev, *Romeo and Juliet*

6. (2:04) Meter: _____ Bach, Brandenburg Concerto No. 5, 1st movement

7. (2:26) Meter: _____ Mozart, *Eine kleine Nachtmusik*, 1st movement

8. (2:46) Meter: _____ Haydn, Symphony No. 94, 3rd movement

9. (3:05) Meter: _____ Bizet, Habanera, from *Carmen*

10. (3:41) Meter: _____ Handel, Minuet, from *Water Music*

 Melody

Watch a video of Craig Wright's Open Yale Course class session 5, "Melody: Notes, Scales, Nuts, and Bolts," at CourseMate for this text.

Listen to an example of a familiar beautiful melody, "Ave Maria," in the iTunes playlist at CourseMate for this text.

A **melody**, simply put, is the tune. It's the part we sing along with, the part we like, the part we're willing to listen to again and again. TV promos try to entice us to buy CD sets of "The Fifty All-Time Greatest Melodies"—yet there are no similar collections devoted to rhythms or harmonies. Needless to say, Josh Groban, Andrea Bocelli, Celine Dion, Katy Perry, and Renée Fleming sing the melody. They, and it, are the stars.

Every melody is composed of a succession of pitches, usually energized by a rhythm. **Pitch** is the relative position, high or low, of a musical sound. We traditionally assign letter names (A, B, C, and so on) to identify specific pitches. When an instrument produces a musical tone, it sets into motion vibrating sound waves that travel through the air to reach the listener's ears. A faster vibration will produce a higher pitch, and a slower one a lower pitch. Pressing the lowest key on the piano sets a string vibrating back and forth 27 cycles (times) per second, while the highest key does the same at a dizzying 4,186 times per second. Low pitches lumber along and sound "fuzzy," whereas high ones are fleetingly clear. A low note can convey sadness, a high one excitement (we don't usually hear a high-pitched piccolo as sad, for example). In Western music, melodies move along from one discrete pitch to another. In other musical cultures—Chinese, for example—melody often "slides," and much of its beauty resides *between* the pitches.

Have you ever noticed, when singing a succession of tones up or down, that the melody reaches a tone that sounds like a duplication of an earlier pitch, but higher or lower? That duplicating pitch is called an **octave,** for reasons that will become clear shortly, and it's usually the largest distance between notes that we encounter in a melody. Pitches an octave apart sound similar because the frequency of vibration of the higher pitch is precisely twice that of the lower. The ancient Greeks, from whom much of our Western civilization derives, knew of the octave and its 2:1 ratio, and they divided it into seven pitches using other ratios. Their seven pitches plus the eighth (the octave) yield the white keys of the modern keyboard. When early musicians reached the repeating pitch, the octave, they began to repeat the A, B, C letter names for the pitches. Eventually, five additional notes were inserted. Notated with symbols called flats (♭) and sharps (♯), they correspond to the black keys of the keyboard.

Example 2-7 ➤

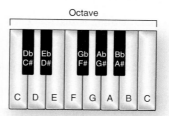

When a tune moves from one pitch to another it moves across a melodic **interval.** Some of these distances are small, others large. Melodies with large leaps are usually difficult to sing, whereas those with repeated or neighboring pitches are easier. Below is the beginning of a well-known melody based on a large interval; both phrases of the tune begin with an ascending leap of an octave. To hear the octave, try singing "Take me . . ." to yourself.

Example 2-8 >

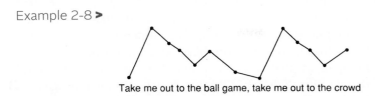

Take me out to the ball game, take me out to the crowd

Now, here's the opening to Beethoven's famous "Ode to Joy" from his Symphony No. 9 (1823), in which almost all of the pitches are adjacent. It is known and beloved around the world because it is tuneful and singable. Try it—you'll recognize the melody. If you're not comfortable with the words, try singing the syllable "la" to each pitch. You can also hear it at (Intro)/5.

Example 2-9 >

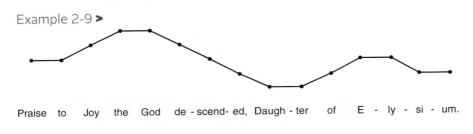

Praise to Joy the God de - scend- ed, Daugh - ter of E - ly - si - um.

Ray of mirth and rap - ture blend - ed, God - dess to thy shrine wel - come.

"Take Me out to the Ball Game" and Beethoven's "Ode to Joy" are very different in both intervallic structure and mood. Indeed, using all possible combinations of rhythms and pitches, an almost endless number of melodies can be created. But can you explain what makes melodies like these memorable and others quickly forgettable? If you can, you've solved one of the biggest mysteries of music: What makes a great melody?

Watch a video of Craig Wright's Open Yale Course class session 6, on what makes a great melody, "Melody: Mozart and Wagner," at CourseMate for this text.

Listening Cue

Hearing Melodies

WHAT TO LISTEN FOR: Practice recognizing the melodic contour of ten famous classical melodies.

Take online Listening Exercise 3 at CourseMate or in the eBook.

Melodic Notation

The type of notation used above for "Take Me out to the Ball Game" and "Ode to Joy" is useful if we need only to be reminded of how a melody goes, but it isn't precise enough to allow us to sing it if we don't already know it. When the melody goes up, how *far* up does it go? Around the year AD 1000, even before the advent of rhythmic notation, church musicians added precision to pitch notation in the West. They started to write black and, later, white circles on horizontal lines and spaces so that the exact distance between these notes could be judged immediately. This gridwork of lines and spaces came to be called a **staff.** The higher on the staff a note is placed, the higher its pitch.

Example 2-10 ➤

Over the course of centuries, the note heads also came to imply different durations, by means of stems and flags. Example 2-11A shows low, slow pitches that become gradually higher and faster, while Example 2-11B shows the reverse:

Example 2-11A ➤

Example 2-11B ➤

In notated music the staff is always provided with a **clef** sign to indicate the range of pitch in which the melody is to be played or sung. One clef, called the **treble clef,** designates the upper range and is appropriate for high instruments such as the trumpet and the violin, or a woman's voice. A second clef, called the **bass clef,** covers the lower range and is used for lower instruments such as the tuba and the cello, or a man's voice.

Example 2-12 ➤

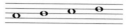

Treble clef   Bass clef

For a single vocal part or a single instrument, a melody could easily be placed on either of these two clefs. But for two-handed keyboard music with greater range, both clefs are used, one on top of the other. The performer looks at this combination of clefs, called the **great staff** (also **grand staff**), and relates the notes to the keys beneath the fingers. The two clefs join at middle C (the middlemost C key on the piano).

Example 2-13 >

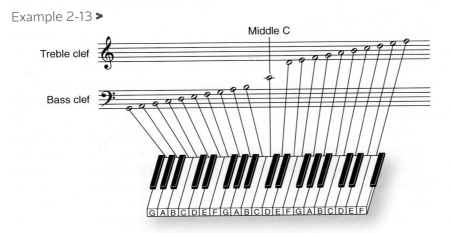

Each musical pitch can be represented by a particular line or space on the great staff as well as by a letter name (like C). We use only seven letter names (in ascending order A, B, C, D, E, F, and G) because, as we've seen, melodies were made up of only seven pitches within each octave. As a melody reaches and extends beyond the range of a single octave, the series of letter names is repeated (see Ex. 2-13). The note above G, then, is an A, which lies exactly one octave above the previous A. Here "Twinkle, Twinkle, Little Star" is notated on the great staff with the pitches doubled at the octave, as might happen when male and female voices sing together, the women an octave higher than the men.

Example 2-14 >

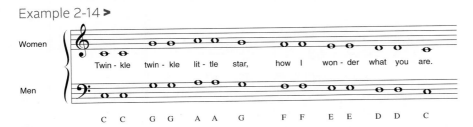

Scales, Modes, Tonality, and Key

When we listen to music, our brain hears a succession of pitches spaced out on a grid. That grid is a **scale,** a fixed pattern of tones within the octave that ascends and descends. Think of the scale as a ladder with eight rungs, or steps, between the two fixed points, low and high, formed by the octave. You can go up or down the ladder, but not all the steps are an equal distance apart. Five are a full step apart, but two are only a half step. For example, the distance between A and B is a full step, but between B and C it's only a half step—that's just the way the ancient Greeks built their musical ladder, an odd arrangement that Western musical culture retains to the present day.

The position of the two half steps tells us two important things: what kind of scale is in play and where we are within that scale. Since the seventeenth century, almost all Western melodies have been written following one of two

Listen to a podcast on hearing major and minor at CourseMate for this text.

Hear the difference between major and minor in CourseMate's Elements of Music melody demo.

seven-note scale patterns: the major one and the minor one. The **major scale** follows a seven-pitch pattern moving upward 1-1-½-1-1-1-½. The **minor scale** goes 1-½-1-1-½-1-1. Once the eighth pitch (octave) is reached, the pattern can start over again.

The choice of the scale (whether major or minor)—and our ability to hear the difference—is crucial to our enjoyment of music. To Western ears, melodies based on major scales sound bright, cheery, and optimistic, whereas minor ones come across as dark, somber, and even sinister. Go back to the end of Chapter 1 and compare the bright, heroic sound of Richard Strauss's *Also sprach Zarathustra,* built on a major scale, with the almost-threatening sound of Beethoven's Symphony No. 5, written in a minor one. Switching from major to minor, or from minor to major, is called a change of **mode**. Changing the mode affects the mood of the music. To prove the point, listen to the following familiar tunes (your instructor can play them for you). In each the mode has been changed from major to minor by inserting a flat into the scale near the last pitch (C), thereby switching from the beginning of the major scale (1-1-½) to that of the minor (1-½-1). Notice how this alteration sucks all the happiness, joy, and sunshine out of these formerly major melodies.

Example 2-15 ➤

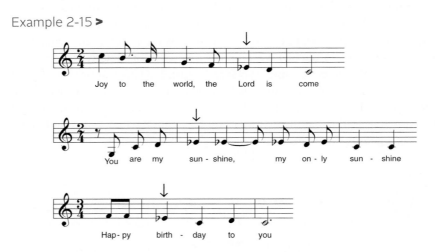

Joy to the world, the Lord is come

You are my sun-shine, my on-ly sun-shine

Hap-py birth-day to you

Listening Exercise 4

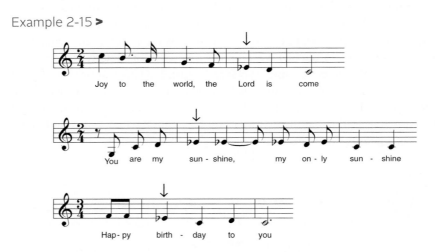

Intro

6

To take this Listening Exercise online and receive feedback, go to CourseMate or the eBook.

Hearing Major and Minor

On your Intro CD, track 6, you will find ten musical excerpts that will help you begin to differentiate major from minor. Pieces in major usually sound bright, cheerful, and sometimes bland, whereas those in minor seem darker, more somber, mysterious, perhaps even exotic. In the blanks below, indicate whether each melody is in major or minor. Five are in major and five in minor.

1. **(0:00) Key:** _____ Musorgsky, "Polish Ox-Cart" from *Pictures at an Exhibition*
2. **(0:28) Key:** _____ Musorgsky, "Great Gate of Kiev" from *Pictures at an Exhibition*
3. **(0:45) Key:** _____ Musorgsky, "Goldenburg and Schmuyle" from *Pictures at an Exhibition*

Finally, a third, special scale sometimes sounds in music: a **chromatic scale,** which makes use of all twelve pitches, equally divided, within the octave. *Chromatic* (from the Greek *chroma,* "color") is a good word for this pattern because the additional five pitches do indeed add color to the music. Unlike the major and minor scales, the chromatic scale is not employed for a complete melody, but only for a moment of twisting intensity.

Example 2-16 ➤

Chromatic scale

I'm   dream - ing   of   a   white   Christ - mas

When listening to any music, we take pleasure, consciously or not, in knowing where we are. Here again the steps of the scale play a crucial role, orienting us during the listening experience. Virtually all the melodies we've heard since birth have been in major or minor, so these two patterns are deeply ingrained. Intuitively, our brain recognizes the mode and hears one pitch as central and the others as gravitating around it. That central, or home, pitch is called the tonic. The **tonic** is the first of the seven pitches of the scale and, consequently, the eighth and last as well. Melodies almost always end on the tonic, as can be seen in the familiar tunes given in Example 2-15, all of which happen to end on the pitch C. The organization of music around a central pitch, the tonic, is called **tonality.** We say that such and such a piece is written in the tonality, and similarly the **key,** of C or of A (musicians use the terms *tonality* and *key* almost interchangeably). Composers—classical composers in particular—like to move temporarily from the home scale and home tonality to another, just for the sake of variety. Such a change is called a **modulation.** In any

∨ Planets rotate around and are pulled toward the sun, just as outlying pitches are pulled toward the tonic pitch.

Courtesy NASA/JPL

musical journey, we enjoy traveling away from our tonic "home," but we experience even greater satisfaction arriving back home. Again, almost all music, pop or classical, ends on the tonic pitch.

 ## Harmony

Western music is exceptional among musical cultures of the world in its emphasis on harmony. Simply said, **harmony** is the sound of one or more pitches that support and enhance a melody. Almost always, the pitches of the melody are higher than those of the accompanying harmony. At the piano, for example, our "higher" right hand usually plays the melody and our left the harmony (see Ex. 2-17). Although a melody can stand by itself, an accompanying harmony adds a richness to it, just as the dimension of depth adds a rich backdrop to a painting.

Example 2-17 ➤

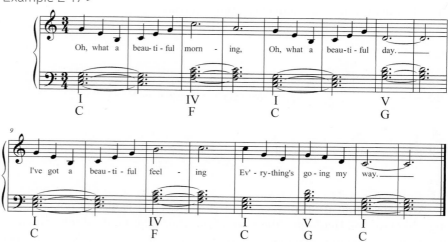

By definition, every harmony must be harmonious. From this truism we can see that there are two meanings of harmony. First, *harmony* means "a general sense that things work or sound well together"; second, *harmony* specifically

➤ Claude Monet, *Waterlily Pond: Pink Harmony* (1900). Monet's painting of this famous bridge at Giverny, France, reveals not only the harmonious qualities of nature but also the painter's ability to harmonize various colors into a blend of pastels.

denotes an exact musical accompaniment, as when we say "the harmony changes here to another chord."

Building Harmony with Chords

Chords are the building blocks of harmony. A **chord** is simply a group of two or more pitches that sound at the same time. The basic chord in Western music is the **triad,** so called because we construct it using three pitches arranged in a very specific way. Let's start with a C major scale beginning with the tonic note C. To form a triad we take one, skip one, take one, skip one, and take one—in other words, we select the pitches C, E, G (skipping D and F) and sound them together.

Watch a video of Craig Wright's Open Yale Course class session 7, "Harmony: Chords and How to Build Them," at CourseMate for this text.

Example 2-18 ➤

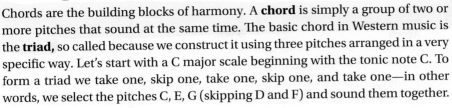

Triads can be constructed in a similar fashion on every pitch of the scale. But given the irregularity of the scale (not all steps are the same distance apart), some triads will be major and others minor. A major triad has its middle pitch a half step closer to its top pitch than to its bottom one; conversely, a minor triad has its middle pitch a half step closer to its bottom pitch than its top one. While this may seem complicated, the difference between a major and a minor triad is immediately apparent. To hear it, go to a piano and build a triad on middle C and then one on the D above. Major triads sound bright; minor ones dark. Example 2-19 shows triads built on every note of the C major scale. Each is assigned a Roman numeral to indicate on which pitch of the scale it is built. These triads provide all the basic chords necessary to harmonize a melody in C major.

Example 2-19 ➤

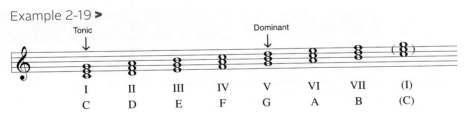

But why do we need more than one chord to harmonize a melody? Why is it necessary to change chords? The answer lies in the fact that the pitches of a melody continually change, sometimes moving through all the notes of a scale. But a single triadic chord can be harmonious, or consonant, only with the three notes of the scale that it contains. In order to keep the harmony consonant with the melody, then, chords must continually change.

As chords change in a purposeful fashion beneath a melody they create what is called a **chord progression.** The individual chords in a chord progression seem to "pull" each other along, one giving way to the next, with all ultimately gravitating toward the powerful tonic triad. The end of a chord progression is called a **cadence.** Usually at a cadence a triad built on degree V of the scale, called the **dominant** triad, will yield to the tonic triad. This is a powerful harmonic move, one conveying a strong feeling of conclusion, as if to say, "THE END."

To sum up: In Western music melodies are supported by an enriching, chordal accompaniment—a harmony. The harmony gains force and enriches the melody as the chords move in a purposeful progression. It is necessary to change chords in a harmony so as to avoid unwanted dissonance.

Consonance and Dissonance

Listen to a podcast on consonance and dissonance at CourseMate for this text.

One reason the human spirit craves music is that this art expresses, through sounds alone, all of the emotional content of life itself. Just as our lives are full of consonance and dissonance, so, too, with music.

You've undoubtedly noticed, when pressing the keys of the piano at one time or another, that some combinations of keys produce a harsh, jarring sound, whereas others are pleasing and harmonious. The former chords are characterized by **dissonance** (pitches sounding momentarily disagreeable and unstable) and the latter by **consonance** (pitches sounding agreeable and stable). Generally speaking, chords that contain pitches that are very close to one another, just a half or a whole step apart, sound dissonant. On the other hand, chords built with the somewhat larger interval of a third (C joined to E, for example) are consonant, as is the case for each triad in Example 2-19. But culture, and even personal taste, plays a role in dissonance perception, too; what might be a hot, spicy, distasteful dissonance to one listener might be a delight to another. While some, for example, find the loud, aggressive distortion of heavy metal bands such as Metallica intolerable, others thrive on it.

But whatever the music, dissonance adds a feeling of tension and anxiety, while consonance produces a sense of calmness and stability. Dissonant chords are unstable, and thus they seek out—want to move to—consonant resolutions. The continual flux between dissonant and consonant chords gives Western music a sense of drama, as a piece moves between moments of tension to longed-for resolution. We humans try not to end the day with an unresolved argument; nor do we end our music with unresolved dissonance.

Listening Cue

Consonance and Dissonance; Cadences

Intro
7

WHAT TO LISTEN FOR: A demonstration of consonance and dissonance, as well as chord progressions

 Listen to streaming music in an Active Listening Guide at CourseMate or in the eBook.

Hearing the Harmony

Listen to a podcast on hearing the bass line at CourseMate for this text.

If you were asked to listen to a new song by your favorite pop artist and sing it back, you'd undoubtedly sing back the melody. The tuneful melody is invariably the line with the highest-sounding pitches. Thus we've become trained, subconsciously, to focus on the top part of any musical texture. To hear and appreciate harmony, however, we've got to "get down" with the bass. Chords are usually built on the bass note, and a change in the bass from one pitch to another may signal a change of chord. The bass is the foundation of the chord and determines where the harmony is going, more so than the higher melody. Some pop artists, such as Paul McCartney and Sting, control both the upper melody and the lower harmony simultaneously. While they sing the tune, they play electric bass, setting the bass pitches for the lead guitar to fill out as accompanying triads.

To begin to hear the harmony beneath a melody, let's start with two alluring pieces, one from the world of popular music, the other a well-known classical favorite. First, a bit of soul music called doo-wop. **Doo-wop** emerged in the 1950s as an outgrowth of the gospel hymns sung in African American churches in urban Detroit, Chicago, Philadelphia, and New York. Often doo-wop was improvised a cappella on the street because it was direct and repetitive—the accompanying singers could easily hear and form a harmony against the melody. And because the lyrics that the accompanying singers sang were often little more than "doo wop, doo wah," the name "doo-wop" stuck to describe these songs. Finally, doo-wop harmony used a short chord progression, mostly commonly a sequence of triads moving I-VI-IV-V-(I) that repeated over and over again (for these four repeating chords, see the Listening Cue below). In music any element (rhythm, melody, or harmony) that continually repeats is called an **ostinato** (from the Italian word meaning "obstinate thing"). In the doo-wop song "Duke of Earl," we hear the bass voice lead, not with "doo, doo, doo," but with "Duke, Duke, Duke," setting the foundation for the chords that soon enter in the other voices. The tempo is moderately fast, and each of the four chords lasts for four beats. Every time the harmony sings the word "Earl," the chords change. The I-VI-IV-V-(I) chord progression lasts for about nine seconds and then repeats over and over again. As you listen to this doo-wop classic, sing along with the bass, no matter what your vocal range. Anyone can hear this harmony change.

Watch a video of Craig Wright's Open Yale Course class session 8, "Bass Patterns: Blues and Rock," at CourseMate for this text.

Listen to a podcast on chord changes at CourseMate for this text.

Listening Cue

Harmony (Chord Changes)

Gene Chandler, "Duke of Earl" (1962)

Intro 8

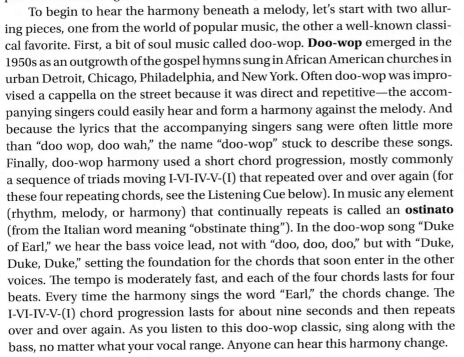

WHAT TO LISTEN FOR: A harmony that repeats as a four-bar ostinato. The bass singer first sets the bass line, and the other singers then add a chordal harmony in support of the melody.

Listen to streaming music in an Active Listening Guide at CourseMate or in the eBook.

Finally, for a similar, but slightly more complex, piece from the classical repertoire, we turn to the famous Pachelbel Canon. (For more on Pachelbel's Canon, see p. 77.) Johann Pachelbel (1653–1706), who lived in Germany and was a mentor to musicians in the Bach family, composed this piece for four musical lines. The top three, here played by violins, are performed as a **canon** (a "round" in which one voice starts out and the others duplicate it exactly, as in "Three Blind Mice"). Below the three-part canon is a harmonic ostinato, this one consisting of eight chords (see Listening Exercise 5). So popular has Pachelbel's harmony become that it has been "borrowed" by The Beatles ("Let It Be"), U2 ("With or Without You"), and Celine Dion (chorus of "To Love You More").

See an amusing rant by comedian Rob Paravonian about the excessive popularity of Pachelbel's famous eight-bar harmony, in the YouTube playlist at CourseMate for this text.

Listening Exercise 5

To take this Listening Exercise online and receive feedback, go to CourseMate or the eBook.

Hearing the Bass Line and Harmony
Johann Pachelbel, Canon in D major (c. 1690)

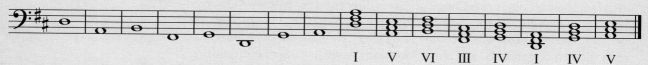

I   V   VI   III   IV   I   IV   V

Focus on the bass and answer the following questions:

1. The bass enters first. At what point does the first violin enter?
   a. 0:00   b. 0:12   c. 0:21

2. Listen again to the beginning. How many pitches do you hear before the violin enters and the bass begins to repeat? In other words, how many pitches are there in the bass pattern?
   a. 4   b. 6   c. 8

3. Are all the pitches within the pattern of the bass held for the same duration?
   a. yes   b. no

4. Do you also hear chords (played on a harpsichord) along with the bass notes?
   a. yes   b. no

5. Therefore, the rate of harmonic change in Pachelbel's Canon is what?
   a. regular   b. irregular

6. Listen now to more of the composition. The bass is highly repetitive as the pattern recurs again and again. Each statement of the pattern lasts approximately how long?
   a. 12 seconds   b. 15 seconds   c. 20 seconds

7. A melody, harmony, or rhythm that repeats again and again in music is called what? (Consult the Glossary for the meanings of all these terms, if you need to.)
   a. pizzicato   b. legato   c. tempo   d. ostinato

8. Now listen up to 1:54 of the recording. Does the bass pattern ever change?
   a. yes   b. no

9. From the beginning of the piece (0:00) to this point (1:54), how many times do you hear the pattern?
   a. 8   b. 10   c. 12   d. 14

10. Listen all the way to the end of the work. Does Pachelbel ever vary his bass and his harmonic pattern?
    a. yes   b. no

chapter **THREE**

Color, Texture, and Form

Listen to a podcast on dynamics at CourseMate for this text.

f rhythm, melody, and harmony are the *what* of music, then color, texture, and form are the *how.* These are the surface details of musical sound that catch our attention and evoke an emotional response, as when a brilliant trumpet suddenly shines forth or a silvery flute floats effortlessly on high. Color, texture, and form, then, refer not so much to the musical idea itself, but instead to the way the musical idea is presented.

Musical **dynamics** (louds and softs) also influence our reaction to music. Heroic themes are usually played loudly and mournful ones quietly, for example, so as to create the desired mood and effect. Because Italian musicians once dominated the Western musical world, most of our musical terminology is drawn from that language. Thus we refer to loud and very loud as *forte* (pronounced FOUR-tay) and *fortissimo,* and soft and softer as *piano* and *pianissimo*. But changes in dynamics need not be sudden and abrupt. They can also be gradual and extend over a long period of time. A gradual increase in the volume of sound is called a **crescendo,** whereas a gradual decrease is called either a **decrescendo** or a **diminuendo.** An impressive crescendo sounds at the beginning of Richard Strauss's *Also sprach Zarathustra* (Intro/2) as the full orchestra enters and gains momentum and force. Spectacular moments like these remind us that in music, as in marketing and communications, the medium (here, powerful dynamics and color) can be the message. When heard as background music for a TV commercial, the viewer is supposed to conclude, "This product *sounds* great!"

 ## Color

Simply stated, **color** in music is the tone quality of any sound produced by a voice or an instrument. **Timbre** (pronounced TAM-ber) is another term for the tone quality of musical sound. We can all hear that a clarinet produces a much different tone quality than does a trombone. Similarly, the voice of pop singer Rihanna has a different timbre than that of opera star Renée Fleming, even when the two produce the same pitch.

The Voice

How many different voices can you recognize? Perhaps as many as a hundred. Each of us has a uniquely constructed set of vocal cords (two folds of mucous membrane within the throat). When we talk or sing, we send air through them, creating vibrations that reach the ear as sounds of a distinctive timbre. We need hear only a few notes of a song to recognize that this is the voice of Elvis, for example, and not that of Bono.

Musical voices are classified by range into four principal parts. The two women's vocal parts are the **soprano** and the **alto,** and the two men's parts the **tenor** and the **bass.** (Men's vocal chords are longer and thicker than women's, and for that reason the sound of the mature male voice is lower.) To hear the sound of a tenor voice, for example, turn to a solo aria from Puccini's *La bohème* (Intro/10). Midway between the soprano and the alto voice is the **mezzo soprano,** and between the tenor and the bass is the **baritone.** To hear the difference between a soprano and a baritone, for example, listen to a duet from Mozart's opera *Don Giovanni* (Intro/14 at 0:00).

Listen to the solo aria streaming in CourseMate Chapter 13.

Listen to the Mozart duet streaming in CourseMate Chapter 9.

Musical Instruments

Have you ever wondered why a flute or violin sounds the way it does—why it has a distinctive timbre? In brief, instruments are constructed in different shapes with different materials of different densities. Even when they sound the same pitch, they emit slightly different vibrations, which our brain perceives as distinctive musical colors.

Musical instruments come in groups, or families—instruments of one general type having the same general shape and made of the same materials. The Western **symphony orchestra** traditionally includes four such groups—the four "food groups" of classical music, so to speak: strings, woodwinds, brasses, and percussion. In addition, there is a fifth group of instruments, the keyboard instruments (piano, organ, and harpsichord), instruments not normally part of the symphony orchestra.

STRINGS

If you travel to Beijing to hear a traditional Chinese orchestra, most of the instruments (erhu, pipa, and qinqin, for example) will be string instruments. If you attend the Bonnaroo Arts & Music Festival in Manchester, Tennessee, the rock bands there play electric bass and a variety of guitars—all string instruments. Visit the Country Music Hall of Fame in nearby Nashville, Tennessee, and you'll likely hear a fiddle and perhaps a mandolin added to the guitar ensemble. Watch the London Symphony Orchestra on stage at the Barbican Centre, and you'll notice the majority of its performers playing, again, string instruments. In sum, string instruments, whether plucked or bowed, dominate musical ensembles around the world.

VIOLIN GROUP

The violin group—violins, violas, cellos, and double basses—constitutes the core of the Western symphony orchestra. A large orchestra can easily include as many as a hundred members, at least sixty of whom play one of these four instruments.

The **violin** (Fig. 3-1) is chief among the string instruments. It is also the smallest—it has the shortest strings and therefore produces the highest pitch. The tune usually sounds in the highest part of the musical texture, so in an orchestra the violin generally plays the melody. Violins are often divided into groups known as firsts and seconds. The seconds play a part slightly lower in pitch and subordinate in function to the firsts. (For the sound of the violin, listen to (Intro)/15 at 0:00.)

The **viola** (Fig. 3-1 left) is about six inches longer than the violin, and it produces a somewhat lower sound. If the violin is the string counterpart of the soprano voice, then the viola has its parallel in the alto voice. Its tone is darker, richer, and more somber than that of the brilliant violin. (For the sound of the viola, listen to (Intro)/15 at 1:37.)

You can easily spot the **cello** (Fig. 3-1 right) in the orchestra because the player sits with the instrument placed between his or her legs. The pitch of the cello is

FIGURE 3-1
This photo of the American group The Brentano String Quartet shows the relative size of the violin (center), viola (left), and cello (right).

Christian Steiner/ Courtesy Brentano String Quartet

FIGURE 3-2
Double bass player, the late Israel "Cachao" Lopez

FIGURE 3-3
The harp's unique special effect is its glissando, a rapid run up and down the strings that seems to fill the atmosphere with energized sound.

well below that of the viola. It can provide a low bass sound as well as a lyrical melody. When played in its middle range by a skilled performer, the cello can produce an indescribably rich, expressive tone. (For the sound of the cello, listen to (Intro)/15 at 2:10.)

The **double bass** (Fig. 3-2) gives weight and power to the bass line in the orchestra. Because at first it merely doubled the notes of the cello an octave below, it was called the double bass. As you can see, the double bass is the largest, and hence lowest-sounding, of the string instruments. Its job in the orchestra, and even in jazz bands, is to help set a solid base/bass for the musical harmony. (For the sound of the double bass, listen to (Intro)/15 at 2:50.)

The members of the violin group all generate pitches in the same way: a bow is drawn across a tight string. This produces the familiar penetrating string sound. In addition, a number of other effects can be created by using different playing techniques.

- **Vibrato:** By shaking the left hand as it stops the string, the performer can produce a sort of controlled "wobble" in the pitch. This adds richness to the tone of the string because, in fact, it creates a blend of two or more pitches. (For an example of a violin playing without vibrato and then with vibrato, listen to (Intro)/15 at 0:31 and 0:51.)
- **Pizzicato:** Instead of bowing the strings, the performer plucks them. With this technique, the resulting sound has a sharp attack, but it dies away quickly. (For an example of pizzicato, listen to (Intro)/15 at 1:13.)
- **Tremolo:** The performer creates a musical "tremor" by rapidly repeating the same pitch with quick up-and-down strokes of the bow. Tremolo creates a feeling of heightened tension and excitement when played loudly, and a velvety, shimmering backdrop when performed quietly. (For an example of tremolo, listen to (Intro)/15 at 1:24.)
- **Trill:** The performer rapidly alternates between two distinctly separate but neighboring pitches. Most instruments, not just the strings, can play trills. (For an example of a trill, listen to (Intro)/15 at 1:30.)

THE HARP

Although originally a folk instrument, the **harp** (Fig. 3-3) is sometimes added to the modern symphony orchestra. Its role is to lend its distinctive color to the orchestral sound and sometimes to create special effects, the most striking of which is a rapid run up or down the strings called a **glissando.** When the notes of a triad are played in quick succession, up or down, an **arpeggio** results, a term derived from the Italian word for harp (*arpa*). (For the sound of the harp and an example of a glissando, listen to (Intro)/15 at 3:35 and 3:44.)

WOODWINDS

The name "woodwind" was originally given to this family of instruments because they emit sound when air is blown through a wooden tube or pipe. Today, however, some of these "wooden" instruments are made entirely of metal. Flutes, for example, are constructed of silver, and sometimes of gold or even platinum. As with the violin group, there are four principal woodwind instruments in every modern symphony orchestra: flute, oboe, clarinet, and

Instruments of the Orchestra: Strings

0:00	Violin plays major scale	1:49	Viola solo: Haydn
0:13	Violin solo: Tchaikovsky	2:10	Cello plays major scale
0:31	Violin plays without vibrato: Haydn	2:30	Cello solo: Haydn
0: 51	Violin plays vibrato: Haydn	2:50	Double bass plays major scale
1:13	Violin plays pizzicato	3:13	Double bass solo: Haydn
1:24	Violin plays tremolo	3:35	Harp plays arpeggio
1:30	Violin plays trill	3:44	Harp solo: Tchaikovsky
1:37	Viola plays major scale		

 Listen to streaming music in an Active Listening Guide at CourseMate or in the eBook.

---

bassoon (Fig. 3-4). In addition, each of these has a close relative that is larger or smaller in size and that possesses a somewhat different timbre and range. The larger the instrument or length of pipe, of course, the lower the sound.

The lovely, silvery tone of the **flute** is probably familiar to you. The instrument can be rich in the lower register and light and airy at the top. It is especially agile, capable of playing tones rapidly and moving quickly from one range to another. (For the sound of the flute, listen to Intro/16 at 0:00.) The smaller cousin of the flute is the **piccolo.** (*Piccolo* comes from the Italian *flauto piccolo,* meaning "little flute.") It can produce higher notes than any other orchestral instrument. And though the piccolo is very small, its sound is so piercing that it can always be heard, even when the full orchestra is playing loudly. (For the sound of the piccolo, listen to Intro/16 at 0:38.)

The **clarinet** produces sound when the player blows air under a single reed fitted to the mouthpiece. The tone of the clarinet is an open, hollow sound. It can be mellow in its low notes but shrill in its high ones. It also has the capacity to slide or glide smoothly between pitches, which allows for a highly expressive style of playing. (For the sound of the clarinet, listen to Intro/16 at 0:54.) A lower, larger version of the clarinet is the bass clarinet.

The **oboe** is equipped with a double reed—two reeds tied together with an air space in between. When the player blows air between them and into the instrument through the double reed, the vibrations create a nasal, slightly exotic sound. It is invariably the oboe that gives the

FIGURE 3-4
(from left to right) A flute, two clarinets, an oboe, and a bassoon. The flute, clarinet, and oboe are about the same length. The bassoon is nearly twice their size.

© Conn-Selmer, Inc.

See a video of all the orchestral instruments, in Benjamin Britten's *Young Person's Guide to the Orchestra,* as well as keyboard videos, at CourseMate for this text.

pitch at the beginning of a symphony concert. Not only was the oboe the first non-string instrument to be added to the orchestra, but it is a difficult instrument to tune (regulate the pitch). Thus, it's better to have the other instruments tune to it than to try to have it adjust to them. (For the sound of the oboe, listen to ⓘ/16 at 1:24.) Related to the oboe is the **English horn.** Unfortunately, it is wrongly named, for the English horn is neither English nor a horn. It is simply a larger (hence lower-sounding) version of the oboe that originated on the continent of Europe.

The **bassoon** functions among the woodwinds much as the cello does among the strings: it adds weight to the lowest sound or acts as a soloist. When playing moderately fast or rapid passages as a solo instrument, it has a dry, almost comic tone. (For the sound of the bassoon, listen to ⓘ/16 at 1:54.) There is also a double bassoon, called the **contrabassoon,** which can play notes lower than any other orchestral instrument.

Listening Cue

Instruments of the Orchestra: Woodwinds

Intro
16

0:00	Flute plays major scale		1:02	Clarinet solo: Berlioz
0:11	Flute solo: Debussy		1:24	Oboe plays major scale
0:38	Piccolo plays major scale		1:33	Oboe solo: Tchaikovsky
0:47	Piccolo solo: Tchaikovsky		1:54	Bassoon plays major scale
0:54	Clarinet plays major scale		2:05	Bassoon solo: Stravinsky

 Listen to streaming music in an Active Listening Guide at CourseMate or in the eBook.

FIGURE 3-5
Members of the Canadian Brass, with the French horn player at the left and the tuba player at the right

Photograph by Martin Reichenthal courtesy of Opening Day Entertainment for the Canadian Brass

BRASSES

Like the woodwind and string groups of the orchestra, the brass family consists of four primary instruments: trumpet, trombone, French horn, and tuba (Fig. 3-5). Brass players use no reeds, but instead blow into their instruments through a cup-shaped **mouthpiece** (Fig. 3-6). By adjusting valves or moving a slide, the performer can make the length of pipe on the instrument longer or shorter, and hence the pitch lower or higher.

Everyone has heard the high, bright, cutting sound of the **trumpet.** Whether in a football stadium or an orchestral hall, the trumpet is an excellent solo instrument because of its agility and penetrating tone. Sometimes the trumpeter is required to play with a **mute** (a plug placed in the bell of the instrument) to lessen its piercing sound. (For the sound of the trumpet, listen to ⓘ/17 at 0:00.)

Although distantly related to the trumpet, the **trombone** (Italian for "large trumpet") plays in the middle range of the brass family. Its sound is large and full. Most important, the trombone is the only brass instrument to generate sounds by moving a slide in and out to produce higher or lower pitches. Needless to say, the trombone can easily slide from pitch to pitch, sometimes for comical effect. (For the sound of the trombone, listen to ⓘ/17 at 0:35.)

The **French horn** (sometimes just called "horn") was the first brass instrument to join the orchestra, back in the late seventeenth century. Because the French horn, like the trombone, sounds in the middle range of the brasses, these two instruments are often almost impossible to distinguish. The French horn, however, has a slightly mellower, more "veiled" sound than does the clearer, "in your face" trombone. (For the sound of the French horn, listen to ⓘ/17 at 0:59.)

The **tuba** is the largest and lowest-sounding of the brass instruments. It produces a full, though sometimes muffled, tone in its lowest notes. Like the double bass of the violin group, the tuba is most often used to set a base, or foundation, for the melody. (For the sound of the tuba, listen to ⓘ/17 at 1:39.)

© Chris Stock/Lebrecht Music & Arts

FIGURE 3-6
Three mouthpieces for brass instruments

Listening Cue

Instruments of the Orchestra: Brasses

0:00	Trumpet plays major scale	0:5	French horn plays major scale
0:09	Trumpet solo: Mouret	1:17	French horn solo: Copland
0:22	Trumpet solo with mute: Mouret	1:39	Tuba plays major scale
0:35	Trombone plays major scale	2:00	Tuba solo: Copland
0:45	Trombone solo: Copland		

Intro
17

🔊)) Listen to streaming music in an Active Listening Guide at CourseMate or in the eBook.

PERCUSSION

Want to make your own percussion instrument? Just find a metal trash can and strike its side with your hand. Percussion instruments are simply resonating objects that sound when hit or scraped with an implement in one fashion or another. Some percussion instruments, like the timpani (kettledrums), produce a specific pitch, while others generate sound that, while rhythmically precise, has no recognizable musical pitch. It is the job of the percussion instruments to sharpen the rhythmic contour of the music. They can also add density to the sounds of other instruments and, when played loudly, can heighten the sense of climax in a piece.

The **timpani** (Fig. 3-7) is the percussion instrument most often heard in classical music. Whether struck in single, detached strokes or hit rapidly to

FIGURE 3-7
Tympanist Jonathan Haas of the American Symphony Orchestra

© Tim Wimborne/Reuters/CORBIS

Instruments of the Orchestra: Percussion

0:00	Timpani	0:19	Bass drum
0:11	Snare drum	0:31	Cymbal

Intro
18

🔊)) Listen to streaming music in an Active Listening Guide at CourseMate or in the eBook.

Listen to a podcast on identifying the different instruments at CourseMate for this text.

produce a thunderlike roll, the function of the timpani is to add depth, tension, and drama to the music. Timpani usually come in pairs, one instrument tuned to the tonic and the other to the dominant. Playing only these pitches, the timpani feature prominently at the beginning of Strauss's *Also sprach Zarathustra* (Intro /2 at 0:26).

The rat-a-tat-tat of the **snare drum,** the dull thud of the **bass drum,** and the crashing ring of the **cymbals** are sounds well known from marching bands and jazz ensembles, as well as the classical orchestra. None of them produces a specific musical tone. (To hear all three in a row, listen to Intro /18 at 0:11.)

KEYBOARD INSTRUMENTS

Keyboard instruments, which are unique to Western music, boast highly intricate mechanisms. The **pipe organ** (Fig. 3-8), the most complex of all musical instruments, traces its origins back to ancient Greece. When the player depresses a key, air rushes into a pipe, thereby generating sound. The pipes are arranged in separate groups, each producing a full range of musical pitches with one particular timbre (the sound of the trumpet, for example). When the organist wants to add a distinctive musical color to a piece, he or she simply pulls a knob, called a **stop.** The most colorful, forceful sound occurs when all the stops have been activated (thus the expression "pulling out all the stops"). The several keyboards of the organ make it possible to play several colorful lines at once, each with its own timbre. There is even a keyboard for the feet to play. The largest fully functioning pipe organ in the world is in the Cadet Chapel of the U.S. Military Academy at West Point, New York. It has 270 stops and 18,408 pipes. (To hear an organ, go to ① /11 at 0:00.)

The **harpsichord** (Fig. 3-9) appeared in northern Italy as early as 1400 but reached its heyday during the Baroque era (1600–1750). When a key is depressed, it drives a lever upward that in turn forces a pick to pluck a string, thereby creating a bright, jangling sound. The harpsichord has one important shortcoming, however: the lever mechanism does not allow the performer to control the force with which the string is plucked. Each string always sounds at the same volume, no matter how hard the player strikes the key. (To hear a harpsichord, go to Intro /9 at 0:00.)

FIGURE 3-8
A three-manual (keyboard) pipe organ with only small pipes visible. Notice the stops (small circular objects on either side of the manual keyboards) and the pedal keyboard below.

© John Haskey

FIGURE 3-9
A two-manual harpsichord built by Pascal Taskin (Paris, 1770), preserved in the Yale University Collection of Musical Instruments, New Haven, Connecticut

FIGURE 3-10
Pianist Lang Lang

The **piano** (Fig. 3-10) was invented in Italy around 1700, in part to overcome the sound-producing limitations of the harpsichord. The strings of a piano are not plucked; they are hit by soft hammers. A lever mechanism makes it possible for the player to regulate how hard each string is struck. Touch lightly and a soft sound results; bang hard and you hear a loud one. Thus the original piano was called the *pianoforte,* the "soft-loud." During the lifetime of Mozart (1756–1791), the piano replaced the harpsichord as the favorite domestic musical instrument. By the nineteenth century every aspiring household had to have a piano, whether as an instrument for real musical enjoyment or as a symbol of affluence.

The Symphony Orchestra

The modern Western symphony orchestra is one of the largest and certainly the most colorful of all musical ensembles. When at full strength, the symphony orchestra can include upward of one hundred performers and nearly thirty different instruments, from the high, piping piccolo down to the rumbling contrabassoon. A typical seating plan for an orchestra is given in Figure 3-11. To achieve the best balance of sound, strings are placed toward the front, and the more powerful brasses at the back.

When it first originated in the seventeenth century, the orchestra had no separate conductor: The group was small enough for the players to play on their own. But around the time of Beethoven (1770–1827), when the orchestra was already two hundred years old and had expanded to include some sixty players, it became necessary to have someone stand before it and direct. Indeed, the **conductor** functions something like a musical traffic cop: he or she makes sure that the cellos don't overshadow the violins and that the oboe yields to

View a video demonstration of the organ, harpsichord, and piano at CourseMate.

Watch a video of Craig Wright's Open Yale Course class session 12, "Guest Conductor: Saybrook Youth Orchestra," at CourseMate for this text.

FIGURE 3-11
Seating plan of a symphony orchestra

© Cengage Learning

the clarinet at the proper moment so the melody can be heard. The conductor reads from an **orchestral score** (a composite of all the parts) and must be able to immediately pick out any incorrectly played pitches and rhythms. To do this, he or she must have an excellent musical ear.

Listening Cue

Hearing the Instruments of the Orchestra: Identifying a Single Instrument

WHAT TO LISTEN FOR: Practice identifying a single solo instrument.

🔊 Take online Listening Exercise 6 at CourseMate or in the eBook.

Listening Cue

Hearing the Instruments of the Orchestra: Identifying Two Instruments

WHAT TO LISTEN FOR: Practice identifying two instruments playing at once, and which one is playing in a higher range.

🔊 Take online Listening Exercise 7 at CourseMate or in the eBook.

Hearing the Instruments of the Orchestra: Identifying Three Instruments

WHAT TO LISTEN FOR: Practice identifying three instruments.

 Take online Listening Exercise 8 at CourseMate or in the eBook.

Texture

When a painter or weaver arranges material on a canvas or loom, he or she creates a texture: **texture** is the density and arrangement of artistic elements. Look at Vincent Van Gogh's *Branch of an Almond Tree in Blossom* (1890), shown on this chapter's opening page. Here the painter has used lines and spaces to create a texture heavy at the bottom but light at the top, projecting an image that is well grounded but airy. So, too, a composer creates effects with musical lines—also called parts or voices, even though they might not be sung. There are three primary textures in music, depending on the number of voices involved: monophonic, homophonic, and polyphonic.

Monophony is the easiest texture to hear. As its name meaning "one sounding" indicates, **monophony** is a single line of music, with no harmony. When you sing by yourself, or play the flute or trumpet, for example, you are creating monophonic music. When a group of men (or women) sings the same pitches together, they are singing in **unison.** Unison singing is monophonic singing. Even when men and women sing together, doubling pitches at the octave, the texture is still monophonic. When we sing "Happy Birthday" with our friends at a party, for example, we are singing in monophony. Monophonic texture is the sparsest of all musical textures. Beethoven uses it for the famous duh-duh-duh-DUHHH opening of his Symphony No. 5 (Intro/1 at 0:00) to create a lean, sinewy effect.

Homophony means "same sounding." In this texture the voices, or lines, all move together to new pitches at roughly the same time. The most common type of homophonic texture is tune plus chordal accompaniment. Notice in Example 3-1 how the melody, which by itself would be monophonic, now joins with vertical blocks of chords to create homophonic texture. Holiday carols, hymns, folksongs, and almost all pop songs have this sort of tune-plus-chordal-accompaniment texture when sung with harmony. Can you hear in your mind's ear a band playing "The Star-Spangled Banner"? That's homophonic texture.

Listen to a podcast on distinguishing the textures at CourseMate for this text.

Example 3-1 Homophony ➤

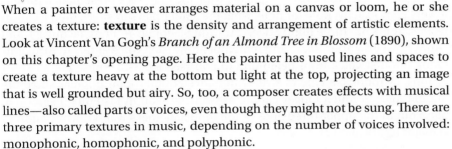

As we might suppose from its name "many sounding," **polyphony** requires two or more lines in the musical fabric. In addition, the term *polyphonic* implies that each of the lines will be free and independent, often entering at different times. Thus polyphonic texture has a strong linear (horizontal) thrust, whereas in homophonic texture the fabric is structured more vertically as blocks of accompanying chords (compare the arrows in Ex. 3-1 and Ex. 3-2). In polyphonic texture the voices are of equal importance, moving against one another to create what is called **counterpoint,** the harmonious opposition of two or more independent musical lines. (Musicians use the terms *polyphony* and *counterpoint* interchangeably.) Finally, there are two types of counterpoint: free and imitative. In free counterpoint the voices are highly independent and go their separate ways; much jazz improvisation is done in free counterpoint. In imitative counterpoint, on the other hand, a leading voice begins, followed by one or more other voices that duplicate what the first voice presented. If the followers copy exactly, note for note, what the leader plays or sings, then a **canon** results. Think of "Three Blind Mice," "Are You Sleeping?" ("Frère Jacques"), and "Row, Row, Row Your Boat," and remember how each voice enters in turn, imitating the first voice from beginning to end (see Ex. 3-2). These are all short canons, or rounds, a type of strictly imitative counterpoint popular since the Middle Ages. A much longer canon, as we have seen in Listening Exercise 5, plays out in the upper three lines of Johann Pachelbel's well-known Canon in D major (Intro/9 at 0:12).

Listen to Pachelbel's Canon streaming in CourseMate Chapter 13.

Example 3-2 Polyphony >

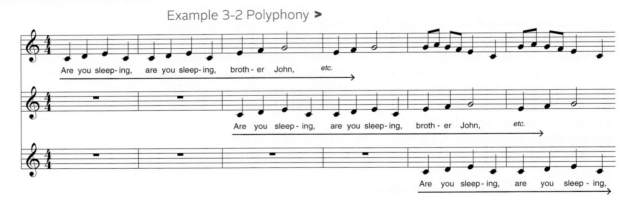

Of course, composers are not limited to just one of these three musical textures in a given piece—they can move from one to another, as George Frideric Handel does brilliantly in the justly famous "Hallelujah" chorus from his oratorio *Messiah*.

Listening Cue

George Frideric Handel, *Messiah,* **"Hallelujah" chorus (1741)**

WHAT TO LISTEN FOR: A skillful manipulation of musical texture to achieve variety and generate excitement

19

 Listen to streaming music in an Active Listening Guide at CourseMate or in the eBook.

To take this Listening Exercise online and receive feedback, go to CourseMate or the eBook..

Hearing Musical Textures

On your Intro CD, track 20, you have ten excerpts that exemplify the three basic textures of music: monophonic, homophonic, and polyphonic. Identify the texture of each of the excerpts by writing an M, H, or P in the appropriate blank.

1. (0:00) _____ Bach, Contrapunctus IX from *The Art of Fugue*

2. (0:44) _____ Beethoven, Symphony No. 5, 1st movement

3. (0:52) _____ Musorgsky, "Promenade" from *Pictures at an Exhibition*

4. (1:02) _____ Musorgsky, "Promenade" from *Pictures at an Exhibition*

5. (1:12) _____ Bach, Organ Fugue in G minor

6. (2:03) _____ Debussy, *Prelude to The Afternoon of a Faun*

7. (2:22) _____ Josquin Desprez, *Ave Maria*

8. (2:48) _____ Dvořák, Symphony No. 9, "From the New World," 2nd movement

9. (3:17) _____ Louis Armstrong, "Willie the Weeper"

10. (3:41) _____ Copland, "A Gift to Be Simple" from *Appalachian Spring*

 # Form

Form in music is the arrangement of musical events. In architecture, sculpture, and painting, objects are situated in physical space to create a pleasing design. Similarly, in music a composer places important sonic events in an order that creates a compelling pattern as sounds pass by in time.

To create form in music, a composer employs one of four processes: statement, repetition, contrast, and variation. A **statement,** of course, is the presentation of an important musical idea. **Repetition** validates the statement by reiterating it. Nothing would be more bewildering for a listener than a steady stream of ever-new music. How would we make sense of it? Recurring musical ideas function as formal markers; each return is an important musical event—and a reassuring return to stability.

Contrast, on the other hand, takes us away from the familiar and into the unknown. Contrasting melodies, rhythms, textures, and moods can be used to provide variety and even to create conflict. In music, as in life, we need novelty and excitement; contrast invigorates us, making the eventual return to familiar ideas all the more satisfying.

Variation stands midway between repetition and contrast. The original melody returns but is altered in some way. For example, the tune may now be more complex, or new instruments may be added against it to create counterpoint. The listener has the satisfaction of hearing the familiar melody, yet is challenged to recognize how it has been changed.

Needless to say, memory plays an important role in hearing musical form. We live forward but we understand backward. Whether in history or in music, our memory puts the pieces together to help us understand relationships among them. To simplify this pattern processing, musicians have developed a system to visualize forms by using letters to represent musical units. The first statement of a musical idea is designated **A**. Subsequent contrasting sections are labeled **B, C, D,** and so on. If the first or any other musical unit returns in varied form, then that variation is indicated by a superscript number—A^1 and B^2, for example. Subdivisions of each large musical unit are shown by lowercase letters **a, b**, and so on. How this works will become clear in the examples used throughout this book.

STROPHIC FORM

This is the most familiar of all musical forms because our hymns, carols, folksongs, and pop tunes invariably make use of it. In **strophic form** the composer sets the words of the first poetic stanza (strophe) and then uses the same entire melody for all subsequent stanzas. Moreover, in many pop songs each strophe begins with a verse of text and ends with a **chorus**—a textual refrain that repeats. In Jay-Z and Alicia Keys's "Empire State of Mind," he raps the verse, and she then sings the refrain. The strophe (verse and chorus) is then repeated two more times, with the music always the same for each strophe. But we can't give the lyrics of "Empire State of Mind" owing to "explicit content," so let's move back to the 1860s to a hymn text that served as a rallying point for the Union (Northern) forces during the American Civil War: "The Battle Hymn of the Republic," text by Julia Ward Howe, 1862.

Strophe 1
(Verse) Mine eyes have seen the glory of the coming of the Lord:
He is trampling out the vintage where the grapes of wrath are stored;
He hath loosed the fateful lightning of His terrible swift sword:
His truth is marching on.

(Chorus) Glory, glory, hallelujah! Glory, glory, hallelujah!
Glory, glory, hallelujah! His truth is marching on.

There are many YouTube clips with different arrangements and video backdrops for the hymn. Explore and find your favorite.

Now listen to the first two strophes of the equally well known *Wiegenlied (Lullaby)* of Johannes Brahms (see Listening Cue on next page). Each strophe, again, is sung to the same music, but here there is no chorus.

A slightly varied version of strophic form, modified strophic form, can be heard in Clara Schumann's "Liebst du um Schönheit" ("If You Love for Beauty"); Intro/22 and Chapter 11.

Johannes Brahms, *Wegenlied (Lullaby;* **1868)**

Intro
21

0:00	Gut' Abend, gut Nacht,	Good evening, good night
	Mit Rosen bedacht,	Covered with roses,
	Mit Näglein besteckt	Adorned with carnations,
	Schlüpf unter die Deck':	Slip under the covers.
	Morgen früh, wenn Gott will,	Tomorrow early, if God so wills,
	Wirst du wieder geweckt.	You will awake again.
0:48	Gut' Abend, gut Nacht,	Good evening, good night
	Von Englein bewacht,	Watched over by angels,
	Die zeigen im Traum	Who in dreams show
	Dir Christkindleins Baum:	You the Christ child's tree.
	Schlaf nun selig und süss,	Now sleep blissful and sweetly,
	Schau im Traum's Paradies.	Behold Paradise in your dreams.

WHAT TO LISTEN FOR: An exact repeat of the music of strophe 1 for strophe 2

 Listen to streaming music in an Active Listening Guide at CourseMate or in the eBook.

THEME AND VARIATIONS

The working of **theme and variations** form is obvious: one musical idea continually returns but is varied in some fashion, by a change in the melody, harmony, texture, or timbre. In classical music, the more variations the composer writes, the more obscure the theme becomes; the listener is increasingly challenged to hear the new as an outgrowth of the old. Theme and variations form can be visualized in the following scheme:

Statement of theme	Variation 1	Variation 2	Variation 3	Variation 4
A	**A^1**	**A^2**	**A^3**	**A^4**

When Mozart was a young man, he lived briefly in Paris, where he heard the French folksong "Ah, vous dirai-je Maman." We know it today as "Twinkle, Twinkle, Little Star." Upon this charming tune (**A**) he later composed a set of variations for piano (discussed in full on pp. 117–119).

Wolfgang Amadeus Mozart, Variations on "Twinkle, Twinkle, Little Star" (c. 1781)

Intro
23

WHAT TO LISTEN FOR: How the theme is varied within each new variation. The familiar theme begins at 0:00 and the variations appear at intervals of thirty seconds thereafter.

 Listen to streaming music in an Active Listening Guide at CourseMate or in the eBook.

> The Opera House in the harbor of Sydney, Australia. Here we see a theme (a rising, pointed arch) that displays a new variation each time it appears in a different position.

my-summit/shutterstock.com

BINARY FORM

As the name indicates, **binary form** consists of two contrasting units, **A** and **B**. In length and general shape, **A** and **B** are constructed so as to balance and complement each other. Variety is usually introduced in **B** by means of a dissimilar mood, key, or melody. Sometimes in binary form, both **A** and **B** are immediately repeated, note for note. Musicians indicate exact repeats by means of the following sign: ‖: :‖. Thus, when binary form appears as ‖: A :‖ ‖: B :‖ it is performed **AABB.** Joseph Haydn created a perfect example of binary form in music for the second movement of his Symphony No. 94, and then wrote a set of variations upon this theme (discussed in full on pp. 119-121).

Listening Cue

Joseph Haydn, Symphony No. 94, the "Surprise" (1792)

Intro
24

Second movement, *Andante* (moving)

WHAT TO LISTEN FOR: A charming **A** theme (repeated at 0:17) followed by a complementary **B** (repeated at 0:50)

 Listen to streaming music in an Active Listening Guide at CourseMate or in the eBook.

Digital Image © 2009 Museum Associates/LACMA/ Art Resource, NY

© Richard Klune/CORBIS

> (left) The essence of binary form, or **AB** form, can be seen in this Japanese wood carving. Here the two figures are distinctly different, yet mutually harmonious. (right) Ternary form, or **ABA** form, can clearly be seen in the architecture of the cathedral of Salzburg, Austria, where Mozart and his father frequently performed.

TERNARY FORM

If the most prevalent form in pop songs is strophic form, in classical music it is ternary form; the musical journey home-away-home (**ABA**) has satisfied composers and listeners for centuries. In the "Dance of the Reed Pipes" from Peter Tchaikovsky's famous ballet *The Nutcracker,* the **A** section is bright and cheery because it makes use of the major mode as well as silvery flutes. However, **B** is dark and low, even ominous, owing to the minor mode and the insistent ostinato (repeated pattern) in the bass.

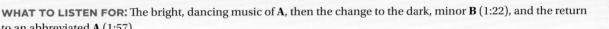

Listening Cue

Peter Tchaikovsky, *The Nutcracker,* "Dance of the Reed Pipes" (1891)

Intro
25

WHAT TO LISTEN FOR: The bright, dancing music of **A**, then the change to the dark, minor **B** (1:22), and the return to an abbreviated **A** (1:57)

🔊 Listen to streaming music in an Active Listening Guide at CourseMate or in the eBook.

RONDO FORM

Rondo form involves a simple principle: a refrain (**A**) alternates with contrasting music. Usually in a rondo, there are at least two contrasting sections (**B** and **C**). Perhaps because of its simple but pleasing design, rondo form has been favored by musicians of every age—medieval monks, classical symphonists such as Mozart and Haydn, and even contemporary pop artists like Sting (see p. 122). Although the principle of a recurring refrain is a constant, composers have written rondos in several different formal patterns, as seen below. The hallmark of each, however, is a refrain (**A**).

ABACA   **ABACABA**   **ABACADA**

◄ The chateau of Chambord, France, has a formal design equivalent to **ABACABA** structure, a pattern often encountered in music in rondo form.

© Charles & Josette Lenars/CORBIS

A B A C A B A

You may already be familiar with a rondo composed by Jean-Joseph Mouret (1682–1738), made famous as the theme music for *Masterpiece Theatre* (now *Masterpiece*), America's longest-running prime-time drama series, on PBS. It is discussed in full on pages 76–77.

Listening Cue

Jean-Joseph Mouret, Rondeau from *Suite de symphonies* (1729)

Intro
26

WHAT TO LISTEN FOR: The regular appearance of theme **A** (0:00, 0:37, and 1:22) played by a brilliant trumpet

 Listen to streaming music in an Active Listening Guide at CourseMate or in the eBook.

Music in the Middle Ages and Renaissance

The term *Middle Ages* is a catch-all phrase that refers to the thousand years of history between the fall of the Roman Empire (476) and the dawn of the Age of Discovery (mid-1400s, culminating in the voyages of Christopher Columbus). It was a period of monks and nuns, of knightly chivalry and brutal warfare, of sublime spirituality and deadly plagues, and of soaring cathedrals amidst abject poverty. Two institutions vied for political control: the Church and the court. From our modern perspective, the medieval period appears as a vast chronological expanse dotted by outposts of dazzling architecture, stunning stained glass, and equally compelling poetry and music.

For the harried inhabitant of the twenty-first century, it is difficult to imagine a life revolving around prayer. But in the Middle Ages a large portion of the population (monks and nuns) defined their lives with two simple tasks: work and prayer. They worked to feed their bodies and they prayed to save their souls. Indeed, the Middle Ages was a profoundly spiritual period, because life on earth was uncertain and often brief. If you got an infection, you likely died (there were no antibiotics); if insects ate your crops, you likely starved (no insecticides); if your village caught fire, it likely burned to the ground (no fire trucks). With seemingly little control over their own destiny, people turned to an outside agent (God) for help. And they did so mainly through organized religion—the Roman Catholic Church, the dominant spiritual and administrative force in medieval Europe.

Music in the Monastery

Watch a video of Craig Wright's Open Yale Course class session 15, "Gregorian Chant and Music in the Sistine Chapel," at CourseMate for this text.

Most medieval society was overwhelmingly agricultural, and thus religion was centered in rural monasteries (for monks) and convents (for nuns). The clergy worked in the fields and prayed in the church. Religious services usually began well before dawn and continued at various other times throughout the day in an almost unvarying cycle. The most important service was **Mass,** a symbolic reenactment of the Last Supper, celebrated at about nine o'clock in the morning. The music for these services was what we today call **Gregorian chant** (or **plainsong**)—a unique collection of thousands of religious songs, sung in Latin, that carry the theological message of the Church. Although this music bears the name of Pope Gregory the Great (c. 540–604), this pontiff actually wrote very little of it. Instead, Gregorian chant was created by many people, male and female, before, during, and after Gregory's reign.

Gregorian chant is like no other music. It has a timeless, otherworldly quality that no doubt arises from its lack of meter and regular rhythms. True, some notes are longer or shorter than others, but pitches do not recur in obvious patterns that would allow us to clap our hands or tap our feet. Because all voices sing in unison, Gregorian chant is monophonic music. There is no instrumental accompaniment, nor, as a rule, are men's and women's voices mixed. For all these reasons, Gregorian chant has a consistently uniform, monochromatic sound, one far more conducive to meditation than to dancing. The faithful are not to hear the music per se, but rather to use the music as a vehicle to enter a spiritual state, to reach communion with God.

The Gregorian Chant of Hildegard of Bingen (1098–1179)

One of the most remarkable contributors to the repertoire of Gregorian chant was Hildegard of Bingen (1098–1179), from whose fertile pen we received seventy-seven chants. Hildegard was the tenth child of noble parents who gave her to the Church as a tithe (a donation of a tenth of one's worldly goods). She was educated by Benedictine nuns and then, at the age of fifty-two, founded her own convent near the small town of Bingen, Germany, on the west bank of the Rhine. Over time, Hildegard manifested her extraordinary intellect and imagination as a playwright, poet, musician, naturalist, pharmacologist, and visionary. Ironically, then, the first "Renaissance man" was really a medieval woman: Hildegard of Bingen.

Hildegard's *O rubor sanguinis (O Redness of Blood)* possesses many qualities typical of her chants, and of chant generally (Ex. 4-1, p. 50). First, it sets a starkly vivid text, which Hildegard herself created. Honoring St. Ursula and a group of 11,000 Christian women believed slain by the Huns in the fourth or fifth century, the poem envisages martyred blood streaming in the heavens and virginal flowers unsullied by serpentine evil. Each phrase of text receives its own phrase of music, but the phrases are not of the same length. Occasionally a passage of **syllabic singing** (only one or two notes for each syllable of text; see "quod divinitas tetigit") will give way to one of **melismatic singing** (many notes sung to just one syllable; see the twenty-nine notes for "num" of "numquam"). Even today some pop singers such as Christina Aguilera, Mariah Carey, and Beyoncé are referred to as "melismatic singers" owing to their penchant for spinning out just one syllable with many, many notes.

Hildegard's chant *O rubor sanguinis* is sweeping yet solidly grounded tonally, as each phrase ends with the first (tonic) or fifth (dominant) degree of the scale, with D or A (colored red in the Ex. 4-1). Notice, too, that after an initial jump (D to A), the chant proceeds mostly in stepwise motion (neighboring pitches). This was, after all, choral music to be sung by the full community of musically unsophisticated nuns or monks, so it had to be easy. Finally, as with most chants, this piece has no overt rhythm or meter. The unaccompanied, monophonic line and the absence of pulsating rhythm allow a restful, meditative mood to develop. Hildegard did not see herself as an "artist" as we think of one today, but in the spirit of medieval anonymity as a mere vessel through which divine revelation came to earth. Indeed, she styled herself simply "a feather floating on the breath of God."

© Erich Lessing/Art Resource, NY

⋀ A twelfth-century illumination depicting Hildegard of Bingen receiving divine inspiration, perhaps a vision or a chant, directly from the heavens. To the right, her secretary, the monk Volmar, peeks in on her in amazement.

© The Art Archive/Biblioteca Civica, Lucca, Italy/Gianni Dagli Orti

◀ (upper frame) A vision of Hildegard revealing how a fantastic winged figure of God the Father, the Son, and the Mystical Lamb killed the serpent Satan with a blazing sword. (lower frame) Hildegard (center) receives the vision and reports it to her secretary (left). This manuscript dates from the twelfth century.

Example 4-1 >

O ___ ru - bor san - gui - nis ___ / qui ___ de ex - cel - so ___

___ il - lo ___ flu - - - xi - sti / quod di - vi - ni - tas te - ti - git:/

tu flos _ es _ / quem hy - - ems de _ fla - - tu ser - pen - - tis _ / num -

quam ___ le - sit.

Listening Cue

Hildegard of Bingen, *O rubor sanguinis* (c. 1150)

Genre: Chant
Texture: Monophonic

WHAT TO LISTEN FOR: A transcendental experience. Does the absence of a beat relax you? Does Hildegard's chant seem to carry you away?

🔊 Listen to streaming music in an Active Listening Guide at CourseMate or in the eBook.

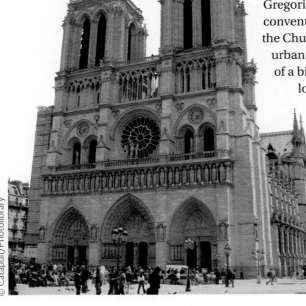

v The cathedral of Notre Dame of Paris, begun c. 1160, was one of the first to be built in the new Gothic style of architecture. Polyphony was composed there as the building was being constructed.

© Catapult/Photolibrary

〰️ Music in the Cathedral

Gregorian chant arose primarily in secluded monasteries and convents around Western Europe. The future of art music within the Church, however, rested not in rural monasteries, but rather in urban cathedrals. Every cathedral served as the "home church" of a bishop, and the bishop could minister to the largest flock by locating himself within Europe's rapidly expanding urban centers. During the twelfth century, cities such as Milan, Paris, and London, among others, grew significantly, as trade and commerce increased. Much of the commercial wealth generated in the cities was used to construct splendid new cathedrals that served as both houses of worship and municipal civic centers. So substantial was this building campaign that the period 1150–1350 is often called the "Age of the Cathedrals." It started in northern France with cathedrals possessing elements of what we now call the Gothic style: pointed arches, high ceiling vaults, flying buttresses, and richly colored stained glass.

Not only was Northern France home to the new Gothic architecture of the Middle Ages, but it was also the birthplace of a new style of music called **polyphony.** Polyphonic music involved multiple, independent voices, and with it came the need for a more precise musical notation. Because monophonic chant had only one line and rhythm played no important role, musicians had found they did not need to notate duration, just pitch. But polyphony required several independent singing parts. With many singing at once, how would the musicians know when to change to another pitch to make good harmony? Thus during the thirteenth century musicians in France devised a system called **mensural notation** (measured notation) to specify musical rhythm as well as pitch. Composers could now write for two, three, or four voices together, and each singer would know how long to sustain his note.

◄ Interior of the cathedral of Reims looking from floor to ceiling. The pillars carry the eye up to the ribbed vaults of the roof, creating a feeling of great upward movement, just as the Mass of Machaut, with four superimposed voices, has a new sense of verticality.

© Craig Wright

Notre Dame of Reims

Thirteenth-century Paris was the first home of the new Gothic polyphony, but by the fourteenth century its primacy, both in music and architecture, was challenged by Reims (pronounced "Rance"). The city of Reims, one hundred miles east of Paris in the Champagne region of France, boasted a cathedral as impressive and, indeed, larger than the one that graced Paris. In the fourteenth century Reims benefited from the service of a poetically and musically talented churchman, Guillaume de Machaut (c. 1300–1377). Judging by his nearly 150 surviving works, not only was Machaut (pronounced "ma-SHOW") the most important composer of his day, he was equally esteemed as a poet. Today, historians of literature place him on a pedestal next to his slightly younger English counterpart, Geoffrey Chaucer (c. 1340–1400), author of *The Canterbury Tales.* Indeed, Chaucer knew and borrowed heavily from the poetic works of Machaut.

Machaut: *Messe de Nostre Dame*

Machaut's *Messe de Nostre Dame (Mass of Our Lady)* is deservedly the best-known work in the entire repertoire of medieval music. It is impressive for its twenty-five-minute length as well as the novel way it applies music to the text of the Mass. Machaut was the first composer to set what is called the **Ordinary of the Mass**—five sung portions of the Mass—specifically, the *Kyrie, Gloria, Credo, Sanctus,* and *Agnus Dei* with texts that did not change from day to day. From Machaut's work onward, composing a Mass meant setting the five texts of the Ordinary and finding some way to shape them into an integrated whole. Bach, Mozart, Beethoven, and Stravinsky were just a few of the later composers to follow Machaut's lead in this regard.

To construct his Mass, Machaut proceeded as follows. First, he took a chant in honor of the Virgin and placed it in long notes in the tenor voice. In fact, because this voice part was often asked to hold out the notes of a preexisting chant, it assumed the name "tenor" (from the Latin *teneo,* French *tenir,* "to hold"). Above the foundational tenor Machaut composed two new lines called the *superius* and the *contratenor altus,* and from these we get our terms *soprano* and *alto,* and below the tenor he composed a *contratenor bassus,* whence our term *bass.* Machaut spread these voices out over two and a half octaves, becoming the first composer to exploit nearly the full vocal range of a chorus. As you listen to the foreign sound of this Gothic work, you likely will be struck by two things: (1) the alternation of chant and polyphony—for some portions of his *Kyrie,* Machaut allowed the monophonic chant to stand unaltered; and (2) the disparity between rhythm and harmony. The rhythmic patterns unfold within a lilting triple meter, but the harmony is mostly dissonant. At the ends of musical phrases, however, Machaut stretches out the dissonances into open, consonant chords (see the asterisk in Ex. 4-2). These longed-for consonances are especially satisfying in an echo-filled medieval cathedral in which the sound can endlessly reverberate around the bare stone walls.

Example 4-2 ➤

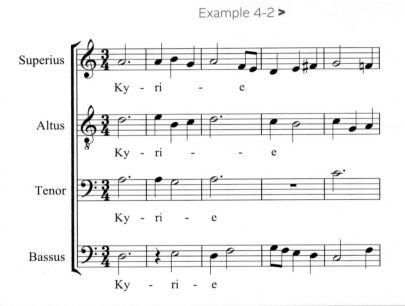

Listening Cue

Guillaume de Machaut, *Kyrie* **of** *Messe de Nostre Dame* **(c. 1360)**

2–4

Genre: Mass
Texture: Polyphonic and monophonic

WHAT TO LISTEN FOR: The alternation between polyphony and chant, and the interplay between passages of dissonant chords and consonant ones, the latter coming at the ends of phrases.

🔊)) Listen to streaming music in an Active Listening Guide at CourseMate or in the eBook.

🔊)) Take online Listening Exercise 10 at CourseMate or in the eBook.

Music at the Court

Outside the walls of the cathedral, there was yet another musical world: one of popular song and dance centered at the court. If the music of the Church was calculated to move the soul toward spiritual reflection, that of the court was meant to move the body to sing and dance. The court emerged as a center for the patronage of the arts during the years 1150–1400, as kings, dukes, counts, and lesser nobles increasingly assumed responsibility for the defense of the land and regulating social behavior. The court embraced forms of public entertainment not permitted by Church authorities. Here, itinerant actors, jugglers, jesters, and animal acts provided welcome diversions at banquets and feasts. Minstrels wandered from castle to castle, playing instruments and bringing with them the latest tunes, along with the news and gossip of the day.

For a modern evocation of royal life at the medieval French castle of Chinon in the twelfth century, watch the greeting of Eleanor of Aquitaine (Katharine Hepburn) by King Henry II (Peter O'Toole) in the YouTube playlist at CourseMate for this text.

Troubadours and *Trouvères*

France was the center of this new courtly art, though French customs quickly spread to Spain, Italy, and Germany as well. The poet-musicians who flourished in the courts of southern France were called **troubadours** and those in the north *trouvères*. These names are distant ancestors of the modern French word *trouver* ("to find"). Indeed, the troubadours and *trouvères* were "finders," or inventors, of a new genre of vocal expression called the **chanson** (French for "song"). In all, the troubadours and *trouvères* created several thousand chansons. Most are monophonic love songs that extol the courtly ideals of faith and devotion, whether to the ideal lady, the just seigneur (lord), or the knight crusading in the Holy Land. The origins of the troubadours and *trouvères* were varied. Some were sons of bakers and drapers, others were members of the nobility, many were clerics who had left the rigors of the Church, and not a few were women.

In the Middle Ages women were not allowed to sing in church, except in convents, owing to the biblical command of St. Paul ("A woman must be silent in the church"). But at court, women often recited poetry, sang, and played musical instruments. A few, such as Beatriz, Countess of Dia, were composers in their own right. Beatriz lived in southern France in the mid-twelfth century. She was married to Count William of Poitiers but fell in love with a fellow troubadour, Raimbaut d'Orange (1146–1173). In her chanson *A chantar m'er (I Must Sing)* Beatriz complains of unrequited love (presumably hers toward Raimbaut) and does so from a woman's perspective. Although lyrics are very worldly, the musical style has much in common with the chant of the Church; the monophonic melody moves essentially by step, and there is no strong rhythmic profile.

▲ Beatriz Countess of Dia as depicted in a manuscript of troubadour and *trouvère* poetry.

Medieval Musical Instruments

In the late Middle Ages the principal musical instrument of the monastery and cathedral was the large pipe organ. In fact, the organ was the only instrument admitted by church authorities. At court, however, a variety of instrumental sounds could be heard. Some, such as the trumpet and early trombone, were rightly identified as loud (*haut*). Others, such as the harp, lute, flute (recorder), fiddle (*vielle*), and small portable organ, were classified as soft (*bas*).

Countess of Dia, *A chantar m'er* (c. 1175)

Genre: Chanson
Texture: Monophonic

WHAT TO LISTEN FOR: An introductory instrumental solo played by a *vielle* (medieval fiddle) and, once the voice enters, a monophonic chanson with a clear **ABABCDB** musical structure

🔊 Listen to streaming music in an Active Listening Guide at CourseMate or in the eBook.

> A thirteenth-century Spanish miniature showing a medieval fiddle (the *rebec* or *vielle*) on the left and a lute on the right. Both instruments were brought into Spain by the Arabs and then carried northward into the lands of the troubadours and *trouvères*.

© The Art Archive/Real Monasterio del Escorial, Spain/Laurie Platt Winfrey

💬 Download another example of a chanson, the song, "Can vei la lauzeta mover," from the iTunes playlist at CourseMate for this text.

The illustration below shows a group of angels playing musical instruments of the late Middle Ages. Moving from left to right we see a straight-pipe trumpet, early trombone, small portative organ, harp, and vielle. The **vielle** (pronounced like the letters "V-L") was a distant ancestor of the modern violin. It usually had five strings that were tuned in a way that made it very easy to play block chords, the same way that guitars today can easily produce basic triads, or "bar chords." In fact, in medieval society the easily portable vielle served the function of our modern guitar: not only could it play a melody, it could also provide a basic chordal accompaniment for songs and dances. To hear the sound of the vielle, return to *A chantar m'er*, where it provides a solo introduction and then an accompaniment to the voice.

💬 A complete Checklist of Musical Style for the Middle Ages can be found at CourseMate for this text.

> Hans Memling (c. 1430–1491), musical angels painted for the walls of a hospital in Bruges, Belgium. The depiction of the instruments is remarkably detailed.

© Scala/Art Resource, NY

Music in the Renaissance, 1450–1600

Renaissance means literally "rebirth." Historians use the term broadly to designate a period of intellectual and artistic flowering that occurred first in Italy, then in France, and finally in England, during the years 1350–1600. Music historians, however, apply the term more narrowly to musical developments in those same countries during the period 1450–1600. The Renaissance was an age in which writers, artists, and architects rediscovered the classical world of Greece and Rome to find models for civic and personal expression. How should city government operate? What should a building look like? What about the sculpture erected within it? How should a poet construct a poem? How ought an orator fashion a speech, or a musician a song? The remains of classical antiquity, some of which were just then being unearthed, provided the answer.

∧ Andrea Palladio's Villa Rotunda (c. 1550) near Vicenza, Italy, clearly shows the extent to which classical architecture was reborn during the Renaissance. Elements of the ancient Greek and Roman style include the columns with capitals, triangular pediments, and central rotunda.

For musicians the process of "rebirth" posed a unique problem: no actual music from Greek and Roman times survived to be rediscovered! Renaissance intellectuals instead turned to the writings of Greek philosophers, dramatists, and music theorists, which contained accounts of how ancient music was constructed and performed. In this way Renaissance musicians came to realize that the ancients had one primary article of faith regarding music: it had enormous expressive power.

To recapture the lost power of music, Renaissance musicians worked to forge a wholly new alliance between text and music, one in which music underscored and enhanced the meaning of the text in an overt, mimetic way. If the verse depicted birds soaring gracefully in the sky, the accompanying music should be in a major key and ascend into a high range; if the text lamented the pain and sorrow of sin, the music ought to be in a minor key, full of dark and dissonant chords. Compared to medieval compositions, those of the Renaissance contained a greater range of expression within each piece, as well as from one piece to the next. A similar development occurred in Renaissance visual arts, which now likewise allowed for a greater range of emotional expression. Compare, for example, the highly contrasting moods of two paintings created within a few years of each other—the peaceful serenity of Leonardo da Vinci's *Madonna, Child, Saint Anne, and a Lamb* and the painful intensity of Mathias Grünewald's *Saint John and the Two Marys* (see p. 56).

Attending the rebirth of the arts and letters of classical antiquity was a renewed interest in humankind itself. We have come to call this enthusiastic self-interest humanism. Simply said, **humanism** is the belief that people are something more than a mere conduit for gifts descending from heaven, that they have the capacity to create many things good and beautiful—indeed, the ability to shape their own world. The culture of the Middle Ages, as we have seen, was fostered by the Church, which emphasized a collective submission to the almighty, hiding the individual human form beneath layers of clothing.

∧ Leonardo da Vinci's *Madonna, Child, Saint Anne, and a Lamb* (c. 1508–1517). Notice the warm human expression and the near-complete absence of religious symbolism, as well as the highly formalistic composition of the painting; the groupings of figures form successively larger triangles.

∧ The expressive grief of the Virgin, Saint John, and Mary Magdalene mark this portion of an altarpiece (1510–1515) painted by Mathias Grünewald.

∧ Michelangelo's giant statue of David (1501–1504) expresses the heroic nobility of man in near-perfect form. Like Leonardo da Vinci, Michelangelo made a careful study of human anatomy.

The culture of the Renaissance, by contrast, rejoiced in the human form in all its fullness, expressed in works such as Michelangelo's *David*. This culture looked outward and indulged a passion for invention and discovery. Today, when college students take courses in the "humanities," they study such arts, letters, and historical events that have enriched the human spirit over the centuries.

During the Renaissance the artist assumed a personal identity and a name, such as "Leonardo," "Michelangelo," or "Josquin"—this in contrast to the faceless, usually anonymous master of the Middle Ages. If inspiration still came from God, it could be shaped in personal ways by an innovative creator. Renaissance artists demanded independence, recognition, and something more: money. Now a gifted artist might vie for the highest-paying commission, just as a sought-after composer might play one patron off against another for the highest salary. Money, it appeared, might prime the pump of creativity and lead to greater productivity. The prolific Michelangelo left an estate worth some $10 million in terms of today's money.

If artists were paid more in the Renaissance, it was because art was now thought to be more valuable. For the first time in the Christian West, there emerged the concept of a "work of art": the belief that an object might not only serve as a religious symbol but also be a creation of purely aesthetic value and enjoyment. Music in the Renaissance was composed by proud artists who aimed to give pleasure. Their music conversed, not with eternity, but with the listener. It was judged good or bad only to the degree that it pleased fellow human beings. Music and the other arts could now be freely evaluated, and composers and painters could be ranked according to their greatness. Artistic judgment, appreciation, and criticism entered Western thought for the first time in the humanistic Renaissance.

Josquin Desprez (c. 1455–1521) and the Renaissance Motet

Watch a video of Craig Wright's Open Yale Course class session 15, "Benedictine Chant and Music in the Sistine Chapel," at CourseMate for this text.

Josquin Desprez (pronounced "josh-CAN day-PRAY") was one of the greatest composers of the Renaissance or, indeed, of any age. He was born somewhere near the present border between France and Belgium about 1455, and died in the same region in 1521. Yet, like so many musicians of northern France, Josquin was drawn to Italy to pursue professional and monetary gain. Between 1484 and 1504, he worked for various dukes in Milan and Ferrara, and in Rome in the **Sistine Chapel,** the pope's private chapel in the Vatican. Evidence suggests that Josquin had a temperamental, egotistical personality, one typical of many artists of the Renaissance. He would fly into a rage when singers tampered with his music; he composed only when he, not his patron, wished; and he demanded a salary twice that of composers only slightly less gifted. Yet Josquin's contemporaries recognized his genius. Martin Luther said of him: "Josquin is master of the notes, which must express what he desires; other composers can do only what the notes dictate." And Florentine humanist Cosimo Bartoli compared him to the great Michelangelo (1475–1564):

> Josquin may be said to have been a prodigy of nature, as our Michelangelo Buonarroti has been in architecture, painting, and sculpture; for just as there has not yet been anyone who in his compositions approaches Josquin, so Michelangelo, among those active in his arts, is still alone and without a peer. Both Josquin and Michelangelo have opened the eyes of all those who delight in these arts or are to delight in them in the future.

Josquin composed in all of the musical genres of his day, but he excelled in writing motets, some seventy of which survive under his name. The Renaissance **motet** can be defined as a composition for a polyphonic choir, setting a Latin text on a sacred subject, and intended to be sung either at a religious service in a church or at home in private devotion. While composers of the Renaissance continued to set the prescribed text of the Mass, they increasingly sought more dramatic texts in the Old Testament of the Bible—specifically, in the expressive Psalms and the mournful Lamentations. A vivid text cried out for an equally vivid musical setting, allowing the composer to fulfill a mandate of Renaissance humanism: use music to heighten the meaning of the word.

▾ Interior of the Sistine Chapel. The high altar and Michelangelo's *Last Judgment* are at the far end; the balcony for the singers, including Josquin Desprez, at the lower right. Josquin carved his name on the door to this balcony and the graffito remains there to this day.

© SuperStock/SuperStock

Josquin's motet *Ave Maria* (*Hail Mary*; c. 1485) honors the Virgin Mary and employs the standard four voice parts: soprano, alto, tenor, and bass (S, A, T, and B in Ex. 4-3). As the motet unfolds, the listener hears the voices enter in succession with the same musical motive. This process is called **imitation,** a polyphonic procedure whereby one or more voices duplicate in turn the notes of a melody.

Example 4-3 ➤

Josquin also sometimes has one pair of voices imitate another—the tenor and bass, for example, imitating what the alto and soprano have just sung.

Example 4-4 ➤

Josquin builds his *Ave Maria* much as a humanistic orator would construct a persuasive speech. The work begins with a salutation to the Virgin, sung in imitation. Thereafter, a key word, "Ave" ("Hail"), sparks a succession of salutes to the Virgin, each making reference to one of her principal feast days during the church year (Conception, Nativity, Annunciation, Purification, and Assumption). Along the way the music overtly mimics the text; for example, on the words "Coelestria, terrestria, nova replet laetitia" ("Fills heaven and earth with new joy") Josquin raises the pitch of all voices excitedly. Then he takes this gesture one step further, literally jumping for joy, by leaping upward an octave on the Latin *laetitia* ("joy"). At the end of the motet comes a final exclamation, "O Mater Dei, memento mei. Amen" ("O Mother of God, be mindful of me. Amen").

These last words are set to striking chords, with each syllable of text receiving a new chord. The chordal, homophonic treatment allows this final phrase to stand out with absolute clarity. Here Josquin reaffirms the key principle of musical humanism: text and music must work together to persuade and move the listener. They must persuade the Virgin Mary as well, for they plead with her to intercede on behalf of the needy soul at the hour of death.

Finally, notice in our recording of Josquin's *Ave Maria* that no instruments accompany the voices. This unaccompanied mode of performance is called **a cappella** singing, and it was a hallmark of the Sistine Chapel. Even today, as in the Renaissance, the pope's Sistine Chapel sings all its religious music—chant, Masses, and motets—without organ or any other instruments. If you belong to an a cappella singing group today, you are perpetuating this ancient style of performance.

Listening Cue

Josquin Desprez, *Ave Maria* **(c. 1485)**

①
5

Genre: Motet
Texture: Polyphonic

WHAT TO LISTEN FOR: Opening using imitation (0:00), five sections (0:46, 1:20, 1:58, 2:26, 3:03) exalting the events in the life of the Virgin, and a final plea for salvation (3:58)

◀)) Listen to streaming music in an Active Listening Guide at CourseMate or in the eBook.

◀)) Take online Listening Exercise 11 at CourseMate or in the eBook.

The Counter-Reformation and Palestrina (1525–1594)

Hear Alessandro Moreschi, the "Last Castrato," in the YouTube playlist at CourseMate for this text.

On October 31, 1517, an obscure Augustinian monk named Martin Luther nailed to the door of the castle church at Wittenberg, Germany, ninety-five complaints against the Roman Catholic Church—his famous ninety-five theses. With this defiant act Luther began what has come to be called the Protestant Reformation. Luther and his fellow reformers sought to bring an end to corruption within the Roman Catholic Church, typified by the practice of selling indulgences (forgiving sin in exchange for money). By the time the Protestant Reformation had run its course, most of

◀ All-male choir with choirboys for the soprano part as depicted in a sixteenth-century Italian fresco. The most common practice was to assign these parts to adult males who sang in what is called "head voice," or **falsetto.** Beginning in 1562, the **castrato** (castrated male) voice was introduced into the Sistine Chapel, mainly as a money-saving measure—one adult castrato could produce as much sound as three choirboys.

© Scala/Art Resource, NY

To hear music in the style of Palestrina sung in one of the Roman churches in which he worked, listen to The Tallis Scholars, Allegri, "Miserere," in the YouTube playlist at CourseMate for this text.

To download Allegri's "Miserere," go to the iTunes playlist at CourseMate for this text.

∧ Portrait of Giovanni Palestrina, the first important composer of the Church to have been a layman rather than a member of the clergy

Listen to a selection from Palestrina's *Missa Papae Marcelli* in the YouTube playlist at CourseMate for this text.

Download another selection by Palestrina, "Con che soavità," from the iTunes playlist at CourseMate for this text.

Germany, Switzerland, and the Low Countries, and all of England, as well as parts of France, Austria, Bohemia, Poland, and Hungary, had gone over to the Protestant cause. The established Roman Catholic Church was shaken to its very foundations.

In response to the Protestant Reformation, the leaders of the Church of Rome gathered in northern Italy to discuss their own reform in what proved to be a two-decades-long conference, the **Council of Trent** (1545–1563). Here began the **Counter Reformation,** a conservative, sometimes austere, movement that changed not only religious practices, but also art, architecture, and music. In the realm of musical composition, the reformers of the Church of Rome were particularly alarmed by the incessant entry of voices in musical imitation; they feared that excessively dense counterpoint was burying the word of the Lord. As one well-placed bishop said mockingly:

> In our times they [composers] have put all their industry and effort into the writing of imitative passages, so that while one voice says "Sanctus," another says "Sabaoth," still another says "Gloria tua," with howling, bellowing, and stammering, so that they more nearly resemble cats in January than flowers in May.

One important composer who got caught up in this debate about the appropriate style for church music was Giovanni Pierluigi da Palestrina (1525–1594). In 1555 Palestrina composed a *Missa Papae Marcelli (Mass for Pope Marcellus)* that conformed to all the requirements for proper church music prescribed by the Council of Trent. His polyphonic Mass was devoid of a strong beat and "catchy" rhythms, and it privileged simple counterpoint over complex, imitative polyphony, all qualities that allowed the text to project with great clarity. Although the fathers of the Council of Trent had once considered banning all polyphony from the services of the Church, they now came to see that this somber, serene style of religious music could be a useful vehicle to inspire the faithful to greater devotion. For his role in securing a place for composed polyphony within the established Church, Palestrina came to be called, perhaps with some exaggeration, the "savior of church music."

Popular Music in the Renaissance

The motets and Masses of Josquin and Palestrina represent the "high" art of the Renaissance—learned music for the Church. But there was popular music as well and, unlike much of the popular music of the Middle Ages, we have a good general sense of how it sounded. During the Middle Ages most popular musicians, like pop musicians today, worked without benefit of written musical notation. In fact, most people in the Middle Ages couldn't read—text or music—and manuscripts (by definition copied by hand) were exceedingly expensive.

All this began to change, however, when Johann Gutenberg invented printing by movable type around 1460. Printing revolutionized the world of information in the late fifteenth century no less than the computer did in the late twentieth century. Hundreds of copies of a book could be produced quickly and cheaply once the type had been set. The first printed book of music appeared in Venice in 1501, and to this important event can be traced the origins of today's music industry. The standard press run for a printed book of music then was usually five hundred copies. Mass production put the music book within reach

© Scala/Art Resource, NY

of the banker, merchant, lawyer, and shopkeeper. "How to" manuals encouraged ordinary men and women to learn to read musical notation, so as to sing and to play an instrument at home. The learned amateur had arrived.

DANCE MUSIC

Our fascination with dance didn't begin with *Dancing with the Stars*. Dancing had existed, of course, since the beginning of time, although almost none of its music survives because it was passed along orally and not in written form. During the Renaissance, however, musicians came to benefit from the growth of literacy. Publishers now issued collections of dance music in notation, rightly assuming that many among the newly emergent middle class could read the notes and were ready to dance at home. Not wishing to miss a single sale, they issued volumes for wind instruments, keyboard instruments, "and any other instruments that might seem appropriate." A favorite ensemble—something akin to the Renaissance dance band—included an early trombone and a predecessor of the modern oboe, called the **shawm.** Its piercing tone made the melody easy to hear.

▲ Musicians in a procession as painted by Denis van Alsloot, c. 1600. The instruments are, from right to left, an early trombone, two shawms, a cornetto, another shawm, and an early bassoon.

© Prado, Madrid/The Bridgeman Art Library International

By far the most popular type of dance of the mid-sixteenth century was the **pavane,** a slow, gliding dance in duple meter performed by couples holding hands. It was often followed by a contrasting **galliard,** a fast, leaping dance in triple meter. (For a painting believed to show Queen Elizabeth I leaping in a galliard, see p. 62.) Around 1550 the French publisher Jacques Moderne issued a collection of twenty-five anonymous dances that included several pavanes and galliards. Moderne titled this collection *Musicque de joye*—listen and you'll understand why.

Listening Cue

Jacques Moderne, publisher, *Musique de joye* **(c. 1550), Pavane and galliard**

Genre: Instrumental dance
Texture: Homophonic

WHAT TO LISTEN FOR: Wind instruments (called shawms) play a succession of symmetrical phrases of four measures plus four measures, making it easy for the dancers to match their steps to the music

◀)) Listen to streaming music in an Active Listening Guide at CourseMate or in the eBook.

THE MADRIGAL

About 1530, a new kind of popular song took Europe by storm: the madrigal. A **madrigal** is a piece for several solo voices (usually four or five) that sets a vernacular poem, most often about love, to music. The madrigal arose in Italy

△ Singers of a four-part madrigal during the mid-sixteenth century. Women were very much a part of this secular, nonreligious music making.

© Giraudon/The Bridgeman Art Library International

but soon spread to northern European countries. So popular did the madrigal become that by 1630 some 40,000 pieces had been printed by publishers eager to satisfy public demand. The madrigal was a truly social art, one that both men and women could enjoy.

Of all the musical genres of the Renaissance, the madrigal best exemplifies the humanist requirement that music express the meaning of the text. In a typical madrigal each word or phrase of poetry receives its own musical gesture. Thus, when the madrigal text says "chase after" or "follow quickly," the music becomes fast, and one voice chases after another in musical imitation. For words such as "pain," "anguish," "death," and "cruel fate," the madrigal composer almost invariably employs a twisting chromatic scale or a biting dissonance. This practice of depicting the text by means of a descriptive musical gesture, whether subtly or jokingly as a musical pun, is called **word painting.** Word painting became all the rage with madrigal composers in Italy and England. Even today such musical clichés as a falling melody for "fainting" and a dissonance for "pain" are called **madrigalisms.**

Although the madrigal was born in Italy, popular favor soon carried it over the Alps to Germany, Denmark, the Low Countries, and to the England of Shakespeare's day. A single madrigal with English text will allow us to explore the "one on one" relationship between music and word.

In 1601 musician Thomas Morley published a collection of twenty-four madrigals in honor of Virgin Queen Elizabeth (1533–1603), which he entitled *The Triumphes of Oriana.* (Oriana, a legendary British princess and maiden, was a poetic nickname of Queen Elizabeth.) Among these madrigals was *As Vesta Was from Latmos Hill Descending* composed by royal organist Thomas Weelkes (1576–1623). The text of the madrigal, likely fashioned by Weelkes himself, is a rather confused mixture of images from classical mythology: the Roman goddess Vesta, descending the Greek mountain of Latmos, spies Oriana (Elizabeth) ascending the hill; the nymphs and shepherds attending the goddess Diana desert her to sing the praises of Oriana. The sole virtue of this verse is that it provides frequent opportunity for word painting in music. As the text commands, the music descends, ascends, runs, mingles imitatively, and offers "mirthful tunes" to the maiden queen. Elizabeth herself played lute and harpsichord, and loved to dance. Weelkes saw fit to end his madrigal with cries of "Long live fair Oriana." Indeed, the fair queen did enjoy a long and glorious reign of some forty-five years—thus our term "Elizabethan Age."

Madrigals such as Weelkes's *As Vesta Was from Latmos Hill Descending* were popular because they were fun to sing. Vocal lines were written within a comfortable range, melodies were often triadic, rhythms were catchy, and the music was full of puns. When Vesta descends the mountain, so, too, her music moves down the scale; when Oriana (Queen Elizabeth) ascends, her music does likewise; when Diana, the goddess of virginity, is all alone—you guessed it, we hear a solo voice. With sport like this to be had, no wonder the popularity of the madrigal endured beyond the Renaissance. Although the genre might not appear often on *Glee*, the madrigal remains today a staple of a cappella singing groups and university glee clubs.

∨ A painting believed to show Queen Elizabeth dancing with the Duke of Leicester.

By kind permission of Viscount De L'Isle from his private collection at Penshurst Place, Kent, England

Thomas Weelkes, *As Vesta Was from Latmos Hill Descending* (1601)

Genre: Madrigal

Texture: Changes according to the dictates of the text

WHAT TO LISTEN FOR: A one-on-one relationship between text and music in which the music acts out, like a mime, each word or phrase of the text

 Listen to streaming music in an Active Listening Guide at CourseMate or in the eBook.

 Take online Listening Exercise 12 at CourseMate or in the eBook.

A complete Checklist of Musical Style for the Renaissance can be found at CourseMate for this text.

chapter FIVE

Baroque Art and Music

Music historians agree, with unusual unanimity, that Baroque music first appeared in Italy in the early seventeenth century. Around 1600 the established equal-voice choral polyphony of the Renaissance receded in importance as a new, more flamboyant style gained popularity. Eventually, the new style was given a new name: Baroque.

Baroque is the term used to describe the arts generally during the period 1600–1750. It derives from the Portuguese word *barroco,* referring to a pearl of irregular shape then used in jewelry and fine decorations. Critics applied the term *baroque* to indicate excessive ornamentation in the visual arts and a rough, bold instrumental sound in music. Thus, originally, *baroque* had a negative connotation: it signified distortion, excess, and extravagance. Only during the twentieth century, with a new-found appreciation of the painting of Peter Paul Rubens (1577–1640) and the music of J. S. Bach (1685–1750), among others, has the term *baroque* come to assume a positive meaning in Western cultural history.

Baroque Architecture and Music

What strikes us most when standing before a monument of Baroque design, such as the basilica of Saint Peter in Rome or the palace of Versailles outside of Paris, is that everything is constructed on the grandest scale. The plazas, buildings, colonnades, gardens, and fountains are all massive. Look at the ninety-foot-high altar canopy inside Saint Peter's (see Fig. 5-1), designed by Gian Lorenzo Bernini (1598–1680), and imagine how it dwarfs the priest below. Outside the basilica, a circle of colonnades forms a courtyard large enough to encompass several football fields. Or consider the French king's palace of Versailles, constructed during the reign of Louis XIV (1643–1715), so monumental in scope that it formed a small independent city, home to several thousand court functionaries (see Fig. 5-7, p. 76).

The music composed for performance in such vast expanses could be equally grandiose. While at first the Baroque orchestra was small, under King Louis XIV it sometimes swelled to more than eighty players. Similarly, choral works for Baroque churches sometimes required twenty-four, forty-eight, or even fifty-three separate lines or parts. These compositions for massive choral forces epitomize the grand or "colossal" Baroque.

Once the exteriors of the large Baroque palaces and churches were built, the artists of the time hastened to fill these expanses with abundant, perhaps even excessive, decoration.

FIGURE 5-1
The high altar at Saint Peter's Basilica, Rome, with baldachin by Gian Lorenzo Bernini. Standing more than ninety feet high, this canopy is marked by twisted columns and curving shapes, color, and movement, all typical of Baroque art.

FIGURE 5-2
Church of the monastery of
Saint Florian, Austria (1686–
1708). The powerful pillars and
arches set a strong structural
framework, while the painted
ceiling and elaborately carved
capitals provide decoration
and warmth.

© Interfoto/Alamy

It was as if the architect had created a large vacuum, and into it raced the painter, sculptor, and carver to fill the void. Examine again the interior of Saint Peter's and notice the ornamentation on the ceiling, as well as the elaborate twists and turns of Bernini's canopy. Or consider the Austrian monastery of Saint Florian (Fig. 5-2); there are massive columns, yet the frieze connecting them is richly decorated, as is the ceiling above. Here elaborate scrolls and floral capitals add warmth and humanity to what would otherwise be a vast, cold space.

Similarly, when expressed in the music of the Baroque era, this love of energetic detail within large-scale compositions took the form of a highly ornamental melody set upon a solid chordal foundation. Sometimes the decoration almost seems to overrun the fundamental harmonic structure of the piece. Notice in Example 5-1 the abundance of melodic flourishes in just a few measures of music for violin by Arcangelo Corelli (1653–1713). Such ornaments were equally popular with the singers of the early Baroque period, when the cult of the vocal virtuoso first emerged.

Example 5-1 ➤

Sonata I

Baroque Painting and Music

Many of the principles at work in Baroque architecture are also found in Baroque painting and music. Baroque canvases are usually large and colorful. Most important, they are overtly dramatic. Drama in painting is created by contrast: bright light is set against darkness; bold colors are pitted against one another; and lines are placed at right angles to one another, evoking tension and energetic movement. Figure 5-3 depicts a horrific scene: the woman Judith visiting retribution upon the Assyrian general Holofernes, as painted by Artemisia Gentileschi (1593–1656). Here the play of light and dark creates a dramatic effect, the stark blue and red colors add intensity, while the head of the victim, set at a right angle to his body, suggests an unnatural motion. Baroque art sometimes delights in the pure shock value of presenting gruesome events from history or myth in a dramatic way.

Music of the Baroque is also highly dramatic. We observed in the music of the Renaissance (1450–1600) the humanistic desire to have music reinforce the text so as to sway, or affect, the emotions. By the early seventeenth century this aim had given rise to a new aesthetic theory called the Doctrine of Affections. The **Doctrine of Affections** held that different musical moods could and should be used to communicate to the listener a specific emotion, or affection—be it rage, revenge, sorrow, joy, or love. Not surprisingly, the single most important new genre to emerge in the Baroque period was opera, which placed intense vocal expression center stage.

Judith and Holofernes (panel), Gentileschi, Artemisia (1597-c. 1651)/Museo e Gallerie Nazionali di Capodimonte, Naples, Italy/The Bridgeman Art Library

Characteristics of Baroque Music

Perhaps more than any other period in the history of music, the Baroque gave rise to a bewildering variety of musical styles, ranging from the expressive monody of Claudio Monteverdi (1567–1643) to the complex polyphony of J. S. Bach (1685–1750). Yet despite the multiplicity of styles, two elements remain constant throughout the Baroque period: an expressive, sometimes extravagant, melody and a strong supporting bass.

FIGURE 5-3
Judith Beheading Holofernes (c. 1615) by Artemisia Gentileschi. The grisly scene of Judith slaying the tyrant general was painted several times by Gentileschi, perhaps as a vivid way of demonstrating her abhorrence of aggressive male domination.

Expressive Melody

Renaissance music, as we saw in Chapter 4, was dominated by polyphonic texture, in which the voices of a choir spin out a web of imitative counterpoint. The nature and importance of each of the lines is about equal, as the following graph suggests,

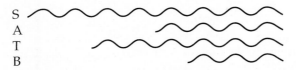

An equal-voice choir might be a useful medium to convey the abstract religious thoughts of the multitudes. To communicate raw human emotions, however, a direct appeal by a soloist seemed more appropriate. In early Baroque music, then, all voices are not created equal. Rather, a polarity develops in which the music projects more strongly from the top and the bottom. In between, the middle voices do little more than fill out the texture.

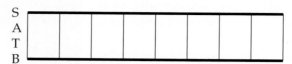

This new structure facilitated a new kind of solo singing called **monody** (from the Greek term meaning "solo song"). A single singer stepped forward, supported only by a bass line and a few accompanying instruments, to project a highly charged text. With the spotlight squarely on the soloist, a more elaborate, indeed showy, style of singing developed. Observe in Example 5-2 how the vocalist ascends rapidly (densely black notes) with a long and difficult melisma. Notice, too, that this heavenly flight underscores the word *paradiso* ("paradise"), the music reinforcing the meaning of the text. As this passage suggests, Baroque melodies generally do not unfold in short, symmetrical units, but rather expand luxuriously, and often unpredictably, over long musical phrases.

Example 5-2 ➤

Tan - ta   bel - lez-za   il pa-ra-di - - - - - - - - - - so ha se - co.
(Wherever so much beauty resides contains paradise.)

For an excellent demonstration of early Baroque violin music, accompanied by a *basso continuo* of harpsichord, cello, and Baroque guitar, go to Ciaccona, "Voices of Music," in the YouTube playlist at CourseMate for this text.

Rock-Solid Harmony

To prevent the high-flying melodies of the Baroque from spinning out of control, a strong harmonic support was needed. If Renaissance music was conceived polyphonically and horizontally, line by line, that of the early Baroque period is organized homophonically and vertically, chord by chord. The chordal accompaniment sounds forth in the **basso continuo** (continuous bass), a small ensemble of usually just two instruments. In Figure 5-4 we see a solo singer, a

FIGURE 5-4
Antonio Visentini (1688–1782), *Concert at the Villa*. Notice how the double bass player at the left turns his head to read the bass (bottom) line in the score on the harpsichord; together they provide the *basso continuo*.

© The Art Archive/Gianni Dagli Orti

large double bass, and a harpsichord. The singer projects the melody while the double bass plays the bass line and the harpsichord fills in the chords above the bass note. Harpsichord and a low string instrument formed the most common *basso continuo* in the Baroque period. Indeed, the continual tinkling of the harpsichord, in step with a strong bass line, signals to the listener that the music being played comes from this era. To hear how Baroque melody and harmony work together for expressive purposes, we turn to a monody (solo song) by Barbara Strozzi.

A Baroque Example: Monody by Barbara Strozzi

Barbara Strozzi (1619–1677) was an exceptional figure. She became a successful composer in an age when female musicians were expected to perform only within the home—and, indeed, where opportunities for women were severely limited in any profession beyond the domestic sphere. Of course there were a few exceptions that proved the "male only" rule: Adriana Basile (c. 1580–c. 1640) became a highly renowned operatic soprano, laying claim to the title "the first diva"; Elena Piscopia (1646–1684) became the first woman to receive a university degree, when she earned the title Doctor of Philosophy at the University of Padua in 1678; and Artemisia Gentileschi (1593–1656; see Fig. 5-3) became a court painter for King Charles I of England. Strozzi's claim to fame rests on her productivity as a composer; she published more sets of chamber cantatas than any other figure of the early Baroque period.

A **chamber cantata** is a "sung thing" (from the Italian *cantata*) for solo voice and a few accompanying instruments, intended to be performed at home or a private chamber; thus it is a type of **chamber music.** While J. S. Bach's later church cantatas would deal with religious subjects (see Chapter 6), the chamber cantata usually described the deeds of the heroes and heroines of classical mythology, or told a tale of unrequited love. Strozzi's cantata *L'amante segreto (The Secret Lover)*, for instance, centers on a hopelessly timid lover. Rather than reveal her passion to the object of her desire, she chooses a painless death. The climax of the cantata comes at "Voglio morire" ("I Want to Die"), a monody for soprano supported by a *basso continuo.* Example 5-3 shows the despondent woman's melody and the chords that accompany it (played by the *basso continuo*). Notice the numbers beneath the bass line. This numerical shorthand is called a **figured bass.** In the original score, only the melody and bass line were written out. A player familiar with Baroque chord formations would look at the

▲ A portrait of Barbara Strozzi painted in the 1630s by Bernardo Strozzi, perhaps a relative

© Erich Lessing/Art Resource, NY

Example 5-3 ➤

basso continuo

basso ostinato → 3   6   7 ♯6 3   3   6   3   3

figured bass ➤

bass and the numbers, and improvise the other notes of the chord (supplied here in smaller note heads). Figured bass is similar in intent to the alphanumerical code found in "fake books" used by jazz musicians today, which suggest which chords to play beneath a written tune. Finally, look again at the bass line and notice how it repeats; in fact, in this song the bass repeats continually from beginning to end. A melody, harmony, or rhythm repeating over and over is called an **ostinato,** a term derived from an Italian word meaning "obstinate," "stubborn," or "pig-headed." Coincidentally, Strozzi's monody, with a soprano voice singing over a repeating, four-chord harmony, has a parallel in the modern-day blues: we often hear contemporary singers like Jennifer Nettles and Adele lamenting above a distinctive, recurrent harmonic progression (the twelve-bar blues harmony).

Listening Cue

Barbara Strozzi, *L'amante segreto* (1651), "Voglio morire," Part 1

1
7

Genre: Monody
Texture: Homophonic

WHAT TO LISTEN FOR: The *basso continuo* of cello and harpsichord introduces the voice. The bass repeats continually, thereby forming a *basso ostinato.*

◀)) Listen to streaming music in an Active Listening Guide at CourseMate or in the eBook.

◀)) Take online Listening Exercise 13 at CourseMate or in the eBook.

 ## Early Baroque Opera

Given the popularity of opera today—and the fact that opera has existed in China and Japan since the thirteenth century—it is surprising that this genre of music emerged comparatively late in the history of Western European culture. Not until around 1600 did opera appear in Europe, and its native soil was Italy.

An **opera,** most basically, is a stage play (a drama) expressed through music. The term *opera* means literally "a work," and it first appeared in the Italian phrase *opera drammatica in musica,* "a dramatic work set to music." Opera demands singers who can act or, in some cases, actors who can sing. Indeed, in opera every word of the text (called the **libretto**) is sung. Such a requirement might strike us as unnatural. After all, we don't usually sing to our roommate, "Get out of the bathroom, I need to get to class this morning." But in opera, what we lose in credibility, we more than recoup in expressive power. Set to music, the text of a song, whether a pop hit or an opera aria, gains emotional force. Find a good drama, add music to the words, call the audience to attention with an opening instrumental piece (an **overture**), throw in a chorus and some instrumental mood music, and you've got a new medium: opera. This is how, in effect, the new genre of opera began. Ironically, its inventors thought they were resurrecting something old—ancient Greek drama.

The origins of opera can be traced to late sixteenth-century Italy. The genre was developed in the cities of Florence, Mantua, and Venice (Fig. 5-5) by progressive musicians and intellectuals who continued to pursue humanist ideals, and sought to re-create the emotive powers of classical Greek theater. They aimed to do so, however, with modern musical means: employing expressive solo song (monody) rather than the old-fashioned choral polyphony of the Renaissance. Among these pioneering musicians were Vincenzo Galilei (1533–1642), a noted music theorist and the father of the famous astronomer Galileo Galilei (1564–1642), and the composer Claudio Monteverdi (1567–1643), who can rightly be called "the father of opera."

Although he built on the experiments of his predecessors, Monteverdi's first opera, *Orfeo* (1607), is generally considered the first true example of the genre. Monteverdi wrote *Orfeo* while employed as a composer and string player at the court of Mantua, Italy, and he would continue to produce operas after moving on to the important basilica of St. Mark in Venice in 1613. Because the aim of early opera was to reproduce elements of ancient Greek drama, it is not surprising that Monteverdi's works draw on stories from classical Greek mythology. *Orfeo* is essentially a "rescue drama." The hero, Orfeo (Orpheus), descends into the realm of Hades (the Greek equivalent of Hell) to rescue his new bride Euridice, who has languished there since her sudden, unexpected death. To accomplish his mission, Orfeo charms and disarms hellish demons with a singularly formidable weapon: his beautiful singing. Indeed, the theme of *Orfeo* is the divine power of music.

Although Monteverdi employed choruses and the occasional instrumental interlude, he conveyed the bulk of his *Orfeo* through monody—expressive solo song. In the hands of Monteverdi and his successors, operatic monody increasingly split into two distinctive types: recitative and aria. **Recitative,** from the Italian word *recitativo* ("something recited"), is musically heightened speech. Generally, an opera composer employs recitative to narrate the plot of the opera. Recitative mirrors the natural rhythms of everyday speech and thus has no perceptible meter or beat—you can't tap your foot to it. In Baroque opera, recitative is accompanied only by the *basso continuo*. Such sparsely accompanied recitative is called **simple recitative** (*recitativo semplice* in Italian; also called *recitativo secco*, "dry recitative"). Later, in the nineteenth century, recitative accompanied by the full orchestra, called *recitativo accompagnato*, would become the norm.

If recitative aims to advance the plot, the aria serves to tell us what the characters are feeling, to showcase the emotional high points of the drama. An **aria** (Italian for "song" or "ayre") is more passionate, more expansive, and more tuneful than a recitative. Here all or part of the orchestra enters to join the

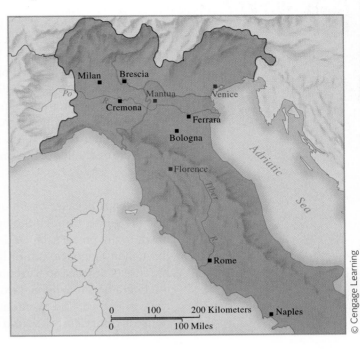

© Cengage Learning

FIGURE 5-5
The major musical centers in northern Italy in the seventeenth century. Opera first developed in Florence, Mantua, and Venice.

© Erich Lessing/Art Resource, NY

▲ Portrait of Claudio Monteverdi by Bernardo Strozzi (1581–1644), who also painted Barbara Strozzi (see p. 69)

Hear three portions of Monteverdi's opera *Orfeo*, in the YouTube playlist at CourseMate for this text: toccata; arioso "Tu se' morta"; and aria "Possente spirto."

basso continuo and thereby provide a strong sonic support, saying, in effect: "Listen, everyone, this solo song is an important moment!" In fact, judging from contemporary accounts, the Baroque audience usually talked during most of the recitatives and listened only during the arias. Finally, whereas a recitative often involves a rapid-fire delivery of text, an aria will work through it at a more leisurely pace; words are repeated to heighten their dramatic effect, and important vowels are extended by means of vocal melismas. These moments not only express feeling, but are moments of musical beauty. Then as now, the audience leaves the opera house humming, not the speech-like recitative, but the tuneful arias.

Perhaps because opera originated in Italy, that country continued to nurture the genre, through the operas of Verdi and Puccini (see Chapter 13), and down to the present day. Indeed, operas have most frequently been written in the Italian language, not only because of the genre's Italian origins, but also because of the pleasing, evenly spaced vowels of this "mother tongue." But early on, opera began to spread from Italy over the Alps to German-speaking countries, to France, and eventually to England. The first English opera worthy of notice is Henry Purcell's *Dido and Aeneas*.

An Opera in English: Henry Purcell's *Dido and Aeneas* (1689)

Henry Purcell (1659–1695) has been called the "greatest of all English composers." Indeed, only the late Baroque composer George Frideric Handel (who was actually German-born) and pop songwriters John Lennon and Paul McCartney can plausibly challenge Purcell for this title. Purcell was born in London, the son of one of the king's singers. In 1679, the younger Purcell obtained the position of organist at Westminster Abbey, and then, in 1682, he became organist for the king's Chapel Royal as well. But London has always been a vital theater town, and Purcell increasingly devoted his attention to works for the public stage.

One of Purcell's stage works that still enjoys public favor today is his opera *Dido and Aeneas*, written not for the royal family, but rather for a private girls' boarding school in the London suburb of Chelsea. The girls presented one major stage production annually, something like the senior class play of today. In *Dido and Aeneas,* they sang the numerous choruses and danced in the equally frequent dance numbers. All nine solo parts save one (the role of Aeneas) were written for female voices. The libretto of the opera, one appropriate for a school curriculum steeped in classical Latin, is drawn from Virgil's *Aeneid.* Surely the girls had studied this epic poem in Latin class, and likely they had memorized parts of it. Surely, too, they knew the story of the soldier-of-fortune Aeneas, who seduces proud Dido, queen of Carthage, but then deserts her to fulfill his destiny—sailing on to found the city of Rome. Betrayed and alone, Dido vents her feelings in an exceptionally beautiful aria, "When I am laid in earth," and then expires. In Virgil's original story, Dido stabs herself with the sword of Aeneas. In Purcell's opera, she dies of a broken heart: her pain is poison enough.

▲ Henry Purcell, by an anonymous painter

◄ A detail from the painting *The Death of Dido* by Guercino (1599–1666). The servant Belinda bends over the dying Dido, who has fallen on her formidable sword.

Dido's final aria is introduced by a brief example of simple recitative (accompanied by *basso continuo* only): "Thy hand, Belinda." Normally, simple recitative is a businesslike process that moves the action along through direct declamation. In this passage, however, recitative transcends its typically routine role. Notice the remarkable way Purcell sets the English language. He understood where the accents fell in the text of his libretto, and he knew how to replicate these effectively in music. In Example 5-4, the stressed words in the text generally appear in long notes and on the downbeat of each measure. Equally important, notice how the vocal line descends a full octave, passing through chromatic notes along the way. (Chromaticism is another device composers use to signal pain and grief.) As the voice twists chromatically downward, we feel the pain of the abandoned Dido. By the end, she has slumped into the arms of her servant Belinda.

Watch a video of Craig Wright's Open Yale Course class session 14, "Ostinato Form in the Music of Purcell, Pachelbel, Elton John, and Vitamin C," at CourseMate for this text.

Example 5-4 ➤

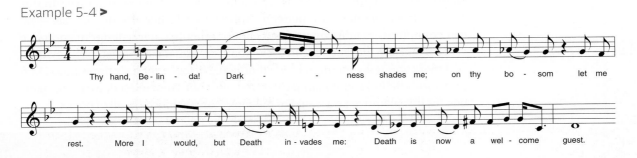

From the recitative "Thy hand, Belinda," Purcell moves imperceptibly to the climactic aria "When I am laid in earth," in which Dido sings of her impending death. Because this high point of the opera is a lament, Purcell chooses, in the Baroque tradition, to build it upon a *basso ostinato* (see p. 68). English composers called the *basso ostinato* the **ground bass,** because the repeating bass provided a solid foundation, or grounding, on which an entire composition could be built. The ground bass that Purcell composed for Dido's lament consists of two sections (Ex. 5-5 on the next page): (1) a chromatic stepwise descent over the interval of a fourth (G, F#, F, E, E♭, D) and (2) a two-measure cadence returning to the tonic G (B♭, C, D, G).

Example 5-5 >

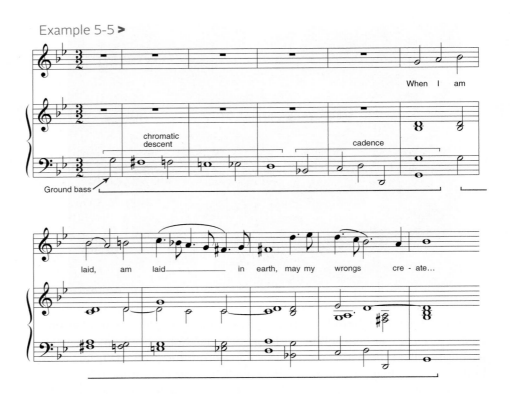

The text of Dido's lament consists of a short, one-stanza poem with an **aba** rhyme scheme. Here brevity begets eloquence.

> When I am laid in earth, may my wrongs create
> No trouble in thy breast.
> Remember me, but ah! Forget my fate.

Each line of text is repeated, as are many individual words and pairs of words. (Such repetition of text is typical of an aria but not of recitative.) In this case, Dido's repetitions are perfectly appropriate to her emotional state—she can communicate in fragments, but cannot articulate her feelings in complete sentences. Here the listener cares less about grammatical correctness, however, and more about the emotion of the moment. No fewer than six times does Dido plead with Belinda, and with us, to remember her. And, indeed, we do remember, for this plaintive aria is one of the most moving pieces in all of opera.

Listening Cue

Henry Purcell, *Dido and Aeneas* **(1689)**

Recitative, "Thy hand, Belinda," and aria, "When I am laid in earth"

1
8–9

WHAT TO LISTEN FOR: Dido's recitative, accompanied by *basso continuo* (cello and large lute), giving way to her mournful aria (track 9), built on a *basso ostinato*

🔊 Listen to streaming music in an Active Listening Guide at CourseMate or in the eBook.

🔊 Take online Listening Exercise 14 at CourseMate or in the eBook.

Middle Baroque Instrumental Music: Three Favorites

When we think of classical music today, we usually think of instrumental music and instrumental performing groups—a symphony orchestra or a string quartet, for example. The equation classical = instrumental, while certainly not entirely true, nonetheless has some validity—about 80 percent of the Western classical repertoire is instrumental. But when and why did this happen? It occurred during the seventeenth century, in part because of the rising popularity of the violin, which now came to enjoy the same position that the piano would in the nineteenth century, as the favorite instrument for making music in the home. Statistics prove the point. During the Renaissance, the number of prints of vocal music outsold those of instrumental music by almost ten to one; by the end of the seventeenth century, on the other hand, instrumental publications outnumbered vocal ones by about three to one. The majority of this instrumental music was intended for members of the violin family.

Accompanying the growth of instrumental music was the emergence of a distinctly instrumental sound. Composers increasingly came to realize not only that voices and instruments were different, but also that the various instruments had different strengths—that a violin, for example, was an excellent instrument to run up and down a scale, whereas a trumpet was particularly good at leaping an octave. Accordingly, they began to engage in **idiomatic writing** (well-suited writing), composing in a way that exploited the strengths and avoided the weaknesses of particular instruments.

Finally, during the Baroque era, the vocabulary of expressive gestures that had developed for vocal music came to be applied to instrumental music as well. Composers realized that the Doctrine of Affections (see p. 67) was valid for instrumental music, too. By adopting devices used in vocal music, composers now made purely instrumental music express rage (with tremolos and rapidly racing scales, for example); despair (with a swooning melody above a lament bass); or a bright spring day (by such means as trills and other "chirps" high in the violins and flutes). Even without the benefit of a text, instrumental music could tell a tale or paint a scene, as Antonio Vivaldi does in his "Spring" Concerto (see p. 79).

The Baroque Orchestra

The symphony orchestra as we know it today had its origins in seventeenth-century Italy and France. Originally, the term *orchestra* referred to the area for musicians in the ancient Greek theater, between the audience and the stage; eventually it came to mean the musicians themselves. By the mid-seventeenth century the core of the orchestra was formed by the violin family—violins, violas, cellos, and the related double bass. To this string nucleus were added woodwinds: oboes and then bassoons and an occasional flute. Sometimes, trumpets would be included to provide extra brilliance. When trumpets appeared, so, too, usually did timpani—trumpets and drums having traditionally sounded together on the battlefield. Finally, by the end of the seventeenth century, a pair of hunting horns (French horns) was sometimes added to the orchestra to give it more sonic resonance. Supporting the entire ensemble was the ever-present *basso continuo*, usually consisting of a harpsichord to provide chords and a low string instrument to play the bass line (Fig. 5-6). The **orchestra** for Western classical

FIGURE 5-6
Detail of an orchestra playing for a Baroque opera, as seen in Pietro Domenico Olivero's *Interior of the Teatro Regio*, Turin (1740). From left to right are a bassoon, two French horns, a cello, a double bass, a harpsichord, and then violins, violas, and oboes.

music, then, can be said to be an ensemble of musicians, organized around a core of strings, with added woodwinds and brasses, playing under a leader.

Most Baroque orchestras were small, usually with no more than twenty performers, and none of the parts was doubled—that is, no more than one instrumentalist was assigned to a single written line. Yet while the typical Baroque orchestra had no more than twenty players, there were exceptions, especially toward the end of the seventeenth century. At some of the more splendid courts around Europe, the orchestra might swell to more than eighty instrumentalists for special occasions. Foremost among these was the court of French king Louis XIV (reigned 1643–1715) and his great-grandson, Louis XV (1715–1774).

Mouret and Trumpet Music for the French Court

FIGURE 5-7
This view of the front of Versailles gives a sense of the grandeur of the palace that King Louis XIV began there in 1669.

Jean-Joseph Mouret (1682–1738) was a minor figure in the history of music. Indeed, he would be totally forgotten today were it not for one small twist of fate: in 1971, PBS's *Masterpiece Theater* chose the Rondeau from Mouret's *Suite de symphonies* (*Succession of Harmonious Pieces*; 1729) to be its theme. *Masterpiece Theater* went on to become the longest-running drama series in television history, and over the course of nearly forty years Mouret's music (but not the composer's name) came to be known by millions. With his *Suite de symphonies* Mouret intended to showcase the newly brilliant French orchestra and thereby grab the attention of his employer, King Louis XV. What surely caught the ear of the king is the same element that appeals to us today: the brilliant color of the trumpet. Imagine if Mouret had orchestrated this Rondeau from beginning to end with only strings and oboes—not very interesting. The moral? In music, as in painting, sometimes we are affected by the color of an idea as much as the idea itself.

Jean-Joseph Mouret, Rondeau from *Suite de symphonies* **(1729)**

Form: Rondo (ABACA)

Texture: Homophonic

WHAT TO LISTEN FOR: The continually returning refrain (A) of the rondo performed by a brilliant trumpet

 Listen to streaming music in an Active Listening Guide at CourseMate or in the eBook.

Pachelbel and His Canon

Today most of us remember the name Johann Pachelbel (rhymes with Taco Bell) only because of a single musical composition, the famous "Pachelbel Canon" in D major. In his day, however, Pachelbel was known as a composer of a great deal of instrumental music and a respected teacher (he taught Bach's older brother). Although almost everyone knows the Pachelbel Canon, there is an oddity about it: we don't hear the imitative canon, or at least we don't focus on it. Pachelbel has not used orchestration to help guide the listener's ear. He composed the three canonic voices all in the same range and assigned a violin to play each one. Because the lines don't stand out from one another by range or color, the unfolding of the canon is difficult to hear.

Instead, we perceive the bass line churning inexorably in the low strings. This bass, together with the harpsichord, form the *basso continuo* (Ex. 5-6). A strong bass is typical of Baroque music generally, but Pachelbel's bass is unforgettable. It has a pleasing intervallic pattern to it (fourths alternate with steps) and it gravitates strongly away from the tonic and back to the tonic in an eight-note cycle. Pachelbel knew he was onto a good thing, so he gives us this bass line twenty-eight times, a classic example of a *basso ostinato*. The allure of the bass is such that later classical composers borrowed it (Handel, Haydn, and Mozart among them), as have pop musicians in recent times, such as Blues Traveler, Vitamin C, and Coolio. The full composition has served as background music in numerous TV commercials and films. Why such popularity? Likely the reason is a play of opposites that we find appealing: the regular, almost plodding *basso ostinato* provides a rock-solid foundation for the violin lines that soar above.

Watch a video of Craig Wright's Open Yale Course class session 14, "Ostinato Form in the Music of Purcell, Pachelbel, Elton John, and Vitamin C," at CourseMate for this text.

Listen to comedian/musician Rob Paravonian rant about Pachelbel's Canon, in the YouTube playlist at CourseMate for this text.

Hear Pachelbel's Canon with *basso continuo* consisting of small organ, cello, and lute—the instruments that might have been used originally—in the YouTube playlist at CourseMate for this text.

Example 5-6 ➤

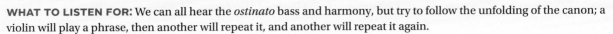

Johann Pachelbel, Canon in D major (c. 1690)

Intro
9

Form: Ostinato
Texture: Polyphonic

WHAT TO LISTEN FOR: We can all hear the *ostinato* bass and harmony, but try to follow the unfolding of the canon; a violin will play a phrase, then another will repeat it, and another will repeat it again.

 Listen to streaming music in an Active Listening Guide at CourseMate or in the eBook.

Vivaldi and the Baroque Concerto

The concerto was to the Baroque era what the symphony would later become to the Classical period: the showpiece of orchestral music. A Baroque concerto emphasizes abrupt contrasts within a unity of mood, just as striking change between the zones of light and darkness often characterizes a Baroque painting (see, for example, Fig. 5-3).

A **concerto** (from the Latin *concertare,* "to strive together") is a musical composition marked by a friendly contest or competition between a soloist and an orchestra. When only one soloist confronts the orchestra, the work is a **solo concerto.** When a small group of soloists works together, performing as a unit against the full orchestra, the piece is called a **concerto grosso.** A concerto grosso consists of two performing forces who work together, a larger group forming the basic orchestra called the concerto grosso (big concert) and a smaller one of two, three, or four soloists called the **concertino** ("little concert"). Playing together, the two groups constitute the full orchestra, called the **tutti** (meaning "all" or "everybody"). The contrast between full group and soloists was desirable, said a contemporary, "so that the ear might be astonished by the alternation of loud and soft . . . as the eye is dazzled by the alternation of light and shade."

As written by Vivaldi and Bach, the solo concerto and the concerto grosso usually have three movements: fast-slow-fast. The fast first movement is invariably composed in ritornello form, a structure popularized by Vivaldi. (The Italian word *ritornello* means "return" or "refrain.") In **ritornello form,** all or part of the main theme—the ritornello—returns again and again, played by the tutti, or full orchestra. Between these orchestra statements, the soloists insert fragments and extensions of the ritornello theme, usually playing in virtuosic fashion. Much of the excitement of a Baroque concerto comes from the tension between the tutti's reaffirming ritornello and the soloists' flights of fancy.

The popularity of the concerto grosso peaked about 1730 and then all but ended around the time of Bach's death (1750). But the solo concerto continued to be cultivated during the Classical and Romantic periods, becoming increasingly a showcase in which a single soloist could display his or her technical mastery of an instrument.

No composer was more influential, and certainly none more prolific, in the creation of the Baroque concerto than Antonio Vivaldi. Vivaldi—like Barbara Strozzi, a native of Venice—was the son of a barber and part-time musician at the basilica of Saint Mark. Young Vivaldi's proximity to Saint Mark's naturally brought him into contact with the clergy. Although he became a skilled performer on the violin, he also entered Holy Orders, ultimately being ordained a priest. For much of his career, Vivaldi served as music director of the *Ospedale della Pietà* (Hospice of Mercy), an orphanage and convent dedicated to the care and education of young women (Fig. 5-8). Vivaldi's life, however, was by no means confined to the realm of the spirit. He concertized on the violin throughout Europe; he wrote and produced nearly fifty operas, which brought him a great deal of money; and he lived for fifteen years with an Italian opera star. The worldly pursuits of *il prete rosso* ("the red-haired priest") eventually provoked a response from the authorities of the Roman Catholic Church. In 1737 Vivaldi was forbidden to practice his musical artistry in papally controlled lands, which then constituted a large portion of Italy. This ban affected his income as well as his creativity. He died poor and obscure in 1741 in Vienna, where he had gone in search of a post at the imperial court.

▲ Portrait of a violinist and composer believed by some to be the musician Antonio Vivaldi

"Spring" Concerto is his most popular piece, and is likely the best-known composition in the entire repertoire of Baroque music today. The "Spring" Concerto is one of a set of four concertos that Vivaldi called *The Four Seasons*. Each of the four works in turn represents the feelings, sounds, and sights of one of the four seasons of the year, beginning with spring. So that there would be no ambiguity as to what sensations and events the music depicts at any given moment, Vivaldi first composed a poem (an "illustrative sonnet" as he called it) about each season. Then he placed each line of the poem at the appropriate point in the music where that particular event or feeling was to be expressed, even specifying at one point that the violins are to sound "like barking dogs." In so

FIGURE 5-8

Foreign visitors attend a concert performed by orphan girls assembled from various orphanages around Venice, as depicted by Gabriele Bella about 1750. The Hospice of Mercy was the most musically intense of the Venetian orphanages. Here girls who showed a special talent for music were placed within a prestigious ensemble of forty musicians. Their musical education included tutelage in singing, ear training, and counterpoint, as well as instruction on at least two musical instruments. Antonio Vivaldi was one of the teachers.

doing, Vivaldi showed that not only voices, but instruments as well, could create a mood and sway the emotions. Vivaldi also fashioned here a landmark in what is called instrumental program music—music that plays out a story or a series of events or moods (for more on program music, see pp. 172–173).

You have no doubt heard the jaunty opening of the "Spring" Concerto. This ritornello consists of two parts (Ex. 5-7A and 5-7B). After the statement of each part, it is repeated at a different volume (here more quietly); such sharp contrasts of volume, common in Baroque music, are called **terraced dynamics.**

Example 5-7A ➤

Example 5-7B ➤

Between appearances of the ritornello, Vivaldi inserts program music depicting spring: solo violins chirp on high, undulating strings suggest a babbling brook, and string tremolos ominously portend a gathering storm. Finally, toward the end of the "Spring" Concerto we hear a musical procedure prominent in Vivaldi's music: melodic sequence. A **melodic sequence** is the repetition of a musical motive at successively higher or lower degrees of the scale, as in Example 5-8, where the pattern is repeated twice, each time a step lower.

Example 5-8 ➤

Although melodic sequence can be found in music from almost all periods, it is especially prevalent in the Baroque. It helps propel the music forward and create the energy we associate with Baroque style. But because hearing the same melodic phrase time and again can become tedious, Baroque composers usually follow the "three strikes and you're out" rule: the melodic unit appears, as in Example 5-8, three times, but no more.

Vivaldi composed more than 450 concertos and in his day was widely admired as both a performer and a composer. But the wheel of fortune can turn quickly. Within a few years of his death, Vivaldi was largely forgotten, a victim of rapidly changing musical tastes. Not until the revival of Baroque music in the 1950s were his scores resurrected from obscure libraries and dusty archives. Now his music is loved for its freshness and vigor, its exuberance and daring. More than 200 professional recordings have been made of *The Seasons* alone. So often is the "Spring" Concerto played that it has passed from the realm of art music into that of "classical pop"—a staple at Starbucks.

Antonio Vivaldi, The "Spring" Concerto (early 1700s), first movement, *Allegro* **(fast)**

Genre: Concerto
Form: Ritornello

WHAT TO LISTEN FOR: The ritornello played by the tutti alternating and contrasting with the descriptive music of the soloists

 Listen to streaming music in an Active Listening Guide at CourseMate or in the eBook.

 Take online Listening Exercise 15 at CourseMate or in the eBook.

A complete Checklist of Musical Style for the Early and Middle Baroque can be found at CourseMate for this text.

Late Baroque Music:
Bach and Handel

The music of the late Baroque period (1710–1750) is best exemplified in the compositions of the two great figures Johann Sebastian Bach and George Frideric Handel. The most noteworthy works of Bach and Handel are large-scale compositions full of dramatic power, broad gestures, and, often, complex counterpoint. At the same time, they convey to the listener a sense of technical mastery—that Bach and Handel could compose seemingly effortlessly in a variety of musical forms, techniques, and styles, building on the innovations of previous Baroque composers such as Monteverdi, Purcell, and Vivaldi. While rankings are always very personal, a recent appraisal by the *New York Times* put Bach and Handel in the top ten "all-time greatest composers," Bach coming in at number one.

The early Baroque period had witnessed the creation of several new musical genres, such as opera, chamber cantata, and concerto. The late Baroque, by contrast, is a period, not of musical innovation, but of refinement. Neither Bach nor Handel invented new forms, styles, or genres; these composers instead gave greater weight, length, and polish to those established by their musical forebears. Bach and Handel approached the craft of composition with unbounded self-confidence. Their music has a sense of rightness, solidity, and maturity about it. Each time we choose to listen to one of their compositions, we offer further witness to their success in bringing a hundred years of musical innovation to a glorious culmination.

Aspects of Late Baroque Musical Style

Melody in late Baroque music is governed by the principle of progressive expansion; an initial theme is set forth and then continually spun out over an ever-lengthening line. Glance ahead to Examples 6-2 and 6-4 where you will see two famous melodies of Bach. The first runs five measures, the second twelve (seven of which appear here), and both seem to gain momentum as they unfold. The sense of endless forward motion comes in part from the rhythmic energy of late Baroque music. Rhythm, too, is ruled by the principle of progressive development. A piece typically begins with one prominent rhythmic idea that propels the music forward in a purposeful, sometimes relentless fashion. Example 6-1 highlights another of Bach's melodies, this one drawn from his first orchestral suite. Once the sixteenth-note pattern gets started, it chugs along irrepressibly. Thus, although late Baroque melodies can be long and winding, rhythmic patterns are recurrent and downbeats are clearly audible. The beat is always easy to hear.

Example 6-1 ➤

Finally, the music of this late Baroque period is usually denser in texture than that of the early Baroque. By the heyday of Bach and Handel, around 1725, composers had returned to polyphonic writing, mainly to add richness to the middle range of what had been in the early Baroque a top-bottom (soprano-bass)–dominated texture (see p. 68). The gradual reintegration of counterpoint into the fabric of Baroque music culminates in the rigorously contrapuntal music of J. S. Bach.

Johann Sebastian Bach (1685–1750)

▲ The only authentic portrait of Johann Sebastian Bach, painted by Elias Gottlob Haussmann in 1746. Bach holds in his hand a six-voice canon, or round, which he created to symbolize his skill as a musical craftsman.

For a period of more than two hundred years, roughly 1600 to 1800, nearly one hundred musicians with the name of Bach worked in central Germany—the longest of all musical dynasties. In fact, the name Bach (German for "brook") was nearly a brand name, like our Kleenex and Xerox: "a Bach" meant "a musician." J. S. Bach was simply the most talented and industrious member of the clan. Although arguably the greatest composer who ever lived, Bach was largely self-taught. To learn his craft, he studied, copied, and arranged the compositions of Vivaldi, Pachelbel, and even Palestrina. He also learned to play the organ, in part by emulating others, once traveling on foot 400 miles round-trip to hear a great performer. Soon Bach became the most renowned organ virtuoso in Germany, and his improvisations on that instrument became legendary.

The organ has traditionally been called "the king of instruments," owing to its antiquity, power, and capacity to create a variety of colorful sounds. It is also the most suitable for playing polyphonic counterpoint, the kind of music in which Bach excelled. Most organs have at least two separate keyboards for the hands and an additional one for the feet (see photo, and Fig. 3-8). Thus the instrument has the capacity to play several lines simultaneously. More important, each of these keyboards can be set to engage a different group (rank) of pipes, and each of these has its own color—allowing the ear to more readily follow the individual lines of a polyphonic piece. For these reasons, "the king" is the instrument *par excellence* for playing fugues.

▼ The organ in the choir loft at Bach's St. Thomas Church in Leipzig, Germany. It was from this loft that Bach played and conducted.

Fugue

A **fugue** is a musical form that originated in the Baroque era, and in it polyphonic texture reigns supreme. The word *fugue* itself comes from the Latin *fuga*, meaning "flight." Within a fugue, one voice alone presents a theme—here called the **subject**—and then "flies away," as another voice enters with the same subject. Usually a fugue will have from three to five "voices." These may be actual human voices (soprano, alto, tenor, and bass of a choir) or they may simply be lines played by a group of instruments, or even by a solo instrument like the piano, guitar, or organ, which has the capacity to play several "voices" simultaneously. As the voices enter, they do not imitate or pursue each other exactly—this would produce a canon or a round such as "Row, Row, Row Your Boat" (see p. 40). Rather, after each has its turn with the subject, it goes more or less its own way in free counterpoint. The opening section of a fugue, during which each voice presents the subject successively, is called the **exposition.** A typical exposition of a fugue is suggested by the beginning of Figure 6-1.

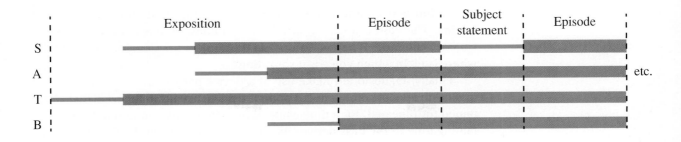

= subject

= counterpoint

FIGURE 6-1
An example of a typical formal plan of a fugue

Once all voices of the fugue have entered with the subject, there ensues a section of totally free counterpoint called the **episode.** In an episode the subject is not heard in its entirety, only brief allusions to it. And whereas the subject is firmly *in* a key, an episode modulates from one key to another. To sum up: a fugue begins with an exposition, follows with an episode, and then continues by alternating subject statements, in one voice or another, with modulating episodes, right to the very end. Fortunately, fugues are easier to hear than to describe.

ORGAN FUGUE IN G MINOR (C. 1710)

Bach's favorite instrument was the organ, and in his day he was known more as an organ virtuoso than as a composer—his fame as a composer came, ironically, years after his death. Indeed, Bach composed his G minor organ fugue, one of the nearly fifty that he wrote for that instrument, while working as a court organist and chamber musician for the duke of Weimar. This fugue has four voices—we'll call them soprano, alto, tenor, and bass—and it begins with a statement of the subject in the soprano:

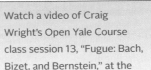

Watch a video of Craig Wright's Open Yale Course class session 13, "Fugue: Bach, Bizet, and Bernstein," at the text website.

Example 6-2 ➤

As fugue subjects go, this is a rather long one, but it is typical of the way Baroque composers liked to "spin out" their melodies. It sounds very solid in tonality because the subject is clearly constructed around the notes of the tonic triad in G minor (G, B♭, D), not only in the first measure but on the strong beats of the following measures as well. The subject also conveys a sense of gathering momentum, like a train pulling out of the station. It starts moderately with quarter notes and then seems to gain speed as eighth notes and finally sixteenth notes are introduced. This feeling of acceleration is typical of fugue subjects. After the soprano introduces the subject, it is then presented, in turn, by the alto, the tenor, and the bass. In a fugue the voices need not appear in any particular order; here Bach simply decided to have them enter in succession from top to bottom. Once all voices are in, the

To hear another of Bach's fugues, download Toccata and Fugue in D minor from the iTunes playlist at CourseMate for this text.

exposition is over, and the alternation of episodes and subject statements begins. Thereafter, tracking aurally what follows is like playing the musical equivalent of "Where's Waldo?" Is the subject in? Can you hear it? If so, where is it? In which voice is it sounding?

Finally, fugues often make use of a device particularly well suited to the organ—the pedal point. A **pedal point** is a pitch, usually in the bass, that is sustained (or repeated) for a time while harmonies change around it. Such a sustaining tone in the bass derives its name, of course, from the fact that on the organ the note is sounded by a foot holding down a key on the pedal keyboard. In his G minor fugue Bach prominently inserts a pedal point toward the middle of the piece. Your online Listening Exercise asks you to identify where this occurs—where a bass note holds for a very long time.

➤ *Fugue* (1925) by Josef Albers. Albers's design suggests the "constructivist" quality of the fugue, one full of repeating and reciprocal relationships. The black-and-white units seem to allude to subject and episode, respectively.

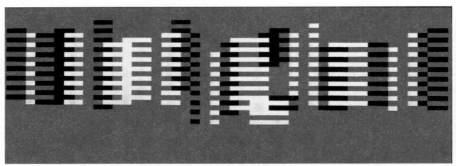

Listening Cue

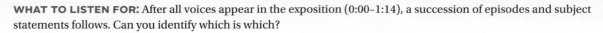

Johann Sebastian Bach, Organ Fugue in G minor (c. 1710)

1
11

Form: Fugue
Texture: Polyphonic

WHAT TO LISTEN FOR: After all voices appear in the exposition (0:00–1:14), a succession of episodes and subject statements follows. Can you identify which is which?

🔊 Listen to streaming music in an Active Listening Guide at CourseMate or in the eBook.

🔊 Take online Listening Exercise 16 at CourseMate or in the eBook.

Watch a video of Craig Wright's Open Yale Course class session 16, "Baroque Music: The Vocal Music of Johann Sebastian Bach," at CourseMate for this text.

The Church Cantata

In 1723 Bach moved to the central German city of Leipzig, population then about 30,000, to assume the coveted position of cantor of Saint Thomas's church and choir school. Here he stayed until he died at age sixty-five in 1750. Although his new post was prestigious, it was also demanding. As an employee of the town council of Leipzig, the composer was charged with superintending the music of the four principal churches of that city. He also played organ for all funerals, composed any music needed for ceremonies at the University of Leipzig, and sometimes taught Latin grammar to the boys at the choir school of

Saint Thomas. But by far the most difficult part of his job was composing new music for the church each Sunday and every religious holiday. In so doing, Bach brought an important genre of music, the church cantata, to the highest point of its development.

Like opera, the **cantata** (recall that it means "a sung thing") first appeared in Italy during the seventeenth century in the form we call chamber cantata (see p. 69), a genre in which a soloist sang about some aspect of love or a topic drawn from classical mythology. During the early eighteenth century, however, composers in Germany increasingly came to see the cantata as a useful vehicle for religious music in the church. Bach and his contemporaries created the **church cantata,** a multimovement sacred work, lasting roughly twenty-five minutes, which included recitatives, arias, and choruses, all accompanied by a small orchestra. The church cantata became the musical soul of the Lutheran Church, the Protestant religion that then dominated spiritual life in German-speaking lands. Bach wrote nearly three hundred cantatas for the citizens of Leipzig. Surrounded by a dozen singers and a small orchestra, all situated in the choir loft above the west door (see p. 84), Bach conducted his cantatas himself, beating time with a roll of paper.

▲ Leipzig, Saint Thomas's Church (center) and choir school (left) from an engraving of 1723, the year in which Bach moved to the city. Bach's large family occupied 900 square feet of the second floor of the choir school.

WACHET AUF, RUFT UNS DIE STIMME (AWAKE, A VOICE IS CALLING, 1731)

Bach composed his cantata *Wachet auf, ruft uns die Stimme* in 1731 for a Sunday immediately before Advent (thus five Sundays before Christmas). The text, drawing upon the Gospel of Matthew (25:1–13), speaks opaquely of a bridegroom (Christ) who is arriving to meet the Daughters of Zion (the Christian community). For every good Lutheran of Leipzig, however, the message was a personal mandate: get your spiritual house in order and prepare for the coming of Christ.

Like most of Bach's cantatas, *Wachet auf* makes use of a **chorale,** a spiritual melody or religious folksong, of the Lutheran church. (In other denominations such a melody is called simply a hymn.) Just as many people today know hymn tunes well, so most Lutherans of Bach's era knew their chorales by heart. Chorales were meant to be easy to remember and sing; indeed, many of the melodies had begun life as folksongs and popular tunes. And, in keeping with their common origins, the musical forms of these chorales were generally straightforward. *Wachet auf* (see Ex. 6-3, p. 88), unfolds in **AAB** form, and the seven musical phrases are allocated in the following way: **A** (1, 2, 3) **A** (1, 2, 3) **B** (4–7, 3). The last phrase of section **A** returns at the end of **B** to round out the melody.

◄ Looking across the parishioners' pews and toward the high altar at Saint Thomas's Church, Leipzig, as it was in the mid-nineteenth century. The pulpit for the sermon is at the right. In Bach's day, nearly 2,500 people would crowd into the church.

Example 6-3 >

chorale tune

Wa- chet auf! ruft uns die Stim - me der Wäch- ter sehr hoch auf der Zin - ne: wach'
Mit- ter - nacht heisst die- se Stun - de; sie ru - fen uns mit hel- lem Mun- de: wo

auf, du Stadt Je - ru - sa - lem! Wohl - auf! der Bräut'gam kommt, steht auf! die Lam- pen nehmt.
seid ihr klu- gen Jung- frau - en?

Al - le - lu - ja! macht euch be - reit zu der Hoch - zeit, ihr müs- set ihm ent - ge - gen gehn!

Bach uses the chorale *Wachet auf* to create a clear, large-scale structure for his cantata. Notice the formal symmetry across all seven movements of the cantata. The chorale is sung three times to three different stanzas of text, and these presentations come at the beginning, middle, and end of the work. Between statements of the chorale tune are linked pairs of recitative and aria, each joyfully announcing the divine love that Christ would bring to the Christian community.

Movement						
1	2	3	4	5	6	7
Chorus chorale 1st stanza	Recitative	Aria (duet)	Chorus chorale 2nd stanza	Recitative	Aria (duet)	Chorus chorale 3rd stanza

With an overview of the structure of cantata *Wachet auf* now in mind, we turn to the crucial fourth movement. Here the text of the chorale speaks of the meeting of Christ and the daughters of Zion (true believers); they enter the banquet hall to share the Lord's Supper. For this spiritual vision Bach constructs a musical tapestry for chorus and orchestra. The main thread is the chorale tune *Wachet auf,* which Bach places in long notes in the tenor voice of his choir. The tenors represent the watchmen of Jerusalem (Leipzig) calling on the people to awaken. Around the chorale tune Bach weaves a second, exquisitely beautiful melody, one of the loveliest that he or any other composer ever created (Ex. 6-4). All the violins and violas play this melody in unison—their togetherness symbolizing the unifying love of Christ for his people.

Example 6-4 >

Beneath both this melody and the chorale tune the bass plays regularly recurring quarter notes on the beat as it moves up and down the scale. This is called a **walking bass,** one that moves in equal note values step by step to neighboring pitches. The walking bass in this movement enhances the meaning of the text, underscoring the steady approach of the Lord. This movement was one of Bach's own favorites and the only cantata movement that he published—all the rest of his Leipzig cantata music was left in handwritten scores at the time of his death.

Listening Cue

Johann Sebastian Bach, *Wachet auf, ruft uns die Stimme* **(1731), fourth movement**

1
12

Genre: Cantata movement
Form: **AAB**

WHAT TO LISTEN FOR: Three-part polyphonic texture: melody in violins and violas, chorale tune in tenor voices, and walking bass. Note that the text that begins "Wachet auf" is the first strophe of the chorale (like the first stanza of a hymn); movement four contains the second strophe, beginning "Zion hört die Wächter singen" ("Zion hears the watchmen singing").

🔊 Listen to streaming music in an Active Listening Guide at CourseMate or in the eBook.

🔊 Take online Listening Exercise 17 at CourseMate or in the eBook.

In the last movement of his cantatas, Bach often ends with a simple four-voice setting of the chorale tune. The seventh and final movement of *Wachet auf* is typical of Bach's approach. Here he assigns the chorale tune to the soprano (top) part and supports it with homophonic chords in the three lower voices (Ex. 6-5). The instruments of the orchestra have no line of their own and merely double the four vocal parts.

Example 6-5 >

Most important, in this final movement of the cantata the members of Bach's congregation would have joined in the singing of the chorale tune. Martin Luther had ordained that the community should not merely witness but also participate in communal worship. At this moment, all of the spiritual energy of Leipzig was concentrated into this one emphatic declaration of faith. The coming Christ reveals to all true believers a vision of life in the celestial kingdom.

In his last decades Bach withdrew from the grind of producing a new cantata for every Sunday and retreated into a realm of large-scale contrapuntal projects, including *The Well-Tempered Clavier* and the encyclopedic *The Art of Fugue.* Bach left the latter work incomplete at the time of his death in 1750—the result of a stroke following unsuccessful surgery to remove a cataract. Ironically, the same eye surgeon who operated on Bach also operated on Handel at the end of that composer's life—with the same unsuccessful result.

George Frideric Handel (1685–1759)

Bach and Handel were born in the same year, 1685, in small towns in central Germany. Other than that commonality, and the fact that they shared the same incompetent eye doctor, their careers could not have been more different. While Bach spent his life confined to towns in the region of his birth, the cosmopolitan Handel traveled the world—from Rome, to Venice, to Hamburg, to Amsterdam, to London, to Dublin. Though Bach was most at home playing organ fugues and conducting church cantatas from the choir loft, Handel was a musical entrepreneur working in the theater, by training and temperament a composer of opera. And though Bach fell into obscurity at the end of his life, retreating into a world of esoteric counterpoint, Handel's stature only grew larger on the international stage. During his lifetime he became the most famous composer in Europe and a treasured national institution in England.

George Frideric Handel was born in the town of Halle, Germany, in 1685, and died in London in 1759. Although his father demanded that he become a lawyer, young Handel managed to cultivate his intense interest in music, sometimes secretly in the attic. At the age of eighteen, he left for the city of Hamburg, where he took a job as second violinist in the orchestra of the city opera. But because the musical world around 1700 was dominated by things Italian, he set off for Italy to learn his trade and broaden his horizons. After a decade in Italy, Handel returned to North Germany to accept the post of court music director for the Elector of Hanover, but on the condition that he be given an immediate leave of absence to visit London. Arriving in London in 1710 Handel conveniently "forgot" about his obligation to the Hanoverian court. London became the site of his musical activity and the place where he won fame and fortune.

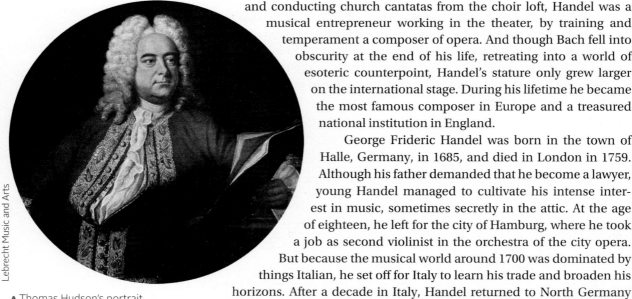

⋀ Thomas Hudson's portrait (1749) of Handel with the score of *Messiah* visible in the composer's left hand. Handel had a quick temper, could swear in four languages, and liked to eat.

London in the early eighteenth century was the largest and richest city in Europe, boasting a population of 500,000. It was the capital city not only of a country but also of a burgeoning empire of international commerce and trade. London may not have possessed the rich cultural heritage of Rome or Paris, but it offered opportunity for financial gain. As a friend of Handel then said, "In France and Italy there is something to learn, but in London there is something to earn."

As fate would have it, Handel's continental employer, the Elector of Hanover, became King George I of England in 1714, when the Hanoverians acceded to the throne on the extinction of the Stuart line. (A direct descendant a of those same Hanoverians, Queen Elizabeth II, sits on the throne of England today.) Fortunately for Handel, the new German-speaking king bore his truant musician no grudge, and Handel was called on frequently to compose festival music to entertain the court or provide a "soundtrack" for its events. For these occasions, Handel produced such works as *Water Music* (1717), *Music for the Royal Fireworks* (1749), and the Coronation Service (1727) for King George II and Queen Caroline, parts of which have been used at the coronation of every English monarch since then.

Handel and Opera

Handel emigrated from Germany to England not for the chance to entertain the king, and certainly not for the cuisine or the climate. Rather, he went to London to make money producing Italian opera. With the rare exception of a work such as Purcell's *Dido and Aeneas* (see pp. 72–74), there was no opera in London at this time. The legacy of Shakespeare in England remained strong, and the occasional sonic interlude was about as much music as English audiences tolerated in their spoken plays. Handel aimed to change this. London audiences, he reasoned, were daily growing wealthier and more cosmopolitan, and would welcome the "high art" of imported Italian opera, the way New Yorkers welcome Gucci bags or shoes today. Guaranteeing himself a healthy share of the profits, Handel formed an opera company, the Royal Academy of Music, for which he served as composer, director, and producer. His first opera, *Rinaldo* (1711), was first performed at the Queen's Theatre, the same theater in which Andrew Lloyd Webber's *The Phantom of the Opera* premiered in 1986.

The type of Italian opera Handel produced in London is called **opera seria** (literally, "serious—as opposed to comic—opera"), a style that then dominated the operatic stage throughout continental Europe. These were long, three-act works that chronicled the triumphs and tragedies of kings and queens, or gods and goddesses, and they appealed to an audience of society's upper crust, namely the nobility. In Handel's day, the leading male roles in *opera seria* were sung by castrati (castrated males with the vocal range of a female); Baroque audiences associated high social standing on stage with a high voice, male or female. From 1710 until 1728, Handel had great artistic and some financial success, producing two dozen examples of Italian *opera seria*. Foremost among these was *Giulio Cesare* (*Julius Caesar*, 1724), a recasting of the story of Caesar's conquest of the army of Egypt and Cleopatra's romantic conquest of Caesar. As was typical, the male hero (Julius Caesar) was portrayed by a castrato and sang in a high, "womanly" register.

But opera is a notoriously risky business, and in 1728 Handel's Royal Academy of Music went bankrupt, a victim of the exorbitant fees paid to the star singers and

▲ In 1730 Handel tried (unsuccessfully) to hire the celebrated castrato Farinelli, whose life was chronicled in a film of the same name. For the film, the now-extinct castrato voice was simulated by synthesizing a female soprano with a male falsetto voice.

To hear a Handel aria from the film *Farinelli*, listen to "Lascia ch'io pianga" from *Rinaldo* (1711) in the YouTube playlist at CourseMate for this text.

the fickle tastes of English theatergoers. Handel continued to write operas into the early 1740s, but he turned his attention increasingly to a musical genre less financially volatile than opera: oratorio.

Handel and Oratorio

An **oratorio** is literally "something sung in an oratory," an oratory being a hall or chapel used specifically for prayer and sometimes prayer with music. Thus the oratorio in seventeenth-century Italy had something in common with today's gospel music: It was sacred music sung in a special hall or chapel and was intended to inspire the faithful to greater devotion. By the time it reached Handel's hands, however, the oratorio had become close to an unstaged opera with a religious subject.

Both Baroque oratorio and Baroque opera begin with an overture, are divided into acts, and are composed primarily of recitatives and arias. Both genres are also long, usually lasting two to three hours. But there are a few important differences between opera and oratorio, aside from the obvious fact that oratorio treats a spiritual subject. Oratorio, being a quasi-religious genre, is performed in a church, a theater, or a concert hall, but it makes no use of acting, staging, or costumes. Because the subject matter is almost always sacred, there is more of an opportunity for moralizing, a dramatic function best performed by a chorus. Thus the chorus assumes greater importance in an oratorio. It sometimes serves as a narrator but more often functions, like the chorus in ancient Greek drama, as the voice of the people commenting on the action that has transpired.

By the 1730s, oratorio appeared to Handel to be an attractive alternative to the increasingly unprofitable opera in London. He could do away with the irascible and expensive castrati and prima donnas. He no longer had to pay for elaborate sets and costumes. He could draw on the longstanding English love of choral music, a tradition that extended well back into the Middle Ages. And he could exploit a new, untapped market—the faithful of the Puritan, Methodist, and growing evangelical sects in England, who had viewed the pleasures of foreign opera with distrust and even contempt. And in contrast to the Italian opera, the oratorio was sung in English, contributing further to the genre's appeal to a large segment of English society.

MESSIAH (1741)

Beginning in 1732 and continuing over a twenty-year period, Handel wrote upward of twenty oratorios. The most famous of these is his *Messiah,* composed in the astonishingly short period of three and a half weeks during the summer of 1741. It was first performed in Dublin, Ireland, the following April as part of a charity benefit, with Handel conducting. Having heard the dress rehearsal, the local press waxed enthusiastic about the new oratorio, saying that it "far surpasses anything of that Nature, which has been performed in this or any other Kingdom." Such a large crowd was expected for the work of the famous Handel that ladies were urged not to wear hoop skirts and gentlemen were admonished to leave their swords at home. In this way, an audience of seven hundred could be squeezed into a hall of only six hundred seats.

Buoyed by his artistic and Baroque financial success in Dublin, Handel took *Messiah* back to London, made minor alterations, and performed it in Covent Garden Theater. In 1750, he offered *Messiah* again, this time in the chapel of the

Foundling Hospital, an orphanage in London, and again there was much popular acclaim for Handel, as well as profit for charity. Thereafter, and down to the present day, Handel's oratorio *Messiah* is equally at home in church, chapel, concert hall, and public theater.

In a general way, *Messiah* tells the story of the life of Christ. It is divided into three parts (instead of three acts): (I) the prophecy of His coming and His Incarnation, (II) His Passion and Resurrection, and the triumph of the Gospel, and (III) reflections on the Christian victory over death. Most of Handel's oratorios recount the heroic deeds of characters from the Old Testament; *Messiah* is exceptional because the subject comes from the New Testament, though much of the libretto is drawn directly from both Old and New Testaments. There is neither plot action nor "characters" in the dramatic sense, nor are there costumes or staging. The drama is experienced in the mind of the listener.

While *Messiah* possesses many beautiful arias, including "Ev'ry valley shall be exalted" and "He shall feed His flock," the power of this oratorio is to be found in its nineteen choruses. Handel is arguably the finest composer for chorus who ever lived. As a world traveler with an unsurpassed ear, he absorbed a variety of musical styles from throughout Europe: In Germany, he acquired knowledge of the fugue and the Lutheran chorale; in Italy, he immersed himself in the styles of the oratorio and the chamber cantata; and during his years in England, he became familiar with the idioms of the English church anthem (a sacred song for chorus sung in English). Most important, having spent a lifetime in the opera theater, Handel had a flair for the dramatic.

Nowhere is Handel's dramatic mastery more evident than in the justly famous "Hallelujah" chorus that concludes Part II of *Messiah*. We have moved from the peaceful adoration of the lamb ("He shall feed His flock") to a triumphant resurrection, and now a variety of choral styles are displayed in quick succession: chordal, unison, fugal, and fugal and chordal together. The opening word "Hallelujah" recurs throughout as a powerful refrain, yet each new

◄ The chapel of the Foundling Hospital, London, where *Messiah* was performed annually for the benefit of the orphans. Handel himself designed and donated the organ seen on the second story at the back of the hall.

The Art Archive/Private Collection/Eileen Tweedy

phrase of text generates its own distinct musical idea. Among them are the following:

Example 6-6A Chordal (homophonic) texture ➤

Hal - le - lu - jah,   Hal - le - lu - jah,

Example 6-6B Unison (monophonic) texture ➤

For the Lord God om-ni - po- tent   reign-eth,

Example 6-6C Fugal (polyphonic) texture ➤

and he shall   reign for ev - er and   ev - er,

The vivid phrases speak directly to the listener, making the audience feel like a participant in the drama. So moved was King George II when he first heard the great opening chords, the story goes, that he rose to his feet in admiration, thereby establishing the tradition of the audience standing for the "Hallelujah" chorus—for no one sat while the king stood. But whether the audience stands or sits, Handel's eternally popular "Hallelujah" chorus has given rise to more praises of God than any other musical work.

Listening Cue

George Frideric Handel, *Messiah,* **"Hallelujah" chorus (1741)**

Genre: Oratorio chorus

WHAT TO LISTEN FOR: The masterful use of contrasting textures (monophonic, homophonic, and polyphonic) to create drama—for, in every art, vivid contrast creates drama.

🔊 Listen to streaming music in an Active Listening Guide at CourseMate or in the eBook.

🔊 Take online Listening Exercise 18 at CourseMate or in the eBook.

The "Hallelujah" chorus is a strikingly effective work because the large choral force creates a variety of exciting textures. In fact, however, Handel's chorus for the original Dublin *Messiah* was much smaller than those used today. It included only four singers on the alto, tenor, and bass parts, and six choirboys singing the soprano. The orchestra was equally slight, with only about sixteen players. For the Foundling Hospital performances of the 1750s, however, the orchestra grew to thirty-five. Then, over the next hundred years, the chorus progressively swelled to as many as four thousand with a balancing orchestra of five hundred, in what were billed as "Festivals of the People" in honor of Handel.

Just as there was a continual increase in the performing forces for his *Messiah,* so, too, did Handel's fortune and reputation grow. Toward the end of his life, he occupied a squire's house in the center of London; bought paintings, including a large and "indeed excellent" Rembrandt; and, on his death, left an enormous estate of nearly £20,000—that of a millionaire in today's money. He had become the first musical impresario to make a fortune from a paying public. More than three thousand attended his funeral in Westminster Abbey on April 20, 1759, and a sculpture of the composer holding an aria from *Messiah* was erected above his grave and is still there. As a memento of Handel's music, *Messiah* was an apt choice, for it is still performed each year at Christmas and Easter by countless amateur and professional groups throughout the world.

Lebrecht Music & Arts

◄ Eighteenth-century London was a place of biting satire. Here, in William Hogarth's *The Oratorio Singer* (1732), the chorus of an oratorio is the object of parody. But there is an element of truth here: the chorus for the first performance of *Messiah*, for example, numbered about eighteen males, with choirboys (front row) taking the soprano part. Women, however, sang soprano and alto for the vocal solos.

Listen to another part of Handel's *Messiah*, "Worthy is the lamb that was slain," in the YouTube playlist at CourseMate for this text.

A complete Checklist of Musical Style for the late Baroque can be found at CourseMate for this text.

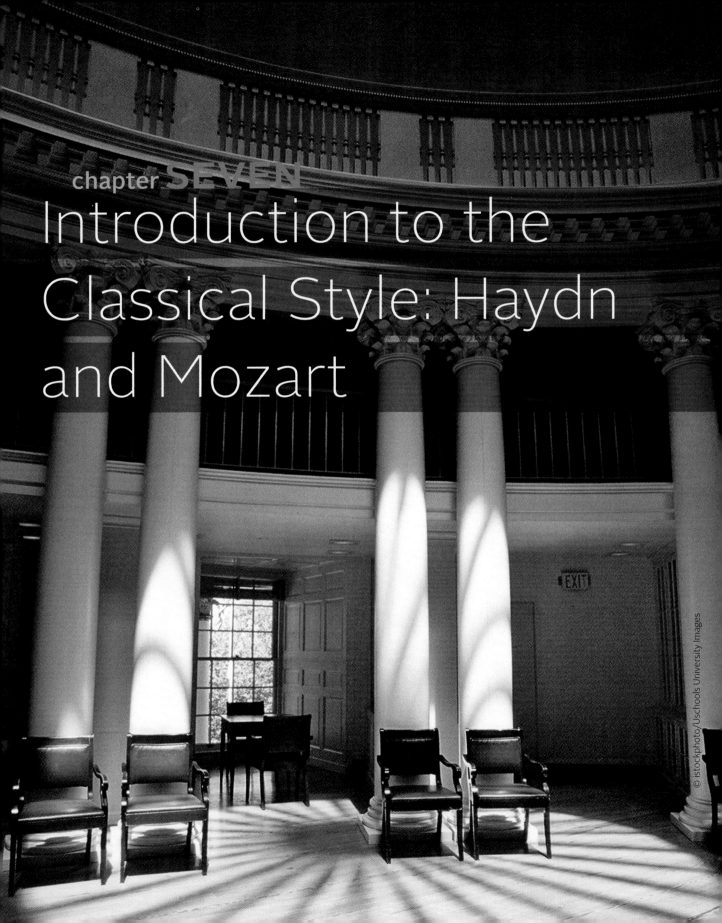

chapter **SEVEN**

Introduction to the Classical Style: Haydn and Mozart

arketing pitchmen encourage us every day, on TV and in print, to buy a particular watch or automobile by saying that it has "classical styling," suggesting that the product possesses a certain timeless beauty. When applied to music, "classical styling" also implies a "high-end" product. We use the word *classical* to signify the "serious" or "art" music of the West as distinguished from popular music. We call this art music "classical" because there is something about the excellence of its form and style that makes it enduring. Yet in the same breath, we may refer to "Classical" music (now with a capital C), and by this we mean the music of a specific historical period, 1750–1820, a period of the great works of Haydn and Mozart, and the early masterpieces of Beethoven. The creations of these artists have become so identified with musical proportion, balance, and formal correctness—with standards of musical excellence—that this comparatively brief period has given its name to all music of lasting aesthetic worth.

"Classical" derives from the Latin *classicus*, meaning "something of the first rank or highest quality." To the men and women of the eighteenth century, no art was more admirable, virtuous, and worthy of emulation than that of ancient Greece and Rome. Other periods in Western history also have been inspired by classical antiquity—the Renaissance heavily so (see Chapter 4)—but no era more than the eighteenth century. Classical architecture, with its geometric shapes, balance, symmetrical design, and lack of clutter, became the preferred style for public buildings, not only in Europe but also in the fledgling United States. Thomas Jefferson, while serving as American ambassador to France (1784–1789), traveled to Italy and brought Classical design back home with him. The U.S. Capitol, many state capitols, and countless other governmental and university buildings abound with the well-proportioned columns, porticos, and rotundas of the Classical style.

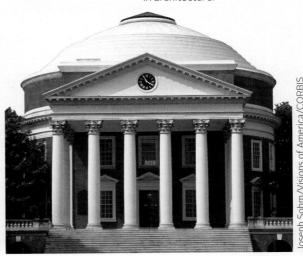

The Enlightenment

The Classical era in music, art, and architecture coincides with the period in philosophy and letters known as the **Enlightenment.** During the Enlightenment, also referred to as the Age of Reason, thinkers gave free rein to the pursuit of truth and the

v The Pantheon in Rome and the library of the University of Virginia, designed by Thomas Jefferson (above). Jefferson had visited Italy and studied ancient ruins while ambassador to France. The portico, with columns and triangular pediment, and central rotunda are all elements of Classical style in architecture.

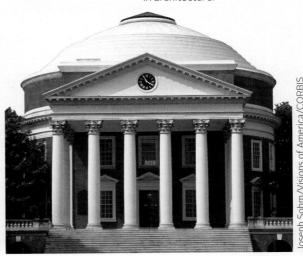

discovery of natural laws. Science now began to provide as many explanations for the mysteries of life as did religion. In many churches around Europe the medieval stained glass depicting saintly stories was replaced by clear glass that let in natural light—a literal example of "enlightenment." This is also the age of such scientific advances as the discovery of electricity and the invention of the steam engine. The first *Encyclopedia Britannica* (1771) was inspired by the French *Encyclopédie* (1751–1772), a twenty-four-volume set that aimed to replace medieval faith with modern, scientific reasoning. French encyclopedists Voltaire (1694–1778) and Jean-Jacques Rousseau (1712–1778) espoused the principles of social justice, equality, religious tolerance, and freedom of speech. These Enlightenment ideals subsequently became fundamental to democratic government and were enshrined in the American Constitution.

Needless to say, the notion that all persons are created equal and should enjoy full political freedom put the thinkers of the Enlightenment on a collision course with the defenders of the existing social order, namely the Church and the aristocracy. Spurred on by economic self-interest and the principles of the Enlightenment philosophers, an expanding, more confident middle class in France and America rebelled against the monarchy and its supporters. The American colonists issued a Declaration of Independence in 1776, and French citizens stormed the Bastille in 1789 to seize weapons, thereby precipitating a civil war among classes. By the end of the eighteenth century, the Age of Reason gave way to the Age of Revolution.

The Democratization of Classical Music: Public Concerts

Music was not exempt from the social changes sweeping eighteenth-century Europe and America. In fact, the century witnessed something of a democratization of classical music. The "audience base" for such music expanded greatly, extending now to the newly affluent middle class. In an earlier day, when art music was performed in only two venues (church and court), the average citizen heard very little of it. By mid-century, however, the bookkeeper, physician, cloth merchant, and stock trader collectively had enough disposable income to organize and patronize their own concerts. In Paris, then a city of 450,000 residents, one could attend, as proclaimed, "the best concerts every day with complete freedom." The most successful Parisian concert series was the *Concert spirituel* (founded in 1725), at which the West's first non-court orchestra played a regular schedule of performances. The *Concert spirituel* advertised its performances by means of flyers distributed in the streets. To make its offerings accessible to several strata of society, it instituted a two-tiered price scheme for a subscription series (4 livres for boxes and 2 livres for

▾ A performance at the Burgtheater in Vienna in the late 1700s. The nobility occupied the frontmost seats on the floor, but the area behind them was open to all. So, too, in the galleries, the aristocracy bought boxes low and close to the stage, while commoners occupied higher rungs, as well as the standing room in the fourth gallery. Ticket prices depended, then as now, on proximity to the performers.

Erich Lessing/Art Resource, NY

the pit, roughly $200 and $100 in today's money). Children under fifteen were admitted for half price. Thus we can trace to the middle of the eighteenth century the commercialization of a shared musical experience. The institution of the "concert" as we know it today dates from this time.

Public concerts sprang up in London, in the Vauxhall Gardens, an eighteenth-century amusement park drawing as many as 4,500 paying visitors daily. Here symphonies could be heard inside in the orchestra room or outside when the weather was good. When Leopold Mozart took his young son Wolfgang to concerts there in 1764, he was surprised to see that the audience was not segregated by class. Likewise in Vienna, the Burgtheater (City Theater) opened in 1759 to any and all paying customers, as long as they were properly dressed and properly behaved. Although the nobility still occupied the best seats, the doors of the concert hall were now open to the general public, fostering a leveling between classes with respect to all the fine arts. The middle class was wresting away from the aristocracy control of high culture. Classical music was not only becoming commercial, it was also becoming fully public entertainment.

Watch a video of Craig Wright's Open Yale Course class session 17, "Mozart and His Operas," at CourseMate for this text..

The Rise of Popular Opera

Social reform in the eighteenth century affected not only the people who went to concerts, but also the characters who populated the operatic stage. A new musical genre, comic opera, appeared and soon drove the established *opera seria* (see p. 91) to the wings. Baroque *opera seria* had portrayed the deeds of heroic rulers and glorified the status quo, making it, in essence, an aristocratic art. By contrast, the new **comic opera,** called *opera buffa* in Italy, exemplified social change and championed middle-class values. Comic opera made use of everyday characters and situations; it typically employed spoken dialogue and simple songs in place of recitatives and lengthy arias; and it was liberally spiced with sight gags, bawdy humor, and social satire.

Even a "high-end" composer like Mozart embraced the more natural, down-to-earth spirit of the comic style. Mozart was not always treated fairly by his noble employers, and several of his operas are rife with anti-aristocratic sentiment. In *Don Giovanni* (1787), for example, the villain is a leading nobleman of the town (see p. 135). In *Le nozze di Figaro* (*The Marriage of Figaro,* 1786) a barber outsmarts a count and exposes him to public ridicule. So seriously did the king of France and the Holy Roman Emperor take the threat of such theatrical satire that they banned the play on which *The Marriage of Figaro* was based. Comic theater and comic opera, it seemed, not only reflected social change, but could also inspire it.

Hear Mozart's aria "Se vuol ballare," from *Le nozze di Figaro*, in the YouTube playlist at CourseMate for this text.

▾ Bryn Terfel as the combative and cunning barber Figaro performs in an English National Opera production of *The Marriage of Figaro.*

Robbie Jack/CORBIS

The Advent of the Piano

Finally, the newly affluent middle class was not content merely to attend concerts and operatic performances; they also wished to make their own music at home. Most of this domestic music-making centered around an instrument that first entered public consciousness in the Classical period: the piano. Invented in Italy about 1700, the piano gradually replaced the harpsichord as the keyboard

instrument of choice—and with good reason, for the piano could play at more than one dynamic level (hence the original name **pianoforte,** "soft-loud"). Compared with the harpsichord, the piano could produce gradual dynamic changes, more subtle contrasts, and—ultimately—more power.

Those who played this new domestic instrument were mostly amateurs, and the great majority of these were women. A smattering of French, an eye for needlepoint, and some skill at the piano—these were signs of status and gentility that rendered a young woman suitable for marriage. For the nonprofessional woman to play in the home, however, a simpler, more homophonic style of keyboard music was needed, one that would not tax the presumed technical limitations of the performer. The spirit of democracy may have been in the air, but this was still very much a sexist age. It was assumed that ladies would not wish, as one publication said, "to bother their pretty little heads with counterpoint and harmony," but would be content with a tuneful melody and a few rudimentary chords to flesh it out. Collections such as *Keyboard Pieces for Ladies* (1768) were directed at these new musical consumers.

▲ Marie Antoinette, in 1770 at the age of fifteen, seated at an early piano. In 1774, this Austrian princess became queen of France, but in 1793, at the height of French Revolution, she was beheaded.

Elements of Classical Style

Fashions change. At the beginning of the eighteenth century, sophisticated men powdered their faces, painted on "beauty spots," and wore elaborate wigs (see George Frideric Handel in Chapter 6). By century's end a simpler, more natural style was in vogue (see Thomas Jefferson's appearance earlier in this chapter). So, too, did musical style evolve during the eighteenth century. Compared with the relentless, ornate, and often grandiose sound of the Baroque era, Classical music is lighter in tone, more natural, yet still full of high drama. It is even capable of humor and surprise, as when Joseph Haydn explodes with a thunderous chord in a quiet passage in his "Surprise" Symphony (1791). But what in precise musical terms creates the levity, grace, clarity, and balance characteristic of Classical music?

Melody

Perhaps most striking about the music of Haydn and Mozart is the fact that the melody is usually tuneful, catchy, even singable. Not only are melodies simple and short, but the phrases are balanced, often organized into matching antecedent–consequent, or "question–answer" pairs. **Antecedent** and **consequent phrases** are units that operate together: one opens, the other closes. To see how this works, think of the first two phrases (the first ten words) of "Twinkle, Twinkle Little Star," the folk song set by Mozart. During the eighteenth century the simple structure of the folksong came to influence the organization of melody in art music. As a result, classical melodies tend to be short, balanced phrases of 2 + 2 measures, or 3 + 3, or 4 + 4. The brevity of the phrases, and the frequent pauses at the end, allow for ample light and air to penetrate the melodic line.

Example 7-1 is the theme from the second movement of Mozart's Piano Concerto in C major (1785). It is composed of two three-bar phrases—an antecedent phrase followed by a consequent one. The melody is light and airy, yet perfectly balanced. It is also singable and quite memorable—indeed, it has been turned into a popular movie theme often played in airports and shopping malls. Contrast this to the long, asymmetrical melodies of the Baroque that were often instrumental in character (see Exs. 6-1, 6-2, and 6-4).

Example 7–1 ➤

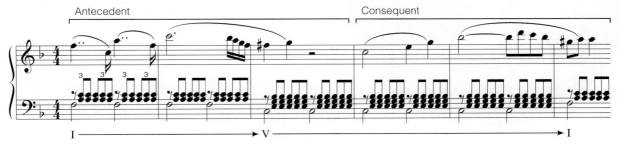

Harmony

In Classical music, harmony often plays a subservient role to the now-prominent melody. Notice in Example 7-1 that only two chords—tonic (I) and dominant (V)—support Mozart's lovely theme. The heavy bass and *basso continuo* of the Baroque era have disappeared entirely. The bass still generates the harmony, but it does not always move in the regular, constant fashion typified by the Baroque walking bass. Rather, the bass might sit on the bottom of one chord for several beats, even several measures, then move rapidly, and then stop again. Thus, the rate at which chords change—the "harmonic rhythm," as it is called—is much more fluid and flexible with Classical composers.

To avoid a feeling of inactivity when the harmony is static, Classical composers invented new "filler" patterns for accompaniment. Sometimes, as in Example 7-1, they simply repeat the accompanying chord in a uniform triplet rhythm (groups of three). More common is the pattern called the **Alberti bass,** named after the minor Italian keyboard composer Domenico Alberti (1710–1740), who popularized this figure. Instead of playing the pitches of a chord all together, the performer spreads them out to provide a continual stream of sound. Mozart used an Alberti bass at the beginning of his famous C major piano sonata (1788).

Example 7–2 ➤

The Alberti bass serves essentially the same function as both the modern "boogie-woogie" bass and the process of "tapping" on a guitar (made famous by

Eddie Van Halen). It provides an illusion of harmonic activity for those moments when, in fact, the harmony is not changing.

Rhythm

Rhythm, too, is more flexible in the hands of Haydn and Mozart than it was in the music of Bach and Handel, animating the stop-and-go character of Classical music. Rapid motion may be followed by repose and then further quick movement, but there is little of the driving, perpetual motion of Baroque musical rhythm.

Texture

The music of the latter half of the eighteenth century assumed a more homophonic, less polyphonic character than that of the late Baroque era. No longer are independent polyphonic lines superimposed, layer upon layer, as in a fugue of Bach or a polyphonic chorus of Handel. This lessening of counterpoint made for a lighter, more transparent sound, especially in the middle range of the texture (see Ex. 7-1, where chords repeat quietly in the middle between melody and bass). Mozart, after a study of Bach and Handel in the early 1780s, infused his symphonies, quartets, and concertos with greater polyphonic content, but this seems to have caused the pleasure-loving Viennese to think his music too dense!

▲ Many major artists of the eighteenth century journeyed to Rome to absorb the ancient classical style, and what they created in painting and architecture we now call "Neoclassicism." Among such classically inspired painters was the Englishwoman Angelica Kauffmann (1741–1807), whose *The Artist [Angelica Kauffmann] in the Character of Design Listening to the Inspiration of Poetry* (1782) shows classical balance (two women and two columns). Not coincidentally, the complementary figures in this painting function as do antecedent–consequent phrases in Classical music: they are somewhat different, but they balance each other.

The Dynamic Mood of Classical Music

What's perhaps most revolutionary in the music of Haydn, Mozart, and their younger contemporary, Beethoven, is its capacity for rapid change and endless fluctuation. Recall that in earlier times, a work by Vivaldi or Bach would establish one "affect," or mood, to be rigidly maintained from beginning to end—the rhythm, melody, and harmony all progressing in a continuous, uninterrupted flow. Such a uniform approach to expression is part of the "singlemindedness" of Baroque art. Now, with Haydn, Mozart, and the young Beethoven, an energetic theme in rapid notes might be followed by a second one that is slow, lyrical, and tender. Similarly, textures might change quickly from light and airy to dense and more contrapuntal, thereby adding tension and excitement. For the first time, composers began to specify crescendos and diminuendos, gradual increases or decreases of the dynamic level, so that the volume of sound might continually fluctuate. When skilled orchestras made use of this technique, audiences were fascinated and rose to their feet. Keyboard players, too, now took up the crescendo and diminuendo, assuming that the new, multidynamic piano was at hand in place of the older, less flexible harpsichord. These rapid changes in mood, texture, color, and dynamics give to Classical music a new sense of urgency and drama. The listener feels a constant flux and flow, not unlike the natural swings of mood that we all experience.

Vienna: Home to Classical Composers

New Orleans jazz, Hollywood film music, and the Broadway musical of New York—these are all names that suggest that a particular city gave rise to a distinctive kind of music. So, too, with the Viennese Classical style. The careers of Haydn, Mozart, Beethoven, and the young Franz Schubert all unfolded in Vienna, and from Vienna radiated their powerful musical influence. For that reason, we often refer to them collectively as the **Viennese School** and say that their music epitomizes the "Viennese Classical style."

Vienna was then the capital of the old Holy Roman Empire, a huge expanse covering much of Western and Central Europe (Fig. 7-1). In 1790, the heyday of Haydn and Mozart, Vienna had a population of 215,000, which made it the fourth-largest city in Europe, after London, Paris, and Naples. Surrounded by vast farmlands ruled by an aristocratic gentry, it served as a cultural mecca, especially during the winter months when there was little agricultural work to be supervised. Vienna boasted a greater percentage of noblemen among its population than did London or Paris, and here the aristocratic hold on high culture loosened only gradually—but loosen it did. Haydn was a court employee, but Mozart and Beethoven became independent operators. And while Viennese nobles still patronized music, they often enjoyed it with middle-class citizens at public concerts. There were theaters for German and Italian opera, concerts in the streets

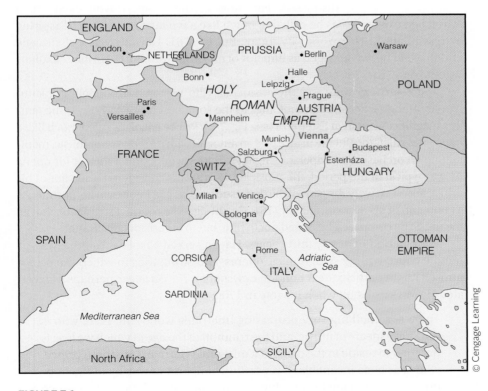

FIGURE 7-1
A map of eighteenth-century Europe showing the Holy Roman Empire and the principal musical cities, including Vienna, Austria

on fine summer nights, and ballroom dances where as many as two thousand couples might sway to a minuet or a waltz by Mozart or Beethoven.

With so much music making going on, Vienna attracted musicians from throughout Europe. Haydn moved there from Lower Austria, Mozart from Upper Austria, his rival Antonio Salieri from Italy, and Beethoven from Bonn, Germany. Later, in the nineteenth century, in addition to native-born Franz Schubert, outsiders such Johannes Brahms and Gustav Mahler would spend their most productive years there. Even today Vienna remains the capital of a nation (Austria) that spends nearly as much money on its state opera as it does on national defense.

Franz Joseph Haydn (1732–1809)

Courtesy of Professor Daniel Heartz

▲ Portrait of Joseph Haydn (c. 1762–1763) wearing a wig and the blue livery of the Esterházy court

Joseph Haydn was the first of the great composers to move to Vienna, and his life offers something of a "rags-to-riches" story. Haydn was born in 1732 in a farmhouse in Rohrau, Austria, about twenty-five miles east of Vienna. His father, a wheelwright, played the harp but could not read music. When the choir director of Saint Stephen's Cathedral in Vienna happened to be scouting for talent in the provinces, he heard the boy soprano Haydn sing and brought him back to the capital. Here Haydn remained as a choirboy, studying the rudiments of composition and learning to play the violin and keyboard. After nearly ten years of service, his voice broke and he was abruptly dismissed. For most of the 1750s, Haydn eked out a "wretched existence," as he called it, much like a freelance musician or aspiring actress might in New York City today. But in 1761, Haydn's years of struggle ended when he was engaged as director of music for the court of Prince Nikolaus Esterházy (1714–1790).

The **Esterházy** were wealthy aristocrats who wintered in Vienna and summered on their extensive landholdings to the southeast (see Fig. 7-1). At the family's magnificent court at Esterháza (see Fig. 7-2), Prince Nikolaus ruled much like a benevolent dictator. But the prince was an autocrat with a fondness for music, maintaining an orchestra, a chapel for singing religious works, and a theater for opera. As was typical of the period, the musician Haydn was considered a servant of his prince and even wore the garb of the domestic help, as can be seen in his portrait. As a condition of his appointment in 1761, Haydn signed a contract stipulating that all the music he composed belonged not to him, but to his aristocratic master.

For a period of nearly thirty years, Haydn served Nikolaus Esterházy at his remote court, writing symphonies, operas, and string trios in which the prince himself might participate. A London newspaper, *The Gazeteer,* perhaps exaggerated Haydn's isolation when it wrote in 1785:

There is something very distressing [that] this wonderful man, who is the Shakespeare of music, and the triumph of the age in which we live, is doomed to reside in the court of a miserable German [Austrian] prince, who is at once incapable of rewarding him, and unworthy of the honour. . . . Would it not be an achievement equal to a pilgrimage, for some aspiring youths to rescue him from his fortune and transplant him to Great Britain, the country for which his music seems to be made?

As it turns out, that is precisely what happened. Prince Nikolaus died in 1790, leaving Haydn a pension for life and freedom to travel. Heeding the call of an enterprising impresario, Johann Solomon—and the promise of a substantial fee—Haydn journeyed to London in 1791. For this capital, then the richest of all European cities, Haydn wrote his last twelve symphonies. The composer himself conducted the premieres of these fittingly named **London Symphonies** in a series of concerts at the Hanover Square Rooms, a new public concert hall that catered to the growing middle-class demand for classical music. By the time he returned to Vienna in 1795, Haydn had earned a total of 24,000 Austrian gulden, the equivalent of about $1.2 million today—not bad for the son of a wheelmaker. Haydn died on May 31, 1809, at the age of seventy-seven, the most respected composer in Europe.

Imagno/Getty Images

Haydn's long life, commitment to duty, and unflagging industry resulted in an impressive number of musical compositions: 106 symphonies, about 70 string quartets, nearly a dozen operas, 52 piano sonatas, 14 Masses, and 2 oratorios. He began composing before the death of Bach (1750) and did not put down his pen until about the time Beethoven set to work on his Symphony No. 5 (1808). Thus, Haydn not only witnessed but, more than any other composer, helped to create the mature Classical style. Yet, although keenly aware of his own musical gifts, he was quick to recognize talent in others, especially Mozart: "Friends often flatter me that I have some genius, but he [Mozart] stood far above me."

Wolfgang Amadeus Mozart (1756–1791)

Indeed who, except possibly Bach, could match Mozart's diversity, breadth of expression, and perfect formal control? Wolfgang Amadeus Mozart was born in 1756 in the mountain town of **Salzburg,** Austria, then a city of about 20,000 residents. His father, Leopold Mozart, was a violinist in the orchestra of the ruling archbishop of Salzburg and the author of a best-selling introduction to playing the violin. Leopold was quick to recognize the musical gifts of his son, who by the age of six was playing the piano, violin, and organ, as well as composing. In 1762, the Mozart family coached off to Vienna, where Wolfgang and his older sister Nannerl displayed their musical wares before Empress Maria Theresa (1717–1780). They then embarked on a three-year tour of Northern Europe that included extended stops in Munich, Brussels, Paris, London, Amsterdam, and Geneva. In London, Wolfgang sat on the knee of Johann Christian Bach (1735–1782) and improvised a fugue. And here, at the age of eight, he wrote his first two symphonies. Eventually, the Mozarts made their way back to Salzburg. But in 1768, they were off again to Vienna, where the now twelve-year-old Wolfgang staged a production of his first opera, *Bastien und Bastienne,* in the home of the famous Dr. Franz Anton Mesmer (1734–1815), the

Alinari/The Bridgeman Art Library

▲ An unfinished portrait of Mozart painted by his brother-in-law Joseph Lange during 1789–1790

inventor of the theory of animal magnetism (hence, "to mesmerize"). The next year father and son visited the major cities of Italy, including Rome, where, on July 8, 1770, the pope dubbed Wolfgang a Knight of the Order of the Golden Spur (see top, next page). Although the aim of all this globe-trotting was to acquire fame and fortune, the result was that Mozart, unlike Haydn, was exposed at an early age to a wealth of musical styles—French Baroque, English choral, German polyphonic, and Italian vocal. His extraordinarily keen ear absorbed them all, and his creative mind synthesized them into a new, international style. Today Mozart is still widely recognized as "the most universal composer in the history of Western music."

A period of relative stability followed Mozart's youthful travels: For much of the 1770s he resided in Salzburg, where he served as violinist and composer to the reigning archbishop, Colloredo. But the archbishop was a stern, frugal man who had little sympathy for Mozart, genius or not (the composer referred to him as the "Archboobie"). Mozart was paid modestly and, like the servant-musicians at the court of Esterházy, ate with the cooks and valets. For a Knight of the Golden Spur who had hobnobbed with kings and queens across Europe, this was humble fare indeed, and Mozart chafed under this system of aristocratic patronage. But he couldn't just quit—servants of the court had to obtain a release from their employer before they could move on. So in the spring of 1781 Mozart precipitated several unpleasant scenes, effectively forcing the archbishop to fire him. Twenty-five-year-old Mozart then established himself in

British Library Board, London/The Bridgeman Art Library

▲ The child Mozart at the keyboard, with his sister, Nannerl, and his father, Leopold, in Paris in 1764 during their three-year tour of Europe

Vienna, attempting to do something that no musician before him had accomplished: make his fortune as a freelance artist.

Mozart chose Vienna because the city had a vibrant musical life and passion for the two things he did best: compose and play the keyboard. In a letter to his sister in the spring of 1782, Mozart spells out how he juggled his time between composition, teaching, and performing.

> My hair is always done by six o'clock in the morning and by seven I am fully dressed. I then compose until nine. From nine to one I give lessons. Then I lunch, unless I am invited to some house where they lunch at two or even three o'clock. . . . I can never work before five or six o'clock in the evening, and even then I am often prevented by a concert. If I am not prevented, I compose until nine.

The years 1784–1787 witnessed the peak of Mozart's success in Vienna and the creation of many of his greatest works. He had a full complement of pupils, played several concerts a week, and enjoyed lucrative commissions as

See "Mozart" presented to the Emperor Joseph II and improvising, from the film *Amadeus*, in the YouTube playlist at CourseMate for this text.

a composer. Piano concertos, string quartets, and symphonies flowed from his fertile pen, as did his two greatest Italian operas, *The Marriage of Figaro* and *Don Giovanni.* He also found time to join the **Freemasons,** an Enlightenment fraternity, which espoused tolerance and universal brotherhood. Many view Mozart's last opera, *Die Zauberflöte* (*The Magic Flute,* 1791) as a hymn in praise of Masonic ideals.

During his best years, Mozart made a great deal of money, about $325,000 annually by one estimate. But money flew out the door as fast as it came in—he lived well and loved fine clothes in particular. When a war with the Turkish Empire broke out and a Europe-wide recession ensued, the Viennese had far less money to spend on luxuries like musical entertainment. Mozart's income plummeted, and he was reduced to begging from his fellow Freemasons. But the composer's economic prospects revived by 1791. In the summer and fall of that year, Mozart received handsome commissions for an opera at court (*La Clemenza di Tito*) and a Requiem Mass. Such good fortune, however, was to be tragically short-lived. Indeed, the Mass became Mozart's own requiem when he died unexpectedly on December 5, 1791, at the age of thirty-five. The precise reason for his death has never been determined, though rheumatic fever and kidney failure, made worse by needless bloodletting, are the most likely causes. No single event in the history of music is more regrettable than the premature loss of Mozart. What he would have given to the world had he enjoyed the long life of a Handel or a Haydn!

⋀ Young Mozart proudly wearing the collar of a Knight of the Order of the Golden Spur, an honor conferred upon him for his musical skills by Pope Clement XIV in July 1770

⋀ This still from the spectacularly good Academy Award–winning film *Amadeus* (1985) shows "Mozart" composing at a billiard table. Mozart did in fact keep a billiard table in his bedroom. But in most other ways, the portrayal of Mozart in *Amadeus* is largely fictitious. Mozart was not an irresponsible idiot-savant who died penniless, but a highly intelligent entrepreneur whose income fluctuated wildly from year to year; moreover, he was not poisoned by his rival, composer Antonio Salieri (1750–1825). But *Amadeus* does pose an intriguing question: What does a mediocre or even somewhat gifted person (Salieri) do when faced with an absolute genius (Mozart)?

Classical Forms

When we use the term *form*, whether discussing a building or a piece of music, we refer to that artifact's external shape or the way it is positioned in physical space. The forms of Classical architecture were consistent and widespread; around 1800, for example, buildings might look much the same in Vienna as in Virginia (see the beginning of Chapter 7). Moreover, the forms of Classical architecture are still very much with us today. Consider, for example, the windows in the dance auditorium at the emperor's court in Vienna (see image below), where Mozart and his wife often waltzed. Windows of precisely this design still can be seen in this chapter's opening photo, the concert hall of your author's university, and even his living room. Look for others next time you walk around your campus. Musical form during the Classical period was similarly well traveled. A few musical designs shaped most Classical music, no matter who the composer or where the concert. Some of these forms predated the Classical period, and some were created during it. And as in architecture, these forms have proved timeless, serving composers down to the present day.

◄ A ball at the Redoutensaal (dancing hall) in the emperor's palace in Vienna, c. 1800. Mozart, Haydn, and, later, Beethoven composed minuets and "German dances" for these events, which sometimes attracted nearly four thousand fee-paying dancers. The orchestra can be seen in the gallery to the left. The Redoutensaal still provides a venue for concerts and balls today.

Erich Lessing/Art Resource, NY

Form, Mood, and the Listener's Expectations

Today when we attend a concert of classical music—of a symphony orchestra, for example—most of the music on the program (perhaps an overture by Mozart, a symphony by Haydn, and a concerto by Beethoven) will have been played by that orchestra and in that hall many times over the years. These favorite overtures, symphonies, and concertos belong to the **canon** (standard repertoire) of Western classical music. When concertgoers stepped into a hall in the late eighteenth century, however, they expected all of the music to be new and up to date—why would anyone want to hear old music? But while the late-eighteenth-century audience didn't know the pieces in advance, listeners did come with certain expectations with regard to the form as well as the mood of the music. For a symphony, for example, they might anticipate the following:

	Four-Movement Symphony			
Movement	1	2	3	4
Form	Sonata–allegro	Large ternary, theme and variations, or rondo	Minuet and trio in ternary form	Sonata–allegro, theme and variations, or rondo
Mood	Serious and substantive despite fast tempo	Lyrical and tender	Usually light and elegant, sometimes spirited	Bright, lighthearted, sometimes humorous
Tempo	Fast	Slow	Lively	Fast

Thus, during the Classical era composers used certain forms for certain movements within a symphony. The same expectations also held true for a sonata and a concerto. But how do composers make a "form" out of music—something you hear but can't see? They do so, as mentioned in Chapter 3, through statement, repetition, contrast, and variation.

Watch a video of Craig Wright's Open Yale Course class session 9, on ternary and sonata–allegro forms, at CourseMate for this text.

Ternary Form

In **ternary form (ABA)**, the idea of statement-contrast-repetition is obvious. Think of it as kind of musical "home–away–home" if you wish. To demonstrate the point in the simplest possible terms, consider again the French folk song known to us as "Twinkle, Twinkle, Little Star."

A Twinkle, twinkle, little star, how I wonder what you are.

B Up above the world so high, like a diamond in the sky.

A Twinkle, twinkle, little star, how I wonder what you are.

Minuet and Trio in Ternary Form

Dance music is generally straightforward and symmetrical in form, so that the mind and body can more easily grasp and perform the steps. During the Baroque and Classical eras, most dances were written in simple forms, such as binary (see p. 44) and ternary. The latter provides the structure of the **minuet,** a stately dance in triple meter. The minuet began life in the Baroque era as a popular dance and was used, during the Classical period, as a movement within a symphony or a string quartet. In this case "dance music" became stylized "listening music."

When set in the high-art genres of symphony and quartet, minuets were usually presented in pairs. Because the second minuet of the set had originally been played by only three instruments, it was called the **trio,** a name that persisted into the nineteenth century, no matter how many instruments were required. Once the trio was finished, convention dictated a return to the first minuet, now performed without repeats. Because the trio also was composed in ternary form, an **ABA** pattern was heard three times in succession. (In the following, the **ABA** structure of the trio is represented by **CDC,** to distinguish it from the minuet.)

◀ Couples in the late eighteenth century dancing the stately minuet. In some areas of Europe at this time, women were forbidden to dance the minuet because it was thought to involve excessive body contact.

And, because the trio was different from the surrounding minuet, the entire minuet–trio–minuet movement formed an **ABA** arrangement.

A (minuet)	B (trio)	A (minuet)
‖: A :‖‖: BA :‖	‖: C :‖‖: DC :‖	**ABA**

Mozart's *Eine kleine Nachtmusik (A Little Night Music),* written in the summer of 1787, is among his most popular works. It is a **serenade,** a light, multimovement piece for strings alone or small orchestra, one intended for an evening's entertainment and often performed outdoors. Although we do not know the precise occasion for which Mozart composed it, we might well imagine *Eine kleine Nachtmusik* providing the musical backdrop for a torch-lit party in a formal Viennese garden. The *Menuetto* appears as the third of four movements in this serenade and is a model of grace and concision.

Example 8-1 ➤

(continued)

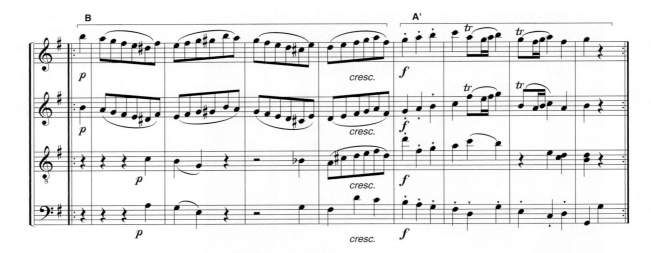

As you can see, the contrasting **B** section interjects rapid motion, but is only four measures long, and the return to **A** does not reproduce the full eight bars of the original but only the last four—thus, this pattern might be viewed as **ABA′**. Formal symmetry, of course, is reflected here also in a simple equation: **A** (8 bars) = **B** (4 bars) + **A′** (4 bars).

Listening Cue

Wolfgang Amadeus Mozart, *Eine kleine Nachtmusik* (*A Little Night Music,* **1787**)

Third movement, Minuet and trio

Genre: Serenade
Form: Ternary

WHAT TO LISTEN FOR: The formal divisions between sections of the minuet (**ABA**) as well as that of the trio (at 0:39) and return to the minuet (at 1:33); also the much thinner texture of the trio

 Listen to streaming music in an Active Listening Guide at CourseMate or in the eBook.

Having now mastered ternary form (**ABA**), let's proceed to a far greater challenge: hearing sonata–allegro form.

Sonata–Allegro Form

Sonata–allegro form is the most complex of all musical structures, and it tends to result in the longest pieces. Yet it is also the most important. In the Classical era, more movements of symphonies, quartets, and the like were written in this form than in any other, and its popularity endured throughout the nineteenth century as well. But first, an important distinction: the difference between the *genre* called sonata and the *form* called sonata–allegro. A sonata is a genre of music usually involving a solo instrument; sonata–allegro, however, is a form giving structure to a single movement of any one of several genres: sonata, string quartet, serenade, symphony, even a one-movement overture.

To see how this works, consider the movements in two different works in two different genres, Mozart's serenade *Eine kleine Nachtmusik* and Haydn's Symphony No. 94. Each work is comprised of four movements, and each movement has its own form. We get the term **sonata–allegro form** from the fact that most sonatas employ this form in the first movement, and the first movement almost always goes fast, or "allegro."

Mozart, *Eine kleine Nachtmusik* (1787)				
Movement	1	2	3	4
Tempo	Fast	Slow	Minuet and trio	Fast
Form	Sonata–allegro	Rondo	Ternary	Rondo
Haydn, Symphony No. 94 (1791)				
Movement	1	2	3	4
Tempo	Fast	Slow	Minuet and trio	Fast
Form	Sonata–allegro	Theme and variations	Ternary	Sonata–allegro

The Shape of Sonata–Allegro Form

To get a sense of what might happen in a typical first movement of a sonata, string quartet, symphony, or serenade, look at the following diagram. Although not every sonata–allegro movement follows this ideal scheme, the diagram provides a useful overall model.

SONATA–ALLEGRO FORM

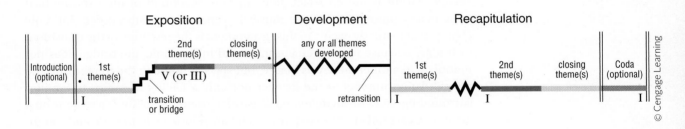

In its broad outline, sonata–allegro form looks much like ternary form. It consists of an **ABA** plan, with the **B** section providing contrast in mood, key, and thematic treatment. The initial **A** in sonata–allegro form is called the exposition, the **B** the development, and the return to **A** the recapitulation. But sonata–allegro is a larger, more dynamic, and more dramatic form than ternary. As with a play or a film, the drama unfolds in three principal parts: setup, complication, and resolution, with perhaps a "fadeout" at the end.

EXPOSITION

In the **exposition,** the composer presents the main themes, or musical personalities, of the movement. It begins with the first theme or theme group, which is always in the tonic key. Next comes the **transition,** or **bridge** as it is sometimes called, which carries the music from the tonic to a new key, usually the dominant, and prepares for the arrival of the second theme. The second theme typically contrasts in character with the first; if the first is rapid and assertive, the second may be more languid and lyrical. The exposition usually concludes with a closing theme, often simply oscillating between dominant and tonic chords—not much is happening harmonically, so we must be near the end. After the final cadence, the exposition is repeated in full. We've now met all the "characters" of the piece; let's see how things develop.

DEVELOPMENT

If sonata–allegro is a dramatic musical form, most of the drama comes in the **development.** As the name indicates, a further working out, or "developing," of the thematic material occurs here. The themes can be extended and varied, or wholly transformed; a character we thought we knew can turn out to have a completely different personality. Dramatic confrontation can occur, as when several themes sound together, fighting for our attention. Not only are developments dramatic, they are unstable and unsettling, the harmony typically modulating quickly from one key to the next. Only toward the end of the development, in the passage called the **retransition,** is tonal order restored, often by means of a stabilizing pedal point on the dominant note. When the dominant chord (V) finally gives way to the tonic (I), the recapitulation begins.

RECAPITULATION

After the turmoil of the development, the listener greets the return of the first theme and the tonic key of the exposition with welcome relief. Though the **recapitulation** is not an exact, note-for-note repetition of the exposition, it nonetheless presents the same musical events in the same order. The only change that regularly occurs in this restatement is the rewriting of the transition, or bridge. Because the movement must end in the tonic, the bridge does not modulate to a different key as before, but stays at home in the tonic. Thus, the recapitulation imparts to the listener not only a feeling of return to familiar surroundings but also an increased sense of harmonic stability. We've gone on a great musical (and emotional) journey and are now back home safe and sound.

The following two elements are optional to sonata–allegro form, functioning something akin to a preface and an epilogue.

INTRODUCTION

About half the mature symphonies of Haydn and Mozart have a brief introduction, like a curtain raiser before the real drama begins. Introductions are, without exception, slow and stately, and usually filled with ominous or puzzling chords designed to get the listener wondering what sort of musical excursion he or she is about to take.

CODA

As the name **coda** (Italian for "tail") indicates, this is a section added to the end of the movement to wrap things up. Like tails, codas can be long or short. Haydn and Mozart wrote relatively short codas in which a motive might simply be repeated again and again in conjunction with repeating dominant-tonic chords. Beethoven, however, was inclined to compose lengthy codas, sometimes introducing new themes even at the end of the movement. But no matter how long the coda, most will end with a final cadence in which the harmonic motion slows down to just two chords, dominant and tonic, played over and over, as if to say "the end, the end, the end, THE **END**." The more these repeat, the greater the feeling of conclusion.

Hearing Sonata–Allegro Form

Movements in sonata–allegro form tend to be long, lasting anywhere from four minutes in a simple composition from the Classical period to twenty minutes or more in a full-blown movement of the Romantic era. Consequently, they can be difficult to follow. How does one tame this musical beast? First, be sure to memorize the diagram of sonata–allegro form given on page 113. Equally important, think carefully about the four distinctive musical styles found in sonata–allegro form: thematic, transitional, developmental, and cadential (ending). Each has a distinctive sound. A thematic passage has a clearly recognizable melody, often a singable tune. The transition is full of motion, with melodic sequences and rapid chord changes. The development sounds active, perhaps confusing; the harmonies shift quickly, and the themes, while recognizable, often pile one on top of another in a dense contrapuntal texture. Finally, a cadential passage, coming at the end of a section or the end of the piece, sounds repetitive because the same chords are heard again and again in a harmony that seems to have stopped moving forward. Each of these four styles has a specific function within sonata–allegro form: to state, to move, to develop, or to conclude.

To test our ability to follow the unfolding sonata–allegro form, we turn now to the opening movement of Mozart's *Eine kleine Nachtmusik*. The Active Listening Guide available at the text website is essential to a full appreciation of the music. But to whet your appetite, the three principal themes of the movement of the exposition are provided here.

The aggressive, fanfare-like opening that rapidly ascends:

ᴧ Jazz artist and improv singer Bobby McFerrin conducting the St. Paul Chamber Orchestra. McFerrin has conducted orchestras around the world and issued several recordings of Mozart, including his *Eine kleine Nachtmusik*, discussed here.

See a fascinating interaction between Mozart's *Eine kleine Nachtmusik* and the musical style of Bobby McFerrin in the YouTube playlist at CourseMate for this text.

Listen to a series of podcasts on hearing sonata–allegro form at CourseMate for this text.

The quieter, lighter, second theme that begins with a rapid descent:

The cheerful closing theme that ends with repeating pitches:

Although you may not recognize the music simply by looking at this notation, you will when you hear it. Mozart's *Eine kleine Nachtmusik* is a "classic" within the repertoire of classical music; its melodies have been used countless times in radio and TV commercials to market elegant, high-end products. The fame is well deserved, for rarely is sonata–allegro form presented as economically, and almost never as artfully.

Listening Cue

Wolfgang Amadeus Mozart, *Eine kleine Nachtmusik* (1787)

First movement, *Allegro* (fast)

Genre: Serenade
Form: Sonata–allegro

WHAT TO LISTEN FOR: Introduction (none). Exposition (track 13). Development (track 14). Recapitulation (track 15). Coda (track 15 at 1:31).

 Listen to streaming music in an Active Listening Guide at CourseMate or in the eBook.

For two other famous movements in sonata–allegro form (and a Listening Exercise for each), skip ahead to Mozart's Symphony No. 40 (p. 126) and Beethoven's Symphony No. 5 (p. 146).

 Theme and Variations

In the film *Amadeus,* Mozart is shown composing variations on a theme of another composer (Salieri), tossing them off effortlessly like a magician pulling handkerchiefs from his sleeve. The capacity, indeed compulsion, to endlessly reimagine an object or idea is typical of great artists like Mozart, Leonardo da Vinci, and Shakespeare. In music, it is not an image or a vision that is varied, but usually a melody. **Theme and variations** form occurs when a melody is altered, decorated, or adorned in some way by changing pitch, rhythm, harmony, or even mode (major or minor). The object is still recognizable but somehow doesn't seem to sound the same. As we've seen (p. 43), we can visualize this musical process with the following scheme:

Statement of theme	Variation 1	Variation 2	Variation 3	Variation 4
A	A¹	A²	A³	A⁴

For theme and variations to work, the theme must be well known or easy to remember. Traditionally, composers have chosen to vary folk songs and, especially, patriotic songs, such as "God Save the King" (Beethoven) or "America" (Ives). Such tunes are popular in part because they are simple, and this, too, is an advantage for the composer. Melodies that are spare and uncluttered can more easily be dressed in new musical clothing.

Broadly speaking, a musical variation can be effected in either of two ways: (1) by changing the theme itself, or (2) by changing the context around that theme (the accompaniment). Sometimes, these two techniques are used simultaneously. The two examples that follow—one by Mozart and one by Haydn—illustrate a number of techniques for varying a melody and its context. In a set of variations, whether in the fine arts or music, the farther one moves from the initial theme, the more obscure it becomes (see Matisse's sculptures, to the right). For the listener, the primary task is to keep track of the tune as it is altered in increasingly complex ways.

⋀ Henri Matisse's classically inspired series of bronze sculptures of the head of his model, Jeannette Vaderin, executed in 1910, allows us to visualize the process of theme and variations. The image becomes progressively more distant from the original as we move left to right.

Mozart: Variations on "Twinkle, Twinkle, Little Star" (c. 1781)

In the Classical period, it was common for a composer/pianist to improvise in concert a set of variations on a well-known tune, perhaps one requested spontaneously by the audience. Contemporary reports tell us that Mozart was especially skilled in this art of on-the-spot variation. In the early 1780s, Mozart wrote down a set of such improvised variations built on the French folk song "Ah, vous dirai-je, Maman," the melody of which we know today as "Twinkle, Twinkle, Little Star." With a tune as well known as this, it is easy to follow the melody, even as it becomes increasingly ornamented and its accompaniment altered in the course of twelve variations. (Only the first eight bars of the theme are given here; the music through the first five variations can be heard on (Intro)/23.)

Example 8-2A: "Twinkle, Twinkle, Little Star," Basic Theme (0:00) ❯

Variation 1 ornaments the theme and almost buries it beneath an avalanche of sixteenth notes. Would you know that "Twinkle, Twinkle" lurks herein (see the asterisks) if you did not have the tune securely in your ear?

Example 8-2B: Variation 1 (0:30) >

In variation 2, the rushing ornamentation is transferred to the bass (the accompaniment is changed), and the theme surfaces again rather clearly in the upper voice.

Example 8-2C: Variation 2 (0:59) >

In variation 3, triplets in the right hand alter the theme, which is now only recognizable by its general contour.

Example 8-2D: Variation 3 (1:29) >

After the same technique has been applied to the bass (variation 4; 2:00), a thematic alteration again occurs in variation 5. Here the rhythm of the melody is "jazzed up" by placing part of it off the beat, in syncopated fashion.

Example 8-2E: Variation 5 (2:29) >

Of the remaining seven variations, some change the tune to minor, while others add Bach-like counterpoint against it. The final variation presents this duple-meter folk tune reworked into a triple-meter waltz! Yet throughout all of Mozart's magical embroidery, the theme remains audible to our inner ear, so well ingrained is "Twinkle, Twinkle" in our musical memory.

Wolfgang Amadeus Mozart, Variations on "Twinkle, Twinkle, Little Star"

Intro
23

Genre: Keyboard movement
Form: Theme and variations

WHAT TO LISTEN FOR: The theme, or its accompaniment, is varied from one statement to the next, each presentation lasting about thirty seconds.

 Listen to streaming music in an Active Listening Guide at CourseMate or in the eBook.

Haydn: Symphony No. 94 (the "Surprise" Symphony, 1792), Second Movement

Mozart composed his set of variations on "Twinkle, Twinkle, Little Star" as a freestanding, independent piece. Joseph Haydn (1732–1809) was the first composer to take a piece in theme and variations form and make it serve as a movement within a symphony. To be sure, Haydn was an innovative composer—he could "surprise" or "shock" like no other composer of the Classical period. In his "Surprise" Symphony, the shock comes from a sudden *fortissimo* (very loud) chord inserted, as we shall see, in the second movement in the middle of an otherwise very quiet theme. When Haydn's Symphony No. 94 was first heard in London in 1792, the audience cheered this second movement and demanded its immediate repetition. Ever since, this surprising movement has been Haydn's most celebrated composition.

The famous opening melody of the second movement (*Andante*) is written in **binary form,** a simple **AB** arrangement (see also p. 44). Here **A** is an eight-bar antecedent (opening) phrase, and **B** an eight-bar consequent (closing) one—more classical balance! Notice how the beginning of the theme (Ex. 8-3A, p. 120) is shaped by laying out in succession the notes of a tonic triad (I) and then a dominant chord (V). The triadic nature of the tune accounts for its folk song–like quality and makes it easy to remember during the variations that follow. These first eight bars (**A**) are stated and then repeated quietly. And just when all is ending peacefully, the full orchestra, including a thunderous timpani, comes crashing in with a *fortissimo* chord (see asterisk), as if to shock the drowsy listener back to attention. What better way to show off the latent dynamic power of the larger Classical orchestra? The surprise *fortissimo* chord leads into the **B** section of the theme, which also is repeated. With the simple yet highly attractive binary theme now in place, Haydn proceeds to compose four variations on it, adding a superb coda at the end. In his memoirs, dictated in 1809, Haydn explains that he included

< A portrait of Joseph Haydn at work. His left hand is trying an idea at the keyboard while his right is ready to write it down. Haydn said about his compositional process, "I sat down at the keyboard and began to improvise. Once I had seized upon an idea, my whole effort was to develop and sustain it."

The Art Archive/Eileen Tweedy

the surprise blast as something of a publicity stunt, "to make a début in a brilliant manner" and thereby call further attention to his concerts in London.

Example 8-3A: Theme of Second Movement (0:00) ➤

The second violins begin variation 1 with the theme, while the first violins and flute add counterpoint above; following the repeat, the second violins continue with **B** (1:41).

Example 8-3B: Variation 1 (1:06) ➤

In variation 2 Haydn suddenly shifts to a minor key (note the flats in key the signature) and asks the orchestra to play *fortissimo*; the full orchestra then develops **A,** but **B** is entirely omitted.

Example 8-3C: Variation 2 (2:14) ➤

The major (tonic) key returns in variation 3 as the theme is played in rapid notes by the oboe; the strings the play **B** (3:56) with oboe and flute ornamenting above.

Example 8-3D: Variation 3 (3:23) ➤

In the fourth and final variation the strings heavily ornament the original melody with running arpeggios; the repeat of **B** (5:20) is loud and leads to a coda containing reminiscences of the theme in its original form.

Example 8-3E: Variation 4 (4:29) ➤

Joseph Haydn, Symphony No. 94, the "Surprise" Symphony (1791)

Intro
24

Second movement, *Andante* **(moving)**

Genre: Symphony
Form: Theme and variations

WHAT TO LISTEN FOR: A charming, tuneful theme followed by four variations (1:06, 2:14, 3:23, 4:29) and a coda (5:51)

🔊 Listen to streaming music in an Active Listening Guide at CourseMate or in the eBook.

🔊 Take online Listening Exercise 19 at CourseMate or in the eBook.

Listening to this theme and variations movement by Haydn requires hearing discrete units of music. Each block (variation) is marked by some new treatment of the theme. In the Classical period, all the units are usually the same size—that is, have the same number of measures. The variations become progressively more complicated as more ornamentation and transformation are applied, but each unit remains the same length. The addition of a coda after the last variation gives extra weight to the end, so the listener feels that the set of variations has reached an appropriate conclusion. If such extra bars were not appended, the audience would be left hanging, expecting yet another variation to begin.

Rondo Form

Of all musical forms, the rondo is perhaps the easiest to hear, because a single, unvaried theme (the refrain) returns again and again. The rondo is also one of the oldest musical forms, having originated in the Middle Ages. The Baroque era (see pp. 76 and 78) made frequent use of rondo principles, and even contemporary pop songs occasionally employ this form (see p. 122). A true Classical **rondo** must have at least three statements of the refrain (**A**) and at least two contrasting sections (at least **B** and **C**). Often the placement of the refrain creates symmetrical patterns such as **ABACA, ABACABA,** or even **ABACADA.** When Haydn and Mozart set about writing a rondo, they brought to it some of the same musical processes they used when writing in sonata–allegro form, specifically transitional and developmental writing. They thereby created a more elastic, flexible rondo in which the refrain (**A**) and the contrasting sections (**B, C,** or **D**) might develop and expand dramatically.

Watch a video of Craig Wright's Open Yale Course class session 11, "Form: Rondo, Sonata–Allegro, and Theme and Variations (cont.)," at CourseMate for this text.

Hear another concerto by Mozart, Piano Concerto No. 21, in the iTunes playlist at CourseMate for this text.

Mozart: Horn Concerto in E♭ major (1786), K. 495, Third Movement (Finale)

In his short life of thirty-five years, Wolfgang Amadeus Mozart wrote more than 650 compositions, an enormous amount of music. To help us keep track of them, a musicologist in the nineteenth century, Ludwig von Köchel, published a list of Mozart's works in approximate chronological order. Today we continue to identify each of Mozart's compositions with a **Köchel (K.) number.** This is especially handy in the case of Mozart's four concertos for the French horn, three of which he composed in E♭: How else could we differentiate them without a number? Thus, the concerto in E♭ written in Vienna in 1786 is identified as K. 495. All four of Mozart's horn concertos end with a movement in rondo form. Indeed, Classical composers most often chose the rondo form for the **finale** (Italian for "end") of a sonata, quartet, or symphony. The carefree refrain and the easily grasped digressions lend to the rondo finale an "upbeat" feeling, the musical equivalent of a happy ending.

See The Police's "Every Breath You Take," a rondo by Sting, in the YouTube playlist at CourseMate for this text.

Listening Cue

Wolfgang Amadeus Mozart, Horn Concerto in E♭ major (1786), K. 495

1
17

Third movement

Genre: Concerto
Form: Rondo (here **ABACABA** and coda)

WHAT TO LISTEN FOR: The sometimes brilliant, sometimes jovial horn themes, as soloist and orchestra strive together in a friendly competition

◀)) Listen to streaming music in an Active Listening Guide at CourseMate or in the eBook.

(For more discussion of this movement as part of a concerto, and for a cue to an online Listening Exercise, see below, p. 134.)

George De Sota/Getty Images

∧ Sting (Gordon Sumner)

Although rondo form has existed in classical music since the Middle Ages, it appears often in the realm of popular music as well. For example, the pop tune "Every Breath You Take" (1983), composed by Sting, produces the rondo pattern (**ABACABA**), a symmetrical arrangement that would do any Classical composer proud.

The forms popularized during the Classical era—sonata–allegro, theme and variations, and rondo, for example—would continue to regulate the flow of musical works generally until after World War II. So, too, musicians maintained the standard *genres* of Classical music, and it is to these that we now turn.

Classical Genres

n music, the term **genre** simply means the type or class of music to which we listen (see also p. 5). The string quartet is a genre of music just as are the opera aria, country music ballad, twelve-bar blues piece, military march, and rap song. When we listen to a piece of music, we come armed with expectations as to how it will sound, how long it will last, and how we should behave. We may even go to a special place—an opera house or a bar—and dress a certain way—in gown and diamond earrings or black leather jacket and nose rings, for example. It all depends on the genre of music we expect to hear. If you change the genre, you change the audience, and vice versa.

In the age of Haydn and Mozart, there were five main genres of art music: the instrumental genres of symphony, string quartet, sonata, and concerto, and the vocal genre of opera. Whereas the sonata, concerto, and opera emerged during the Baroque era, the symphony and string quartet were entirely new to the Classical period. Thus we begin our exploration of Classical genres with the instrumental symphony and quartet.

Instrumental Music

The Symphony and the Symphony Orchestra

A **symphony** is a multimovement composition for orchestra lasting about twenty-five minutes in the Classical period to nearly an hour in the Romantic era. The origins of the symphony go back to the late-seventeenth-century Italian opera house, where an opera began with an instrumental *sinfonia* (literally, "a harmonious sounding together"). Around 1700, the typical Italian *sinfonia* was a one-movement instrumental work in three sections: fast–slow–fast. Soon, Italian musicians and foreigners alike took the *sinfonia* out of the opera house and expanded it into three separate and distinct movements. A fourth movement, the minuet, was inserted by composers north of the Alps beginning in the 1740s. Thus, by mid-century the **symphony** had assumed its now-familiar four-movement format: fast–slow–minuet–fast (see p. 110). While the movements of a symphony are usually independent with regard to musical themes, all are written in a single key (or set of closely related keys).

As public concerts became more common during the Classical period (see p. 98), so the symphony increased in popularity. The larger public halls accommodated more people, and the bigger audience enjoyed the more robust, colorful sound of the Classical orchestra. The four-movement symphony was the best format by which to convey that sound. The fact that Haydn composed so many (106), and Mozart (given his short life) an even more astonishing number (41), shows that the symphony had become the foremost instrumental genre, the showpiece of the concert hall by the end of the eighteenth century. All but a few of Haydn's last twenty symphonies were composed for public performance in Paris and London, and Mozart's last four symphonies were intended for public concerts that he himself produced. His famous G minor symphony (1788), for example, was apparently first performed in a casino in central Vienna—that's where the people were and that's where the money was. So dominant did the genre of the "symphony" become that it was linked forever with the concert "hall" and the performing "orchestra," thus creating our terms *symphony hall* and *symphony orchestra*.

Erich Lessing/Art Resource, NY

◄ The New Market in Vienna in the late 1700s. The building on the far right (today the Ambassador Hotel) housed the casino, and it was here that Mozart's G minor symphony was apparently first performed in 1788. Even today, famous musicians, such as Placido Domingo and Sting, perform in casinos, because that's where the money is!

THE CLASSICAL SYMPHONY ORCHESTRA

As the symphony orchestra moved from private court to public auditorium the ensemble increased in size to satisfy the demands of its new performance space—and expanding audience. During the 1760s and 1770s, the ensemble at the court of Haydn's patron, Prince Nikolaus Esterházy, was never larger than twenty-five, and the audience at this court was often only the prince and his staff. But when Haydn went to London in 1791, his concert promoters provided him with an orchestra of nearly sixty players in the Hanover Square Rooms. Although this hall normally accommodated 800 to 900 persons, for one concert in the spring of 1792 nearly 1,500 eager listeners crowded in to hear Haydn's latest works.

Deutsches Theatermuseum, Munich/© The Bridgeman Art Library

◄ A watercolor of 1775 shows Haydn leading the small orchestra at the court of the Esterházy princes during a performance of a comic opera. The composer is seated at the keyboard, surrounded by the cellos. The higher strings and woodwinds are seated in two rows at the desk.

Mozart's experience in Vienna was similar. For the public concerts that he mounted in the casino there in the mid-1780s, he engaged an orchestra of 35 to 40 players. But in a letter of 1781, he mentions an orchestra of 80 instrumentalists, including 40 violins, 10 violas, 8 cellos, and 10 double basses. Although this was an exceptional ensemble brought together for a special benefit concert, it shows that at times a very large group could be assembled. It also reveals that a large number of string players could be assigned to play just one string part—as many as 20 might "double" each other on the first violin line, for example.

To balance the growth in the string section, and to increase the variety of color in the orchestra, more winds were added. By the 1790s, a typical symphony orchestra in a large European city might include the instrumentalists listed below. Compared to the Baroque orchestra, this ensemble of up to forty players was larger, more colorful, and more flexible. Moreover, within the Classical orchestra, each instrumental family had a specific assignment: The strings presented the bulk of the musical material; the woodwinds added richness and colorful counterpoint; the French horns sustained a sonorous background; and the trumpets and percussion provided brilliance when a magnificent sound was needed.

Strings	1st violins, 2nd violins, violas, cellos, double basses (about 27 players in all)
Woodwinds	2 flutes, 2 oboes, 2 clarinets, 2 bassoons
Brasses	2 French horns, 2 trumpets (for festive pieces)
Percussion	2 timpani (for festive pieces)

MOZART: SYMPHONY NO. 40 IN G MINOR (1788), K. 550

Mozart's celebrated Symphony in G minor requires all the full instrumental sound and disciplined playing that the late-eighteenth-century orchestra could muster. This is not a festive composition (hence no trumpets and drums), but rather an intensely brooding work that suggests tragedy and despair. Though we might be tempted to associate the minor key and despondent mood with a specific event in Mozart's life, apparently no such causal relationship exists. This was one of three symphonies that Mozart produced in the short span of six weeks during the summer of 1788, and the other two are sunny, optimistic works. Rather than responding to a particular disappointment, it is more likely that Mozart invoked the tragic muse in this G minor symphony by drawing on a lifetime of disappointments and a premonition—as his letters attest—of an early death.

To get the most out of the following discussion, have the diagram of sonata–allegro form (see p. 113) firmly in mind.

FIRST MOVEMENT (MOLTO ALLEGRO)

Exposition (①/18 at 0:00) Mozart begins his G minor symphony with a textbook example of Classical phrase structure (four-bar antecedent, four-bar consequent phrases; Ex. 9-1). Yet an unusual sense of urgency is created immediately by a throbbing accompaniment and the repeating, insistent eighth-note figure in the melody. This melodic motive, the most memorable aspect in the movement, is a falling half step (here E♭ to D), a tight interval used throughout the history of music to denote pain and suffering.

Example 9-1 ➤

Less immediately audible, but still contributing equally to the sense of urgency, is the accelerating rate of harmonic change. At the outset of the movement, chords are set beneath the melody at an interval of one chord every four measures, then one every two bars, then one every measure, then two chords per measure, and finally four. Thus, the "harmonic rhythm" is moving sixteen times faster at the end of this section than at the beginning! This is how Mozart creates the sense of drive and urgency we all feel yet may be unable to explain. After this quickening start, the first theme begins once again but soon veers off its previous course, initiating the transition (0:30). Transitions take us somewhere, usually by means of running scales, and this one is no exception. But a new motive is inserted, one so distinctive that we might call it a "transition theme" (Ex. 9-2).

Example 9-2 ➤

The transition concludes with a strong cadence (0:44) that clears the musical stage for the entry of the soft second theme appearing in a new, major key (0:47; Ex. 9-3).

Example 9-3 ➤

For his closing theme (1:07), Mozart simply alludes to the feverish motive of the first theme.

Development   (①/19 at 0:00) Here Mozart employs only the first theme, but subjects it to a variety of musical treatments. First he pushes it through several distantly related keys, next shapes it into the subject of a brief fugue, then sets it as a descending melodic sequence, and finally turns the motive on its head—what went down now goes up!

Example 9-4 ➤

The retransition (return to the main theme and tonic key) is suddenly interrupted by *sforzandi* (loud attacks). But soon a dominant pedal point sounds in the bassoons (1:05), and above it the flute and clarinets descend, cascading gradually back to the tonic pitch. This use of colorful, solo woodwinds in the retransition is a hallmark of Mozart's symphonic style.

Recapitulation (①/20 at 0:00) As expected, the recapitulation offers the themes in the same order in which they appeared in the exposition. But now the transition theme, which Mozart has left untouched since the exposition, receives extended treatment (0:30), creating something akin to a second development section. When the lyrical second theme finally reappears (1:07), now in the minor mode, its mood is somber and plaintive. Because the repeating figure of the first theme rounds off the recapitulation by way of a closing theme, only the briefest coda (2:05) is needed to end this passionate, haunting movement.

Listening Cue

Wolfgang Amadeus Mozart, Symphony No. 40 in G minor (1788), K. 550

First movement, *Molto allegro* (very fast)

①

18–20

Genre: Symphony
Form: Sonata–allegro

WHAT TO LISTEN FOR: You can listen "formally," paying attention to the passing of the exposition, development, and recapitulation of sonata–allegro form, or "emotionally," experiencing the occasional rays of musical sunlight that emerge within Mozart's dark, passionately brooding landscape.

◀)) Listen to streaming music in an Active Listening Guide at CourseMate or in the eBook.

◀)) Take online Listening Exercise 20 at CourseMate or in the eBook.

SECOND MOVEMENT (*ANDANTE*)

After the feverish excitement of the opening movement, the slow, lyrical *Andante* comes as a welcome change of pace. What makes this movement exceptionally beautiful is the extraordinary interplay between the light and dark colors of the woodwinds against the constant tone of the strings. If there is no thematic contrast and confrontation here, there is nonetheless heartfelt expression brought about by Mozart's masterful use of orchestral color.

THIRD MOVEMENT (*MENUETTO; ALLEGRETTO*)

We expect the aristocratic minuet to provide elegant, graceful dance music. But much to our surprise, Mozart returns to the intense, somber mood of the opening movement. This he does, in part, by choosing to write in the tonic minor key—a rare minuet in minor. This again demonstrates how the minuet had changed from "dance music" to "listening music."

FOURTH MOVEMENT (*ALLEGRO ASSAI*)

The finale (last movement) starts with an ascending "rocket" that explodes in a rapid, *forte* flourish—and only carefully rehearsed string playing can pull off this orchestral special effect. The contrasting second theme of this sonata–allegro form movement is typically Mozartean in its grace and charm, a proper foil to the explosive opening melody. Midway through the development, musical compression takes hold: There is no retransition, only a pregnant pause before the recapitulation; the return dispenses with the repeats built into the first theme; and a coda is omitted. This musical foreshortening at the end produces the same psychological effect experienced at the very beginning of the symphony—a feeling of urgency and acceleration.

The String Quartet

The symphony is the ideal genre for the public concert hall, for it aims to please a large listening public. The **string quartet,** on the other hand, typifies chamber music—music for the small concert hall, for the private chamber, or just for the enjoyment of the performers themselves. Like the symphony, the string quartet normally has four movements, all unified by a common key. But unlike the symphony, which might have a dozen violinists joining on the first violin line, the string quartet features only one player per part: first violinist, second violinist, violist, and cellist. Such an intimate ensemble has no need for a conductor; all performers function equally and communicate directly among themselves. No wonder the German poet Johann Wolfgang von Goethe (1749–1832) compared the string quartet to a conversation among four intelligent people.

Joseph Haydn is rightly called "the father of the string quartet." In the 1760s and 1770s he began to compose music for four string instruments requiring a new, more agile kind of interaction. From the old Baroque model Haydn removed the *basso continuo,* replacing it with a more melodically active bass played by a nimble cello alone. And he enriched the middle of the texture by adding a viola, playing immediately above the cello. If Baroque music had a "top- and bottom-heavy" texture (see p. 68), the newer Classical string quartet style shows a texture covered evenly by four instruments, each of which participates more or less equally in a give and take of theme and motive. Haydn's string quartet could not have pulled off the "big bang" special effect of his "Surprise" Symphony (see p. 119)—it didn't have the fire power. But Haydn's symphony orchestra could not have effectively played all the rapidly moving notes in Example 9-5, from his "Emperor" Quartet—it wasn't agile enough.

⋏ A representation of a string quartet at the end of the eighteenth century. The string quartet was at first an ensemble for playing chamber music in the home. Not until 1804 did a string quartet appear in a public concert in Vienna, and not until 1814 in Paris.

Example 9-5 ➤

The chance to play string quartets together gave rise to a lasting friendship between Haydn and Mozart. During 1784–1785, the two men met in Vienna, sometimes at the home of an aristocrat, and other times in Mozart's own apartment. In their quartet, Haydn played first violin, and Mozart viola. As a result of this experience, Mozart was inspired to dedicate a set of his best works in this genre to the older master, which he published in 1785. Yet in this convivial, domestic music-making, Haydn and Mozart merely joined in the fashion of the day. For whether in Vienna, Paris, or London, aristocrats and members of the well-to-do middle class were encouraged to play quartets with friends, as well as to engage professional musicians to entertain their guests.

HAYDN: OPUS 76, NO. 3, THE "EMPEROR" QUARTET (1797)

Haydn's "Emperor" Quartet, written in Vienna during the summer of 1797, numbers among the best works of the string quartet genre. It is known as the "Emperor" because it makes liberal use of "The Emperor's Hymn," a melody that Haydn composed in response to the military and political events of his day.

In 1796, the armies of Napoleon invaded the Austrian Empire, which ignited a firestorm of patriotism in Vienna, the Austrian capital. But the Austrians were at a musical disadvantage: the French now had the "Marseillaise," and the English had their "God Save the King," but the Austrians had no national anthem. To this end, the ministers of state approached Haydn, who quickly fashioned one to the text "Gott erhalte Franz den Kaiser" ("God Preserve Franz the Emperor"; Ex. 9-6), in honor of the reigning Austrian Emperor Franz II. Called "The Emperor's Hymn," it was first sung in theaters throughout the Austrian realm on the emperor's birthday, February 12, 1797. Later that year, Haydn took the tune and worked it into a string quartet.

∧ (top) Title page of six string quartets by Mozart dedicated to Haydn (1785). Mozart offers them to Haydn as "six children," asking Haydn to be their "father, guide, and friend." (bottom) Franz II (1765–1835), last Holy Roman Emperor, and first emperor of Austria. Haydn composed *The Emperor's Hymn* in his honor.

Example 9-6 ➤

In truth, when Haydn fashioned quartet Opus 76, No. 3, he made use of his imperial hymn not in all four movements, but only in the slow second movement. Here it serves as the basis of a theme and variations set. The noble theme is first presented by the first violin and harmonized in simple chords. Thereafter four variations ensue, and each instrument has its turn at presenting the melody. In each variation the accompaniment (context) changes, but the theme remains unaltered. Presumably, one did not toy with the musical personification of the emperor.

Listening Cue

Joseph Haydn, String Quartet, Opus 76, No. 3, the "Emperor" Quartet (1797)

Second movement, *Poco adagio cantabile* **(rather slow, song-like)**

21–22

Genre: String quartet
Form: Theme and variations

WHAT TO LISTEN FOR: Emperor's theme (0:00) followed by four variations in which the second violin (1:28), cello (2:48), viola (1 /22 at 0:00), and first violin (1:25) present the theme

🔊 Listen to streaming music in an Active Listening Guide at CourseMate or in the eBook.

🔊 Take online Listening Exercise 21 at CourseMate or in the eBook.

The popularity of "The Emperor's Hymn" did not end with the defeat of Napoleon in 1815 or the death of Emperor Franz II in 1835. So alluring is Haydn's melody that with altered text it became a Protestant hymn ("Glorious Things of Thee Are Spoken"), as well as the national anthem of Austria (1853) and Germany (1922). It was also Haydn's own favorite piece, and he played a piano arrangement of it every night before retiring. In fact, "The Emperor's Hymn" was the last music Haydn played before he died in the early hours of May 31, 1809.

The Sonata

Most children who study a Western musical instrument (piano, flute, violin, or cello, for example) will play a sonata at one time or another. A **sonata** (Italian for "something to be sounded") is a genre of chamber music played on a solo instrument or a solo instrument accompanied by piano. Although it originated at the beginning of the Baroque period, the sonata took its definitive shape during the Classical era. The usual format was three movements (fast-slow-fast), and each movement might be in any one of the preferred Classical forms: sonata–allegro, ternary, rondo, or theme and variations.

According to publishers' inventories from the end of the eighteenth century, more sonatas were printed than any other genre of music. The explanation for this sudden vogue is tied to the equally sudden popularity of the piano. Indeed, the word *sonata* has become so closely associated with the piano that unless otherwise qualified as "violin sonata," "cello sonata," or the like, we usually assume that "sonata" refers to a three-movement work for piano.

💬 Watch a video of Craig Wright's Open Yale Course class session 18, "Piano Music of Mozart and Beethoven," at CourseMate for this text.

Bildarchiv Preussischer Kulturbesitz/Art Resource, NY

◄ Mozart's piano, preserved in the house of his birth in Salzburg, Austria. The keyboard spans only five octaves, and the black-and-white color scheme of the keys is reversed, both typical features of the late-eighteenth-century piano. Mozart purchased the instrument in 1784 and on it he played both his piano sonatas privately and piano concertos publicly.

Who played this flood of new sonatas for the piano? Amateur musicians, mostly women, who practiced and performed for polite society in the comfort of their own homes. (Oddly, men in this period usually played not the piano but string instruments such as the violin or cello.) As we have seen (p. 100), in Mozart's time, the ability to play the piano, to do fancy needlework, and to utter a few selected words of French were thought by male-dominated society all that was necessary to be a cultured young lady.

To teach the musical handicraft, instructors were needed. Mozart, Haydn, and Beethoven all served as piano teachers in fashionable circles early in their careers. Their piano sonatas were not intended to be played in public concert halls. Instead, they served two functions: The easier ones provided students with material they might practice at home to develop technique; and the more difficult ones were to be showpieces for the composers themselves, with which they could impress in the homes of wealthy patrons. Among the thirty-two splendid piano sonatas that Beethoven composed, for example, only one was ever performed at a public concert in Vienna during his lifetime.

(An example of a Classical piano sonata by Beethoven, his *"Pathétique"* Sonata, is found on ①/23–25. It is discussed in detail on pp. 142–144.)

The Concerto

The Classical **concerto** was a large-scale, three-movement (fast-slow-fast) work for instrumental soloist and orchestra. We derive our term *concerto* from the Italian word *concertare* ("to strive together"). Indeed, the central drama of the genre results from the interaction between a soloist and an ensemble, who engage in a spirited give and take with thematic material. Like the symphony, the concerto was intended for performance in the public auditorium. While the symphony might have provided the greatest musical substance at a concert, audiences were often lured to the hall by the prospect of hearing a virtuoso performer play a concerto. Then as now, audiences were fascinated with personal virtuosity and all the derring-do that a stunning technical display might bring. Gone was the Baroque tradition of the concerto grosso, in which a group of soloists (concertino) stepped forward from the full orchestra (tutti) and then receded back into it. From this point forward, the concerto was a **solo concerto,** usually for piano but sometimes for violin, cello, French horn, trumpet, or woodwind. In the new concerto, the soloist commanded all the audience's attention.

Mozart composed twenty-three piano concertos, many among the best ever written, securing his reputation as the inventor of the modern piano concerto. Mozart's motivation, however, was not enduring fame, but money. At each of the public concerts he produced, Mozart offered one or two of his latest concertos. But he had to do more: he was responsible for renting the hall, hiring the orchestra, leading rehearsals, attracting an audience, transporting his piano to the hall, and even selling tickets from his apartment—all this in addition to composing the music and appearing as solo virtuoso. But when all went well, Mozart could make a killing, as a music journal of March 22, 1783, reported:

> Today the celebrated Chevalier Mozart gave a musical concert for his own benefit at the Burgtheater in which pieces of his own music, which was already very popular, were performed. The concert was honored by the presence of

v One of the few surviving tickets to a concert given by Mozart in Vienna. These were sold in advance, not from a ticket agency, but from Mozart's own apartment.

Internationale Stiftung Mozarteum (ISM), Salzburg, Austria

an extraordinarily large audience and the two new concertos and other fantasies which Mr. Mozart played on the Forte Piano were received with the loudest approval. Our Monarch [Emperor Joseph II], who contrary to his custom honored the entire concert with his presence, joined in the applause of the public so heartily that one can think of no similar example. The proceeds of the concert are estimated at sixteen hundred gulden.

Sixteen hundred gulden was the equivalent of about $140,000 today, and more than four times the annual salary of Mozart's father. With a take such as this, young Mozart could, at least for a time, indulge his expensive tastes.

MOZART: HORN CONCERTO IN E♭ MAJOR (1786), K. 495, THIRD MOVEMENT (FINALE)

Sometimes, however, Mozart wrote concertos for which he received nothing other than the gratitude of a friend. The French horn player Joseph Leutgeb (1732–1811) was one such recipient of Mozart's generosity. Indeed, during the 1780s Mozart composed four horn concertos for old family friend and always down-on-his luck Leutgeb. In these scores Mozart poked fun at his friend, inserting the remark in the music of K. 417, for example: "Wolfgang Amadé Mozart has taken pity on Leutgeb, ass, ox, and fool."

In Mozart's day the horn was a natural one that lacked valves. Before joining the symphony orchestra around 1700, the French horn had enjoyed life in forest and field as an instrument of sport. It was adept at playing hunting calls but, without valves, it could not play a full scale in its lowest register. For this reason composers wrote for the horn what it could play easily: repeated notes, as well as triads spun out as arpeggios. Below are the themes of the finale of Mozart's horn concerto in E♭, K. 495. **A** and **C** feature repeated pitches and an occasional arpeggio, whereas **B** calls for leaping arpeggios.

∧ A natural French horn of the late eighteenth century, the sort of horn that would have been used in the Classical orchestras of Mozart, Haydn, and Beethoven

Example 9-7A: Theme **A** (1 /17 at 0:00) **>**

Example 9-7B: Theme group **B** (0:15) **>**

Example 9-7C Theme **C** (1:22) **>**

Recall that this movement is in rondo form (see p. 121). All four horn concertos by Mozart end with a jovial rondo. Consider how the "striving together" plays out in this concerto: the horn presents the principal themes (**A, B,** and **C**), while the orchestra accompanies or elaborates upon them. Finally, observe toward the end (2:59) how the orchestra stops and the soloist plays a brilliant fanfare alone. Such a moment of soloistic display at the end of a concerto movement is called a **cadenza,** a final opportunity for the soloist to show off his or her technical skill. During the Baroque period the cadenza was usually improvised on the spot by the soloist; in the Classical era the composer sometimes spelled out in notation precisely what was desired and sometimes not; during the later Romantic epoch the creator notated everything, leaving nothing to chance.

Listening Cue

Wolfgang Amadeus Mozart, Horn Concerto in E♭ major (1786), K. 495

Third movement

Genre: Concerto
Form: Rondo (**ABACABA** and coda)

WHAT TO LISTEN FOR: The sometimes brilliant, sometime jovial horn themes, as soloist and orchestra strive together in a friendly competition

 Listen to streaming music in an Active Listening Guide at CourseMate or in the eBook.

 Take online Listening Exercise 22 at CourseMate or in the eBook.

Vocal Music: Classical Opera

When we consider the genres of vocal music of the Classical period, we turn first and foremost to opera. Then as now, the public embraced opera because, in addition to beautiful music, it had glamour, star appeal, and all the excitement of the theater.

Opera is drama, yes, but drama propelled by music. In the Classical period, opera maintained the essential features it had developed during the Baroque era. It still began with an overture, was divided into two or three acts, and made use of a succession of arias and recitatives, along with an occasional choral number. And, of course, it still was performed in a theater large enough to accommodate both an orchestra and elaborate stage sets.

A central development in the eighteenth century was the rise of comic opera (*opera buffa*), a powerful voice for social change during the Enlightenment (see p. 99). The statue-like gods, goddesses, emperors, and queens of the old Baroque *opera seria* gradually departed the stage, making room for more natural, realistic characters drawn from everyday life—a barber and a maid, for example. Where Baroque opera posed magnificently, Classical opera moves fluidly. Arias and recitatives flow easily from one to another, and the mood of the music changes rapidly to reflect the quick-moving, often comic, events on stage.

Comic opera introduces a new element into the opera house, the **vocal ensemble,** which allows the plot to unfold more quickly. Instead of waiting for each character to sing in turn, three or more characters can express their own particular emotions simultaneously, singing together. One might sing of her love, another of his fear, another of her outrage, while a fourth pokes fun at the other three. If an author attempted this in a spoken play (everyone talking at once), an incomprehensible jumble would result. In opera, however, the end product is both harmonious and dramatically compelling. Composers often placed vocal ensembles at the ends of acts to help spark a rousing conclusion, one in which all the principals might appear together on stage. The vocal ensemble typifies the more democratic spirit, and better dramatic pacing, of the late eighteenth century.

Mozart and Opera

The master of Classical opera, and of the vocal ensemble in particular, was Wolfgang Amadeus Mozart (1756–1791). While Haydn wrote more than a dozen operas and conducted others (see p. 125, bottom image), he lacked Mozart's instinct for what was effective in the theater and what was not. Beethoven wrote only one opera, *Fidelio,* and he labored mightily on it, working through several revisions over the course of nearly ten years. Neither Haydn nor Beethoven had Mozart's talent for lightning-quick changes in mood or his capacity to give each character a distinctly personal set of musical attributes. Mozart's music is inherently dramatic and perfectly suited to the stage.

Mozart wrote Italian *opera seria* of the old Baroque sort, modern *opera buffa,* as well as German comic opera, which was called *Singspiel.* Like a Broadway musical, a *Singspiel* is made up of spoken dialogue (instead of recitative) and songs. Mozart's best work of this type is *Die Zauberflöte* (*The Magic Flute,* 1791). But more important, Mozart created a new kind of opera that mixed serious and comic elements to powerful effect. His *Le nozze di Figaro* (*The Marriage of Figaro,* 1786) is a domestic comedy that nonetheless examines betrayal, adultery, love, and, ultimately, forgiveness; his *Don Giovanni* (1787) sets hilarious moments of comic buffoonery within a story of rape, murder, and, ultimately, damnation. In these two masterpieces, both set to texts (libretti) by Lorenzo da Ponte, Mozart's quickly changing music evokes laughter and tears in almost equal measure.

Don Giovanni has been called not only Mozart's greatest opera but also the greatest opera ever written. It tells the tale of an amoral philanderer, a Don Juan (Juan is Spanish, Giovanni Italian), who seduces and murders his way across Europe before being pursued and finally dragged down to Hell by the ghost of a man whom he has killed. Because the seducer and mocker of public law and morality is a nobleman, *Don Giovanni* is implicitly critical of the aristocracy, and Mozart and da Ponte danced quickly to stay one step ahead of the imperial censor before production. Mozart's opera was first performed on October 29, 1787, in Prague, Czech Republic, a city in which his music was especially popular. As fate would have it, the most notorious Don Juan of the eighteenth century, Giacomo Casanova (1725–1798), was in the audience that first night in Prague. It turns out that he had a small hand in helping his friend da Ponte shape the libretto.

Watch a video of Craig Wright's Open Yale Course class session 17, "Mozart and His Operas," at CourseMate for this text.

Lebrecht/ColouriserAL

ᴧ The man who wrote the librettos for Mozart's most important operas of the 1780s, including *Don Giovanni,* was Lorenzo da Ponte. Da Ponte was an Italian priest who, after the death of Mozart and a stay in London, immigrated to America in 1805. Once there, he ran a dry goods store in Sunbury, Pennsylvania, and worked as a trader, distiller, and occasional gunrunner during the War of 1812. Eventually, he moved to New York City, becoming the first professor of Italian literature at Columbia University in 1825. In 1826 he sponsored a performance of *Don Giovanni,* the first opera by Mozart to be performed in America.

Watch a performance of Mozart, *Don Giovanni*, "Notte e giorno faticar," in the YouTube playlist at CourseMate for this text.

The rape and murder perpetrated by Don Giovanni isn't funny. The comedy in *Don Giovanni* is delivered not by the Don, but rather by his worldly-wise servant, Leporello, who points out the contradictions (the basis of all humor) in his master's life and in society in general. As the curtain rises, we find the reluctant accomplice Leporello keeping watch outside the house of Donna Anna, while his master is inside attempting to satisfy his sexual appetite. Grumbling as he paces back and forth, Leporello sings about how he would gladly trade places with the fortunate aristocrat ("Notte e giorno faticar" ["I would like to play the gentleman"]; Intro/11). Immediately, Mozart works to establish Leporello's musical character. He sets this opening aria in F major, a traditional key for the pastoral in music, showing that Leporello is a rustic fellow; he gives him a narrow vocal range without anything fancy; and he has him sing quick, repeated notes, almost as if stuttering. This last technique, called "patter song," is a stock device used to depict low-caste, inarticulate characters in comic opera.

▲ Don Giovanni (Roderick Williams) tries to seduce Donna Anna (Suzannah Glanville) at the beginning of a 2005 British production of Mozart's *Don Giovanni*. Note the similarity in approach to *The Phantom of the Opera* by Andrew Lloyd Webber. Lloyd Webber drew heavily from Mozart's *Don Giovanni*. For example, the opera that the Phantom composes in Act II is called *Don Juan [Giovanni] Triumphant*, which tries to tell this timeless tale of seduction from Don Juan's point of view.

As Leporello concludes his complaint, the masked Don Giovanni rushes onstage, chased by the virtuous Donna Anna. Here the strings rush up the scale and the music modulates up a fourth (at 1:40) to signify that we are now dealing with the highborn. The victim of Don Giovanni's unwanted sexual advances, Donna Anna wants her assailant captured and unmasked. While the gentleman and lady carry on a musical tug-of-war in long notes above, the cowering Leporello patters away fearfully below. This excellent example of vocal ensemble makes clear the conflicting emotions of each party.

Now Donna Anna's father, the Commandant, enters to confront Don Giovanni. Mozart's music tells us that this bodes ill—there is a troubling tremolo in the strings, and the mode (and mood) shifts from major to minor (3:04). Our fear is immediately confirmed as the Don, first refusing to duel, draws his sword and attacks the aging Commandant. In the brief exchange of steel, Mozart depicts the rising tension by means of ascending chromatic scales and tight, tense chords (3:55). At the very moment Don Giovanni's sword pierces the Commandant, the action stops and the orchestra holds on a painful **diminished chord** (4:00)—a tension-filled chord comprised entirely of minor thirds. Mozart then clears the air of discord with a simple texture and accompaniment as Don Giovanni and Leporello gaze in horror on the dying Commandant.

Now a magical moment that perhaps only Mozart could have created (Intro/12): a vocal ensemble in which three very different sentiments are conveyed simultaneously: surprise and satisfaction (Don Giovanni), the desire to flee (Leporello), and the pain of a violent death (Commandant). At the end, the listener can feel the Commandant expire, his life sinking away through the slow descent of a chromatic scale (0:56). In its intensity and compression, only the opening scene of Shakespeare's *King Lear* rivals the beginning of *Don Giovanni*.

Wolfgang Amadeus Mozart, Opera *Don Giovanni* (1787), K. 527

11–12

Act I, Scene 1

Characters: Don Giovanni, a rakish lord; Leporello, his reluctant servant; Donna Anna, a virtuous noblewoman; the
      Commandant, her father, a retired military man

WHAT TO LISTEN FOR: Leporello's simple aria (/11 at 0:00), a vocal ensemble (1:46) leading to a duel (3:55), and
another vocal ensemble (Intro/12 at 0:00) during which the Commandant dies

🔊 Listen to streaming music in an Active Listening Guide at CourseMate or in the eBook.

When we next meet the unrepentant Don Giovanni (Intro/13 at 0:00), he
is in pursuit of the country girl Zerlina. She is the fiancée of another peasant,
Masetto, and their wedding is to take place the next day. But no matter: Don
Giovanni quickly dismisses Masetto and turns his charm on the naive Zerlina.
First, he tries verbal persuasion carried off in simple recitative. Zerlina, he says,
is too lovely for a country bumpkin like Masetto. Her beauty demands a higher
state: she will become his wife!

Simple recitative now gives way to more passionate expression in the
charming duet "Là ci darem la mano" ("Give me your hand, o fairest"). During
this duet, Don Giovanni persuades Zerlina to extend her hand (and the prospect
of a good deal more). He begins with a seductive melody (**A**) cast squarely in the
Classical mold of two four-bar antecedent–consequent phrases.

> Watch a performance of Mozart,
> *Don Giovanni*, "Là ci darem la
> mano," in the YouTube playlist at
> CourseMate for this text.

Example 9-8 ➤

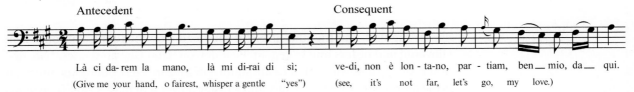

Zerlina repeats and extends the opening theme, but she still sings alone and
untouched. The Don becomes more insistent in a new phrase (**B**).

Example 9-9 ➤

Zerlina, in turn, becomes flustered, and sings in quick sixteenth notes. The
initial melody (**A**) returns but is now sung together by the two principals, their
voices intertwining—musical union accompanies the act of physical embrace
that occurs on stage. Finally, as if to further affirm this coupling through music,
Mozart adds a concluding section (**C**) in which the two characters skip off, arm
in arm ("Let's go, my treasure"), their voices linked together, mainly in paral-
lel-moving thirds. Here musical unity underscores the lovers' unity of feeling

and purpose. These are the means by which a skilled composer like Mozart can intensify, through music, the drama unfolding on the stage.

Example 9-10 >

Listening Cue

Wolfgang Amadeus Mozart, Opera, *Don Giovanni* (1787), K. 527

13–14

Act I, Scene 7

Characters: Don Giovanni and the peasant girl Zerlina
Situation: Don Giovanni apparently succeeding in the seduction of Zerlina

WHAT TO LISTEN FOR: Recitative (Intro/13 at 0:00) gives way to aria (duet; Intro/14 at 0:00) and a gradual unification of the music accompanies the characters' physical union (at 2:10).

◀)) Listen to streaming music in an Active Listening Guide at CourseMate or in the eBook.

In the end, the frightful ghost of the dead Commandant confronts Don Giovanni and orders him to repent. Ever defiant, Don Giovanni cries, "No, no," and is dragged down to Hell to the sounds of Mozart's most demonic music. It is the admixture of divine beauty and sinister power that makes *Don Giovanni* a masterpiece of the highest order. No wonder Andrew Lloyd Webber (see p. 136) paid homage to it in his long-running *Phantom of the Opera*.

Beethoven: Bridge to Romanticism

No composer looms larger as an iconic figure than Ludwig van Beethoven (1770–1827). When we imagine the "musician as artist," most likely it is the angry, defiant, disheveled Beethoven who comes to mind. Is it not the bust of Beethoven, rather than the elegant Mozart or the stalwart Bach, that sits atop Schroeder's piano in the comic strip *Peanuts*? Is it not Beethoven's music that accompanies "the king's speech" in the Academy Award–winning film of that name (2010)? Is it not Beethoven who is one of the "3 B's" of classical music (Bach, Beethoven, and Brahms)? And why is our first listening example (Intro/1) the beginning of Beethoven's Symphony No. 5? Because he and it serve as useful reference points that everyone recognizes. Beethoven is, in short, deeply ingrained in our culture.

But Beethoven was lucky. The period of his maturity (the early nineteenth century) was the first to create the notion that a great artist was an angry, self-absorbed loner, suffering for his art. Beethoven was all these and more, and thus his contemporaries made him something of a poster boy for the "artist as genius." Oblivious to the world, he walked about Vienna humming and scribbling music in a notebook. His last compositions were understood only by a few. At the same time, Beethoven did matter to the people of his day, because he had elevated the stature of the artist and art itself. When he died in March of 1827, 20,000 citizens of Vienna turned out for the funeral. Schools closed, and the army mobilized to control the huge crowd. An artist—and a musician, no less—had become a cult figure.

➤ In this work painted after Beethoven's death by artist Josef Danhauser, a bust of Beethoven looms godlike over the scene as pianist Franz Liszt and other artists of the day look up with reverential respect. For the nineteenth century, Beethoven came to personify the divinely inspired genius, perhaps because Beethoven himself said that he "conversed with God."

Josef Danhauser (1805–1845). *Franz Liszt at the Piano.* 1840. Oil on canvas, 119 × 167 cm. Photo: Juergen Liepe. Nationalgalerie, Staatliche Museen zu Berlin, Berlin, Germany. © Bildarchiv Preussischer Kulturbesitz/Art Resource, NY

Beethoven's Music

Today Beethoven's symphonies (9), piano sonatas (32), and string quartets (16) are performed more in concert and streamed online more frequently than those of any other classical composer. These works, as was Beethoven himself, are sometimes tender and sometimes explosive. And just as the composer struggled to overcome personal adversity—his gradual deafness—so his music imparts a feeling of struggle and ultimate victory. Listeners sense a rightness, even morality, about it. It elevates and inspires all of us.

Historians have traditionally divided Beethoven's music into three periods: early, middle, and late. In his early works in particular Beethoven employed Classical forms (sonata–allegro, rondo, and theme and variations) and throughout his life he honored Classical genres (symphony, sonata, concerto, string quartet, and opera). Yet in all his music Beethoven projects a new spirit, one that foreshadows the musical style of the Romantic era (1820–1900). An intense, lyrical expression is heard in his slow movements, while his allegros abound with pounding rhythms, strong dynamic contrasts, and startling orchestral effects. Although Beethoven stays largely within the bounds of Classical forms, he pushes their confines to the breaking point, so great is his urge for personal expression. Though a pupil of Haydn and a lifelong admirer of Mozart, he nevertheless elevated music to new heights of both lyricism and dramatic power. For this reason, he can rightly be called the prophet of Romantic music.

Watch a video of Craig Wright's Open Yale Course class session 9, "Sonata-Allegro Form: Mozart and Beethoven," at CourseMate for this text.

The Early Years (1770–1802)

Like Bach and Mozart before him, Beethoven came from a family of musicians. His father and grandfather were performers at the court at Bonn, Germany, on the Rhine River, where Beethoven was baptized on December 17, 1770. Seeing great musical talent in his young son, Beethoven's father, a violent alcoholic, forced him to practice the piano, going so far as to chain him to the instrument. Soon he tried to exploit his son as a child prodigy, a second Mozart, telling the world that the diminutive boy was a year or two younger than he actually was; throughout his life Beethoven was convinced that he was born in 1772, two years after his actual birth date.

In 1792 Beethoven moved to Vienna, then the musical capital of Europe, and began to study with the world's most respected composer, Joseph Haydn. Beethoven also bought new clothes, located a wig maker, and found a dancing instructor. His aim was to gain acceptance into the homes of the wealthy of the Austrian capital. And this he soon achieved, owing not to his woeful social skills, but to his phenomenal ability as a pianist.

Beethoven played the piano louder, more forcefully, and even more violently than anyone the Viennese nobility had ever heard. He possessed an extraordinary technique—even if he did hit occasional wrong notes—and this he put to good use, especially in his fanciful improvisations. As a contemporary witness observed, "He knew how to produce such an impression on every listener that frequently there was not a single dry eye, while many broke out into loud sobs, for there was a certain magic in his expression."

The aristocracy was captivated. One patron put a string quartet at Beethoven's disposal, another made it possible for the composer to experiment with a small orchestra, and all showered him with gifts. He acquired well-to-do pupils; he sold his compositions ("I state my price and they pay," he said with pride in 1801); and he requested and eventually received an annuity from three noblemen so that he could work undisturbed. The text of this arrangement includes the following provisions:

> It is recognized that only a person who is as free as possible from all cares can consecrate himself to his craft. He can only produce these great and sublime works which ennoble Art if they form his sole pursuit, to the exclusion of all unnecessary obligations. The undersigned have therefore taken the decision to ensure that Herr Ludwig van Beethoven's situation shall not be embarrassed by his most necessary requirements, nor shall his powerful Genius be hampered.

What a contrast between Beethoven's contract and the one signed by Haydn four decades earlier (see p. 104)! Music was no longer merely a craft and the composer a servant. It had now become an exalted Art, and the great creator a Genius who must be protected and nurtured—a new, Romantic notion of the value of music and the importance of the composer. Beethoven himself promoted this belief that the artistic genius was cut from a different cloth than the rest of humanity. When one patron demanded that he play for a visiting French general, Beethoven stormed out of the salon and responded by letter: "Prince, what you are, you are through the accident of birth. What I am, I am through my own efforts. There have been many princes and there will be thousands more. But there is only one Beethoven!" What Beethoven failed to realize, of course, is that he, too, owed much of his success to "the accident of birth"—coming from a long line of musicians, he had been born with a huge musical talent.

Piano Sonata, Opus 13, the *"Pathétique"* Sonata (1799)

Watch a video of Craig Wright's Open Yale Course class session 18, "Piano Music of Mozart and Beethoven," at CourseMate for this text.

The bold originality in Beethoven's music can be heard in one of his most celebrated compositions, the **"Pathétique" Sonata**. A Classical sonata, as we have seen (p. 131), is a multimovement work for solo instrument or solo instrument with keyboard accompaniment. This particular sonata, for solo piano, is identified as Beethoven's opus 13, denoting that it is the thirteenth of 135 works that Beethoven published. (Composers often use the term **opus**—Latin for "work"—with a number to identify their works.) But Beethoven himself also supplied the sonata with its descriptive title—"*Pathétique*" ("Plaintive")—underscoring the passion and pathos he felt within it. Its great drama and intensity derive in large part from the juxtaposition of extremes. There are extremes of dynamics (from *fortissimo* to *pianissimo*), tempo (*grave* to *presto*), and range (from very high to very low). The piece also requires of the pianist more technical skill and stamina than had any piano sonata of Mozart or Haydn. Displaying his virtuosity, Beethoven frequently performed the "*Pathétique*" in the homes and palaces of the Viennese aristocracy.

FIRST MOVEMENT

Contemporaries recount how Beethoven the pianist played with "super-human" speed and force, and how he banged the keys so hard on one occasion that he broke six strings. The crashing C minor chord that opens the "*Pathétique*" Sonata suggests Beethoven's sometimes violent approach to the instrument. After this startling opening gesture, Beethoven the dramatist takes over, juxtaposing music of wildly differing moods: The *sforzando* chord is immediately followed by the quietest sort of lyricism, only to be interrupted by another chordal thunderbolt (Ex. 10-1). This slow introduction is probably a written-out version of the sort of improvisation that gained Beethoven great fame in Vienna.

Example 10-1 >

The dramatic introduction leads to a racing first theme that rises impetuously in the right hand. The sense of anxiety the listener feels is amplified by the throbbing bass, where the left hand of the pianist plays broken octaves (the alternation of two tones an octave apart) reminiscent of the rumble of distant thunder.

Example 10-2 : ①/23 at 1:25 >

The remainder of the movement now plays out as a contest between the impetuous, racing themes and the stormy chords. But while there is much passion and intensity here, there is also Classical formal control. The crashing chords come back at the beginning of both the development and the coda in this sonata–allegro form movement. Thus the chords set firm formal boundaries and thereby prevent the racing theme from flying out of control. Beethoven's music often conveys a feeling of struggle: Classical forms gave Beethoven something to struggle against.

Listening Cue

Ludwig van Beethoven, Piano Sonata, Opus 13, the *"Pathétique"* Sonata (1799)

First movement, *Grave; Allegro di molto e con brio* (grave; very fast and with gusto)

①
23–25

Genre: Sonata
Form: Sonata–allegro

WHAT TO LISTEN FOR: The drama created not only within the opening chords, but also between the chords and the racing main theme (①/23 at 1:25). Here contrast is the name of the game: loud against soft, slow against fast, high against low

🔊) Listen to streaming music in an Active Listening Guide at CourseMate or in the eBook.

🔊) Take online Listening Exercise 23 at CourseMate or in the eBook.

Listen to "This Night" in the iTunes, Rhapsody, and YouTube playlists at CourseMate for this text.

SECOND MOVEMENT

Eyewitnesses who heard Beethoven at the piano remarked on the "legato" (long and lyrical) style of his playing and contrasted it with Mozart's staccato (light and detached) style. Beethoven himself remarked in 1796 that "one can sing on the piano, so long as one has feeling." We can hear Beethoven sing through the legato melodic line that dominates the slow second movement of the "*Pathétique*" Sonata. Indeed, the expression mark he gave to the movement is *cantabile* (songful). The singing quality of the melody seems to have appealed to pop star Billy Joel, who borrowed this theme for the chorus (refrain) of his song "This Night" on the album *Innocent Man*.

THIRD MOVEMENT

A comparison of the second and third movements of the "*Pathétique*" Sonata will show that musical form does not determine musical mood. Although both the *Adagio* and the fast finale are in rondo form, the first is a lyrical hymn, and the latter a passionate, but slightly comical, chase. The finale has hints of the crashing chords and stark contrasts of the first movement, but the earlier violence and impetuosity have been softened into a mood of impassioned playfulness.

The eighteenth-century piano sonata had been essentially private music of a modest sort—music that a composer-teacher like Mozart or Haydn would write for a talented amateur pupil to be played as entertainment in the home. Beethoven took the modest, private piano sonata and infused it with the technical dazzle of the public stage. The louder sound, wider range, and greater length of Beethoven's thirty-two piano sonatas made them appropriate for the increasingly large concert halls—and pianos—of the nineteenth century. Beginning in the Romantic period, Beethoven's piano sonatas became a staple of the professional virtuoso's repertoire. But there was a downside: Sonatas that had originally been created for all amateurs to play were now becoming too difficult. The virtuoso had begun to run off with the amateur's music, a development that would continue throughout the nineteenth century.

Beethoven Loses His Hearing

Beethoven cut a strange, eccentric figure as he wandered the streets of Vienna, sometimes humming, sometimes mumbling, and sometimes jotting on music paper. Dogs barked and street kids, knowing nothing about genius, sometimes threw stones. Adding to the difficulties of his somewhat unstable personality was the fact that Beethoven was gradually losing his hearing—a serious handicap for any person, but a tragic condition for a musician. Can you imagine a blind painter?

Beethoven first complained about his hearing and a ringing in his ears (tinnitus) in the late 1790s, and he suffered considerable anguish and depression. His increasing deafness did not stop him from composing—most people can hear simple melodies inside their heads, and the gifted Beethoven could generate complex melodies and harmonies in his "inner ear" without need of external sound. However, his condition caused him to retreat even further from society and all but ended his career as a pianist, because he could no longer gauge how hard to press the keys. By late 1802, Beethoven recognized that he would ultimately suffer a total loss of hearing. In despair, he wrote something akin to a last will and testament, today called the **Heiligenstadt Testament** after the Viennese suburb in which he penned it. In this confessional document for posterity, the composer admits that he considered suicide: "I would have ended my life; it was only *my art* that held me back." Beethoven emerged from this personal crisis with renewed resolve to fulfill his artistic destiny—he would now "seize Fate by the throat."

Watch a video of Craig Wright's Open Yale Course class session 20, "The Colossal Symphony: Beethoven, Berlioz, Mahler, and Shostakovich," at CourseMate for this text.

The "Heroic" Period (1803–1813)

It was in this resurgent, defiant mood that Beethoven entered what we call his **"heroic" period** of composition (1803–1813; also simply termed his "middle period"). His works became longer, more assertive, and full of grand gestures. Simple, often triadic, themes predominate, and these are repeated, sometimes incessantly, as the music swells to majestic proportions. When these themes are played *forte* and given over to the brass instruments, a heroic, triumphant sound results.

Beethoven wrote nine symphonies in all, six of them during his "heroic" period. Beethoven's symphonies are few in number because they are so much longer and more complex than those of his predecessors. Beginning with No. 3, his symphonies sometimes go on for forty-five minutes or more, twice the duration of any symphony of Haydn or Mozart. Beethoven's works set the standard for the epic, narrative symphony of the nineteenth century.

Symphony No. 3 in E♭ major ("Eroica") (1803)

As its title suggests, Beethoven's **"Eroica" ("Heroic") Symphony** epitomizes the grandiose, heroic style. More than any other single orchestral work, it changed the historical direction of the symphony. It assaults the ear with startling rhythmic effects and chord changes that were shocking to early-nineteenth-century listeners. It makes mountains of sound out of the simplest triads, by repeating with ever increasing volume. Most novel, the work has biographical content, for the hero of the "Eroica" Symphony, at least originally, was Napoleon Bonaparte.

Austria and the German states were at war with France in the early nineteenth century. Yet the German-speaking Beethoven was taken with the enemy's revolutionary call for liberty, equality, and fraternity. Napoleon Bonaparte became his hero, and the composer dedicated his third symphony to him, writing on the title page "intitolata Bonaparte." But when news that Napoleon had declared himself emperor reached Beethoven, he flew into a rage, saying, "Now he, too, will trample on all the rights of man and indulge his

As a young officer, Napoleon Bonaparte seized control of the government of France in 1799. He established a new form of republican government that emphasized the revolutionary ideals of liberty, equality, and humanity. After Napoleon elevated himself to emperor in 1804, Beethoven changed the title of his Symphony No. 3 from "Bonaparte" to "Eroica." The portrait by Jacques-Louis David shows the newly crowned Napoleon in full imperial regalia. Liberator had become oppressor.

Burstein Collection/CORBIS

▲ The title page of the autograph of Beethoven's "Eroica" Symphony: *Sinfonia grande intitolata Bonaparte.* Note the hole where Beethoven took a knife and scratched out the name "Bonaparte."

Erich Lessing/Art Resource, NY

ambition." Taking up a knife, he scratched so violently to erase Bonaparte's name from the title page that he left a hole in the paper. When the work was published, Napoleon's name had been removed in favor of the more general title "Heroic Symphony: To Celebrate the Memory of a Great Man." Beethoven was not an imperialist; he was a revolutionary.

Symphony No. 5 in C minor (1808)

At the center of Beethoven's symphonic output stands his remarkable Symphony No. 5 (see also pp. 10–11). Its novelty rests in the way the composer conveys a sense of psychological progression over the course of four movements. An imaginative listener might perceive the following sequence of events: (1) a fateful encounter with elemental forces, (2) a period of quiet soul-searching, followed by (3) a further wrestling with the elements, and, finally, (4) a triumphant victory over the forces of Fate. Beethoven himself is said to have remarked with regard to the famous opening motive of the symphony: "There Fate knocks at the door!"

The rhythm of the opening—perhaps the best-known moment in all of classical music—animates the entire symphony. Not only does it dominate the opening *Allegro,* but it reappears in varied form in the three later movements as well, binding the symphony into a unified whole.

Example 10-3 ▸

first movement

second movement

third movement

fourth movement

FIRST MOVEMENT

At the very outset, the listener is jolted to attention, forced to sit up and take notice by a sudden explosion of sound. And what an odd beginning to a symphony—a blast of three short notes and a long one, followed by the same three shorts and a long, all now a step lower. The movement can't quite get going. It starts and stops, then seems to lurch forward and gather momentum. And where is the melody? This three-shorts-and-a-long pattern is more a motive or musical cell than a melody. Yet it is striking by virtue of its power and compactness. As the movement unfolds, the actual pitches of the motive prove to be of secondary importance. Beethoven is obsessed with its rhythm. He wants to demonstrate the enormous latent force lurking within even the most basic rhythmic atom, a power waiting to be unleashed by a composer who understands the secrets of rhythmic energy.

To control the sometimes violent forces that will emerge, the music unfolds within the traditional confines of sonata–allegro form. The basic four-note motive provides all the musical material for the first theme area.

Example 10-4: ①/26 at 0:00 ➤

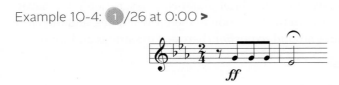

The brief transition played by a solo French horn is only six notes long and is formed simply by adding two notes to the end of the basic four-note motive. As expected, the transition carries us tonally from the tonic (C minor) to the relative major (E♭ major).

Example 10-5: 0:43 ➤

The second theme offers a moment of escape from the rush of the "fate" motive, but even here the pattern of three shorts and a long lurks beneath like a ticking time bomb.

Example 10-6: 0:46 ➤

The closing theme, too, is none other than the motive once again, now presented in a more heroic guise.

Example 10-7: 1:17 ➤

In the development, the opening motive returns, recapturing, and even surpassing, the force it had at the beginning. Beethoven now inverts the motive—he makes it go up as well as down, though the rhythmic shape remains the same.

Example 10-8: ①/27 at 0:22 ➤

As the motive rises, so does the musical tension. A powerful rhythmic climax ensues and then gives way to a brief imitative passage. Soon Beethoven reduces the six-note motive of the transition to merely two notes, and then just one, passing these figures around *pianissimo* between the strings and winds.

Example 10-9: 0:46 ➤

Beethoven was a master of the process of thematic condensation—stripping away all extraneous material to get to the core of a musical idea. Here, in this mysterious *pianissimo* passage, he presents the irreducible minimum of his motive: a single note. In the midst of this quiet, the original four-note motive tries to reassert itself *fortissimo,* yet at first cannot do so. Its explosive force, however, cannot be held back. A thunderous return of the opening pitches signals the beginning of the recapitulation.

Although the recapitulation (①/28) offers a repeat of the events of the exposition, Beethoven has a surprise in store. No sooner has the motive regained its momentum than an oboe interjects a tender, languid, and wholly unexpected solo. A deviation from the usual path of sonata–allegro form, this brief oboe cadenza allows for a momentary release of excess energy. The recapitulation then resumes its expected course.

What is not expected is the enormous coda that follows. It is even longer than the exposition! A new form of the motive appears, and it, too, is subjected to development. In fact, this coda constitutes essentially a second development section, so great is Beethoven's single urge to exploit the latent power of this one simple musical idea.

Listening Cue

Ludwig van Beethoven, Symphony No. 5 in C minor (1808), Opus 67

①

26–28

First movement, *Allegro con brio* (fast with gusto)

Genre: Symphony
Form: Sonata–allegro

WHAT TO LISTEN FOR: How much mileage and how many startling effects Beethoven is able to extract from a simple four-note motive, owing to his extraordinary creative powers. In one form or another, the motive dominates almost every moment of this first movement

🔊 Listen to streaming music in an Active Listening Guide at CourseMate or in the eBook.

🔊 Take online Listening Exercise 24 at CourseMate or in the eBook.

SECOND MOVEMENT

After the pounding we experienced in the explosive first movement, the calm of the noble *Andante* comes as a welcome change of pace. The mood is at first serene, and the melody is expansive—in contrast to the four-note motive of the first movement, the opening theme here runs on for twenty-two measures. The musical form is also a familiar one: theme and variations. But this is not the simple, easily audible theme and variations of Haydn and Mozart (see pp. 116–121). There are two themes: the first lyrical and serene, played mostly by the strings; and the second quiet, then triumphant, played mostly by the brasses. By means of this "double" theme and variations, Beethoven demonstrates his ability to add length and complexity to a standard Classical form. He also shows how it is possible to contrast within one movement two starkly opposed expressive domains—the intensely lyrical (theme 1) and the brilliantly heroic (theme 2).

◀ Original autograph of Beethoven at work on the second movement of his Symphony No. 5. The many corrections in different-colored inks and red pencil suggest the turmoil and constant evolution involved in Beethoven's creative process. Unlike Mozart, to whom finished musical ideas came quickly, Beethoven's art was a continual struggle.

Bildarchiv Preussischer Kulturbesitz/Art Resource, NY

THIRD MOVEMENT

In the Classical period, the third movement of a symphony or quartet was usually a graceful minuet and trio (see p. 111). Haydn and his pupil Beethoven wanted to infuse this third movement with more life and energy, so they often wrote a faster, more rollicking piece and called it a **scherzo,** meaning "joke." And while there is nothing particularly humorous about the mysterious and sometimes threatening sound of the scherzo of Beethoven's Symphony No. 5, it is certainly far removed from the elegant world of the courtly minuet.

Now, a stroke of genius on Beethoven's part: He links the third and fourth movements by means of a musical bridge. Holding a single pitch as quietly as possible, the violins create an eerie sound, while the timpani beats menacingly in the background. A three-note motive grows from the violins and is repeated over and over as a wave of sound begins to swell from the orchestra. Here

Beethoven is concerned only with volume, not melody, rhythm, or harmony. With enormous force, the wave finally crashes down, and from it emerges the triumphant beginning of the fourth movement—one of the grandest "special effects" in all of music.

FOURTH MOVEMENT

When Beethoven arrived at the finale, he was faced with a nearly impossible task. The last movement of a symphony had traditionally been a light sendoff. How to write a conclusion that would relieve the tension of the preceding musical events, yet provide an appropriate, substantive balance to the weighty first movement? To this end, he created a finale that is longer and beefier than the first movement. To bulk up his orchestra, Beethoven adds three trombones, a contrabassoon (low bassoon), and a piccolo (high flute), the first time any of these instruments had been called for in a symphony. He also writes big, bold, and, in most cases, triadic themes, assigning these most often to the powerful brasses. In these instruments and themes, we hear the "heroic" Beethoven at his best. The finale projects a feeling of affirmation, a sense that superhuman will has triumphed over adversity.

Beethoven's Symphony No. 5 reveals his genius in a paradox: from minimal material (the basic cell), he derives maximum sonority. Everywhere there is a feeling of raw, elemental power propelled by the newly enlarged orchestra. Beethoven was the first to recognize that massive sound could be a potent psychological weapon. Mood and emotions could be manipulated by sound alone. No wonder that during World War II (1939–1945) both sides, Fascist as well as Allied, used the music of this symphony to symbolize triumph—in Morse code, short-short-short-long is the letter "V," as in "Victory."

▾ In this engraving of 1823, Martin Tejcek presents Beethoven at his idealized best, walking the streets of Vienna. In fact in later life, as other contemporary observers noted, the composer's hair was usually unkempt, his face unshaven, and his clothes disheveled. In 1821 Beethoven was mistakenly arrested as a tramp.

Snark/Art Resource, NY

The Final Years (1814–1827)

By 1814, Beethoven had lost his hearing entirely and had withdrawn from society. His music, too, took on a more remote, inaccessible quality, placing heavy demands on performer and audience alike. In these late works, Beethoven requires the listener to connect musical ideas over extended spans of time—to engage in long-term listening where the ties between melodies or rhythms are not immediately obvious. This is music that seems intended not for the audience of Beethoven's day, but rather for future generations. Most of Beethoven's late works are piano sonatas and string quartets—intimate, introspective chamber music. But two pieces, the Mass in D major (*Missa Solemnis,* 1823) and the Symphony No. 9 (1824), are large-scale compositions for full orchestra and chorus. In these latter works, Beethoven strives once again to communicate directly to a broad spectrum of humanity.

Symphony No. 9 in D minor (1824)

Beethoven's Symphony No. 9, his last, was the first symphony in the history of music to include a chorus; in the fourth and final movement he turned to choral voices to add an immediate, human appeal. Here a chorus sings a poem in honor of universal brotherhood, *An die Freude* (*Ode to Joy*), written by Friedrich von Schiller (1759–1805). For more than twenty years Beethoven had struggled to craft just the right melody for this text. Example 10-10 gives the final result: Beethoven's complete melody with Schiller's poem in English. Observe the direct, four-square phrase structure of the melody: antecedent, consequent, extension, consequent, or **abcb** form. Notice also that nearly every pitch is adjacent to the next; there are almost no leaps. Everyone can sing this melody—and that was exactly Beethoven's wish.

Example 10-10 >

Having fashioned this simple but inspiring melody, Beethoven used it as the centerpiece of the fourth and final movement. Here *Ode to Joy* becomes the thematic foundation of a magnificent set of variations. Beethoven first sets the melody for instruments alone, beginning with the low strains of the double basses and cellos. The theme is repeated three more times, in successively higher registers, gathering force. In each variation, Beethoven changes the surrounding context, rather than the melody itself. This passage demonstrates how Beethoven, like no composer before him, exploited the power of sound alone, detached from the usual concerns of rhythm or harmony. When the full orchestra with brilliant brasses presents the theme a fourth time, we all feel the power of an overwhelming sonic force.

With this *fortissimo* statement of the theme, the orchestra has done all that it can do alone. Beethoven now bids the chorus to join in, singing Schiller's liberating text. From here to the end of the movement, chorus and orchestra speak with one exalted voice, pressing the tempo, volume, and the range of the pitches to the limits of the performers' abilities. Their message is Beethoven's message: Humanity will be unified and victorious if it strives together, as it does here to create great art. In the course of time, Beethoven's hope has been realized: *Ode to Joy* has been sung at all of the Olympic Games since 1956, was performed to celebrate the fall of the Berlin Wall, and currently serves as the official anthem of the European Union.

Ludwig van Beethoven, *Ode to Joy* **from Symphony No. 9 in D minor (1824)**

Intro
5

Fourth movement (instrumental excerpt only)

Genre: Symphony
Form: Theme and variations

WHAT TO LISTEN FOR: Beethoven's noble melody grows in magnificence from statement in basses and cellos (0:00), to variation 1 with bassoon counterpoint (0:48), to variation 2 with melody in first violins (1:38), to variation 3 with brasses leading the full orchestra (2:22).

 Listen to streaming music in an Active Listening Guide at CourseMate or in the eBook.

 Take online Listening Exercise 25 at CourseMate or in the eBook.

A complete Checklist of Musical Style for the Classical period can be found at CourseMate for this text.

What Is Forward Looking in Beethoven's Music?

Beethoven was a cult figure during his own lifetime, and his image continued to tower over all the arts throughout the nineteenth century. He had shown how personal expression might push against and break free from the confines of Classical form. He had expanded the size of the orchestra by calling for new instruments and had doubled the length of the symphony. He had given music "the grand gesture," stunning effects like the crashing introduction of the "*Pathétique*" Sonata or the gigantic crescendo leading to the finale of the Symphony No. 5. And he had shown that pure sound—sound divorced from melody and rhythm—could be glorious in and of itself. The power and originality of his works became the standard against which composers, indeed all artists, of the Romantic era measured their worth. The painting shown earlier in this chapter (see p. 140) depicts Franz Liszt at the piano surrounded by other writers and musicians of the mid-nineteenth century. A larger-than-life bust gazes down from Olympian heights. It is Beethoven, the prophet and high priest of Romanticism.

Romanticism and Romantic Chamber Music

The mature music of Beethoven, with its powerful crescendos, pounding chords, and grand gestures, announces the arrival of the Romantic era in music. Today we think of a "romantic" as an idealistic person, a dreamer, sometimes fearful, always hopeful, and perpetually in love. This view resonates with and emerges from the values of the Romantic era (1820–1900), when reason gave way to passion, objective analysis to subjective emotion, and "the real world" to a realm of the imagination and of dreams. In all the arts of the nineteenth century, freedom, spontaneity, and personal expression became paramount. And just as Beethoven cast off the face paint, wig, and powdered hair of the eighteenth century (he rarely combed his wild mane) so Romantic artists generally did away with the rules and restrictive forms that had regulated Classical style.

Romantic Inspiration, Romantic Creativity

Romanticism is often defined as a revolt against the Classical adherence to reason and tradition. Whereas artists of the eighteenth century sought to achieve unity, order, and a balance of form and content, those of the nineteenth century leaned toward self-expression, striving to communicate with passion no matter what imbalance, even excess, might result. If Classical artists drew inspiration from the monuments of ancient Greece and Rome, those of the Romantic era looked to the human imagination and the wonders of nature. The Romantic artist exalted instinctive feelings—not those of the masses, but individual, personal ones. As the American Romantic poet Walt Whitman said, "I celebrate myself, and sing myself."

If a single feeling or sentiment pervaded the Romantic era, it was love. Indeed, "romance" is at the very heart of the word *romantic*. The loves of Romeo and Juliet (as seen in the chapter opener), and Tristan and Isolde, for example, captured the public's imagination in the Romantic era. The endless pursuit of an unattainable love became an obsession that, when expressed as music, produced the sounds of longing and yearning heard in so many Romantic works.

Nature and natural feelings were also subjects dear to the Romantics. As Beethoven proclaimed in 1821, "I perform most faithfully the duties that Humanity, God, and Nature enjoin upon me." In his "Pastoral" Symphony (Symphony No. 6), the first important Romantic "nature piece," Beethoven sought to capture both the tranquil beauty and the destructive fury of the natural

▼ *Man and Woman Gazing at the Moon*, by German Romantic artist Casper David Friedrich (1774–1840). The painting projects a sense not only of isolation and a contemplation of nature but also of the slow, evolutionary progress of geological time.

Bildarchiv Preussischer Kulturbesitz/Art Resource, NY

world. Indeed, the Romantic vision of nature, and human nature, had its dark side. Composers, writers, and painters were now increasingly fascinated with the occult, the supernatural, and the macabre. This was the age not only of composer Robert Schumann's *The Happy Farmer,* but also of writer Mary Shelley's *Frankenstein.*

Just how much the range of expression expanded in Romantic music can be seen in the musical "expression marks" that came into being at this time: *espressivo* (expressively), *dolente* (sadly), *presto furioso* (fast and furiously), *con forza e passione* (with force and passion), *misterioso* (mysteriously), and *maestoso* (majestically). Not only do these directives explain to the performer how a passage ought to be played, they also reveal the intense emotions the composer wished to express.

The Musician as "Artist," Music as "Art"

With the Romantic era came the idea that the composer was more than a hired employee and music something more than mere entertainment. Bach had been a municipal civil servant, devoted and dutiful, in the town of Leipzig. Haydn and Mozart had served and been treated as domestics in the homes of the great lords of Europe. But Beethoven began to break the chains of submission. He was the first to demand, and receive, the respect and admiration due a great creative spirit. For the composer Franz Liszt (1811–1886), a great admirer of Beethoven, the duty of the artist was nothing less than "the upbringing of mankind." Never was the position of the creative musician loftier than in the mid-nineteenth century.

Just as the musician was elevated from servant to artist, so the music he or she produced was transformed from entertainment to art. In 1776, noted critic Charles Burney had described music as "an innocent luxury, unnecessary, indeed, to our existence." But to Beethoven, writing in 1812, music was the most important of the arts, the pursuit of which "would raise men to the level of gods." His symphonies, quartets, and piano sonatas sprang to life, not only to give immediate pleasure to listeners, but also to satisfy a deep-seated creative urge within the composer. They became extensions of the artist's inner personality. Such works might not be understood by the creator's contemporaries, as was true of Beethoven's late piano sonatas, for example, but they would be appreciated by posterity, by future generations of listeners. The idea of "art for art's sake"—art free of all immediate functional concerns—was born of the Romantic spirit.

The Style of Romantic Music

The Romantic spirit rebelled against Classical ideals in ways that allow us to generalize these two artistic movements in terms of opposites: rational against irrational, intellect opposed to heart, conformity versus originality, and the masses in contrast to the individual. Yet in purely musical terms, the works of the Romantic composers represent not so much a *revolution* against Classical ideals as an *evolution* beyond them. Throughout the nineteenth century, the

Classical genres of the symphony, concerto, string quartet, piano sonata, and opera remain fashionable, though somewhat altered in shape. The symphony now grows in length, embodying the widest possible range of expression, while the concerto becomes increasingly virtuosic, as a heroic soloist does battle against an orchestral mass. The Romantics introduced no new musical forms and only two new genres: the art song (addressed later in this chapter) and the symphonic poem (see Chapter 12). Instead, Romantic composers took the musical materials received from Haydn, Mozart, and Beethoven, and made them more intensely expressive, more personal, more colorful, and, in some cases, more bizarre.

Romantic Melody

Listen to the love theme from *Romeo and Juliet* in the iTunes and YouTube playlists at CourseMate for this text.

As mentioned in Chapter 1, when a hundred undergraduates were recently asked to choose their favorite piece of music (classical or pop), 85 percent chose a work written in the Romantic style. Why? Likely the answer rests in the surging melodies and rich harmonies of nineteenth-century music. Our love songs and film scores make use of the Romantic sound—not the more dissonant style of modern or postmodern music. Countless melodies of Schubert, Chopin, and Tchaikovsky, for example, have been borrowed and turned into sound tracks of various sorts, a reflection of their great expressive power. Romantic melodies go beyond the symmetrical structure (two plus two measures, or four plus four) of the Classical period, becoming longer, rhythmically more flexible, and more irregular in shape. They sigh, lament, surge, and wax ecstatic. They start haltingly and then build to a grandiose climax, sublime and triumphant. Example 11-1 shows the well-known love theme from Tchaikovsky's *Romeo and Juliet*. As the brackets show, it rises and falls, only to rise higher again, a total of seven times, on the way to a *fortissimo* climax.

Example 11-1 ➤

Colorful Harmony

Part of the emotional intensity of Romantic music was generated by a new, more colorful harmony. Classical music had, in the main, made use of chords built on only the seven notes of the major or minor scale. Romantic composers went further by creating **chromatic harmony,** constructing chords on the five additional notes (the chromatic notes) within the full twelve-note chromatic scale. This lent more colors to their harmonic palette, creating the rich, lush sounds that we associate with Romantic music.

Chromatic harmony likewise encouraged bold chordal shifts—a chord with three sharps might be followed immediately by one with six flats, for example.

Our ears hear these unexpected shifts as enrichments that sometimes border on the bizarre. They exemplify the Romantic desire to express a much wider range of feeling.

Finally, nineteenth-century composers gave a "romantic feel" to music by means of dissonance. Pain, suffering, and the longing of unrequited love are part of the Romantic aesthetic, and all three sentiments have traditionally have been expressed in music by means of dissonance. Although the traditional Rules of musical counterpoint require that dissonance resolve to consonance, Romantic composers frequently prolong moments of dissonance in their works. The more the resolution of the painful dissonance is delayed, however, the greater the feeling of longing.

All three of these qualities of Romantic harmony—chromatic harmony, bold chordal shifts, and prolonged dissonance—can be heard in Frédéric Chopin's Nocturne in C♯ (1835). Neither you nor this author can take in all the music given in the following three examples simply by looking at them. (To hear them, listen to ②/3) We can, however, visualize some of the music's inner workings here— first, the bold harmonic shift from a chord with four sharps to one with four flats, then the chromaticisms (note the many changing sharps and flats), and finally the prolonged dissonances (see arrows). In this way we may begin to understand, when hearing the rich, sensuous sound of Romantic music, how it is created.

Example 11-2: Bold harmonic shift at 2:40 ➤

Example 11-3: Chromatic harmony at 3:20 ➤

Example 11-4: Romantic longing (prolonged dissonances) beginning at 5:05 ➤

Romantic Tempo: *Rubato*

In keeping with an age that glorified personal freedom and tolerated eccentric behavior, tempo in Romantic music was cut loose from the restraints of a regular beat. The term coined for this was *rubato* (literally, "robbed"), an expression mark that the composer wrote into the score for the benefit of the performer. A performer playing tempo **rubato** "stole" some time here and gave it back there, moving faster or slower so as to create an intensely personal performance. This free approach to tempo was often reinforced by fluctuating dynamic levels—slowdowns (ritards) were executed with diminuendos, and accelerations with crescendos—as a way of explaining, even exaggerating, the flow of the music. Whatever excesses might result could be excused under the license of artistic freedom.

The Art Song

Popular song became all the rage during the nineteenth century, in America as well as Europe. In those days a music lover couldn't download an MP3 or M4A or listen to a radio, but he or she could sing, and do so at home from sheet music. The popularity of domestic singing was fed in part by increased accessibility to the piano (see p. 164). Mass production had lowered piano prices, allowing middle-class families to buy a modest, upright instrument, put it in the parlor, and gather around it to sing. What ended in America with the beloved parlor songs of Stephen Foster ("My Old Kentucky Home," "Oh! Susanna," "Beautiful Dreamer"), however, had begun earlier in Europe with a slightly more elevated genre: the art song. An **art song** is a song for solo voice and piano accompaniment, with high artistic aspirations. Because it was cultivated most intensely in German-speaking lands, it is also called the *Lied* (pronounced "leet"; pl., *Lieder*), German for "song."

A song, of course, embodies two art forms: poetry (the lyrics) and music—never call a piece a "song" unless it has lyrics! In the early nineteenth century, publishers churned out odes, sonnets, ballads, and romances by the thousands. This was the great age of the Romantic poets: Wordsworth, Keats, Shelly, and Byron in England, Hugo in France, and Goethe and Heine in Germany, among them. Many of their poems quickly became song lyrics for young Romantic composers, with the prolific Franz Schubert leading the way. His special talent was to fashion music that captured not only the broad spirit, but also the small details of the text, creating a sensitive mood painting. Schubert remarked, "When one has a good poem, the music comes easily, melodies just flow, so that composing is a real joy."

Franz Schubert (1797–1828)

Franz Schubert was born in Vienna in 1797. Among the great Viennese masters—Haydn, Mozart, Beethoven, Schubert, Brahms, and Mahler—only he was native-born to the city. His father was a schoolteacher; thus young Franz was groomed for that profession. Yet the boy's obvious musical talent made it imperative that he also take music lessons; his father taught him to play the violin, and his older brother the piano. At the age of eleven, Schubert was admitted as a choirboy in the emperor's chapel, a group still well known today as the Vienna Boys' Choir.

After his voice changed in 1812, young Franz left the court chapel and enrolled in a teachers' college. He had been spared compulsory military service because he was below the minimum height of five feet and his sight was so poor that he was compelled to wear the spectacles now familiar from his portraits. By 1815, he had become a teacher at his father's primary school. But he found teaching demanding and tedious, and so after three unpleasant years, Schubert quit his "day job" to give himself over wholly to music.

"You lucky fellow; I really envy you! You live a life of sweet, precious freedom, can give free rein to your musical genius, can express your thoughts in any way you like." This was Schubert's brother's view of the composer's new-found freedom. But as many Romantics would find, the reality was harsher than the ideal. Aside from some small income that he earned from the sale of a few songs, he lacked financial support. For most of his adult life, Schubert lived like a bohemian, moving from café to café and helped along by the generosity of his friends, with whom he often lodged when he was broke.

Schubert had exchanged security for freedom. Indeed, he never enjoyed noble patronage, for as he reached artistic maturity, the era of the great aristocratic salon was drawing to an end, replaced by the middle-class parlor or living room. Here, in less formal surroundings, groups of men and women might gather to read poetry, hear parts of a novel, or sing art songs. In Vienna the gatherings at which Schubert appeared, and at which only his compositions were performed, were called **Schubertiads**; today an evening chamber concert devoted exclusively to *Lieder* is called a ***Liederabend*** ("art song evening"). In small, "chamber" assemblies such as these—rather than in large public concerts—most of his best songs were first performed.

In 1822, disaster struck: Schubert contracted syphilis, a venereal disease that, before the advent of antibiotics, was tantamount to a death sentence. Although he completed a great C minor symphony (1828), a more lyrical one in B minor—appropriately called the "Unfinished Symphony"—was left incomplete at his death. When Beethoven died in 1827, Schubert served as a torchbearer at the funeral. The next year, he, too, was dead, the youngest of the great composers to die prematurely.

Although Schubert composed symphonies, piano sonatas, and even operas in the course of his brief career, he was known in his day almost exclusively as a writer of art songs (*Lieder*). Indeed, he composed more than six hundred works in this genre, many of them minor masterpieces. In a few cases, Schubert chose to set several texts together in a series. In so doing, he created what is called a **song cycle** (something akin to today's "concept album")— a tightly structured group of individual songs that tell a story or treat a single theme. *Die schöne Müllerin* (*The Lovely Miller's Daughter;* twenty songs) and *Winterreise* (*Winter Journey;* twenty-four songs), both of which relate the sad consequences of unrequited love, are Schubert's two great song cycles.

▲ Franz Schubert

▾ A small, private assembly known as a Schubertiad, named after the composer, at which artists presented their works. The singer before the piano is Johann Vogl, accompanied by Schubert at the piano, immediately to Vogl's left.

Erlkönig (1815)

Like Mozart, Schubert was a child prodigy. To get an idea of his precocious talent, we need only listen to his song *Erlkönig* (*Elf King*), written when he was just seventeen. According to a friend's account, Schubert was pacing back and forth, reading a book of poetry by the famous poet Johann Wolfgang von Goethe. Suddenly he reached for a pen and began writing furiously, setting all of Goethe's ballad *Erlkönig* to music in one creative act. A folk **ballad** is a dramatic, usually tragic, story told by a narrator (today's "country music ballad" is a distant descendant of such European folk ballads). In Goethe's *Erlkönig,* an evil Elf King lures a young boy to his death, for legend had it that whomever the Elf King touched would die. This tale exemplifies the Romantic fascination with the supernatural and the macabre.

The ballad of the Elf King depicted by Schubert's close friend Moritz von Schwind. The artist had heard Schubert perform the song at many Schubertiads.

The opening line of the poem sets the frightening nocturnal scene: "Who rides so late through night and wind?" With his feverish son cradled in his arms, a father rides at breakneck speed to an inn in an attempt to save the child. Schubert captures both the general sense of terror in the scene and the detail of the galloping horse; he creates an accompanying figure in the piano that pounds on relentlessly just as fast as the pianist can make it go (Ex. 11-5).

Example 11-5: 1/29 at 0:00 >

The specter of death, the Elf King, beckons gently to the boy. He does so in seductively sweet tones, in a melody with the gentle lilt and folksy "um-pah-pah" accompaniment of a popular tune.

Example 11-6: 1:28 >

(Thou dearest boy, come go with me!)

The frightened boy cries out to his father in an agitated line that culminates in a tense, chromatic ascent.

Example 11-7: 1:50 >

(Dear father, my father, say, did'st thou not hear the Elf King whisper promises in my ear?)

This cry is heard again and again in the course of the song, each time at a successively higher pitch and with increasingly dissonant harmonies. In this way the music mirrors the boy's growing terror. The father tries to calm him in low tones that are steady, stable, and repetitive. The Elf King at first charms in sweet, consonant tones, but then threatens in dissonant ones, as seduction gives way to abduction. Thus each of the three characters of the story is portrayed with distinct musical qualities (though all are sung by a single voice). This is musical characterization at its finest; the melody and accompaniment not only support the text but also intensify and enrich it. Suddenly the end is reached: The hand of the Elf King (Death) has touched his victim. Anxiety gives way to sorrow as the narrator announces in increasingly somber (minor) tones, "But in his arms, his child was dead!"

Listening Cue

Franz Schubert, *Erlkönig* (1815)

Genre: Art song
Form: Through-composed

WHAT TO LISTEN FOR: Onomatopoetic music—music that sounds out its meaning at every turn. In this art song, Schubert takes the changing expressive elements of the text (galloping horse, steady reassuring tones of the father, sweet enticements of the Elf King, increasingly frantic cries of the boy) and provides each with characteristic music. Done today, such a treatment likely would be cartoon music; done by a master songwriter like Schubert, it is great art.

Listen to streaming music in an Active Listening Guide at CourseMate and in the eBook.

Take online Listening Exercise 26 at CourseMate and in the eBook.

Just as the tension in Goethe's poem rises incessantly, from the beginning to the very end, Schubert's music unfolds continually, without significant repetition. Such a musical composition featuring ever-changing

In the YouTube playlist at CourseMate for this text, begin exploring how this art song by Schubert can be interpreted in very different ways by different performers.

melodic and harmonic material is called **through-composed,** and Schubert's *Erlkönig,* accordingly, is termed a through-composed art song. For texts that do not tell a story or project a series of changing moods, however, **strophic form** is often preferred. Here a single poetic mood is maintained from one stanza, or strophe, of the text to the next, and the same music can be used for each stanza, resulting in an **AAA** musical form. Most pop songs are written in strophic form, each strophe consisting of a verse and chorus. For a very familiar example of a nineteenth-century art song in strophic form, revisit the famous Brahms *Lullaby* (Intro/21).

Robert Schumann (1810–1856)

While some art songs, such as Schubert's *Erlkönig,* were musical arrangements of dramatic ballads, most were settings of lyrical love poems. The subject of love dominates not only Schubert's *Lieder* but also those of Robert and Clara Schumann, whose life story as a married couple is itself something of an ode to love.

Today the name Robert Schumann denotes a famous composer, the creator of oft-played piano pieces, art songs, and other chamber music. When he met the love of his life, Clara, however, Schumann was a nobody, a failed law student who only hoped that someday he might make a living through music. In 1830 Robert Schumann left law school and began a serious study of the piano with the renowned teacher Friedrich Wieck (1785–1873) in Leipzig, Germany. There he met Wieck's beautiful daughter Clara, a child piano prodigy, who at the age of eleven had already turned heads in Paris. In 1834, when he was twenty-four and she fifteen, the two fell in love. But father Friedrich adamantly opposed their union: Robert seemed to have no prospects, especially since an injury to his right hand had dashed any hopes of a career as a concert pianist. Only after a protracted legal battle and a court decree did Robert and Clara wed, on September 12, 1840. The day Robert Schumann won his court victory for the hand of Clara, he wrote in his diary, "Happiest day and end of the struggle."

Bettmann/CORBIS

▲ Robert and Clara Schumann in 1850, from an engraving constructed from an early photograph

Robert Schumann was something of a "streak" composer. During the 1830s, he wrote music for solo piano almost exclusively. In 1840, perhaps inspired by his marriage to Clara, he composed almost nothing but art songs, most about love. But from his earliest years, Robert had been afflicted with what psychiatrists now call bipolar disorder (likely exacerbated by doses of arsenic that he had taken as a young man to cure a case of syphilis). His moods swung from nervous euphoria to suicidal depression: In some years, he produced a torrent of music; in others, virtually nothing. As time progressed, Schumann's condition worsened. He began to hear voices, both heavenly and hellish, and one morning, pursued by demons within, he jumped off a bridge into the Rhine River. Nearby fishermen pulled him to safety, but from then on, by his own request, he was confined to an asylum, where he died of dementia in 1856.

Clara Wieck Schumann (1819–1896)

Unlike her husband, Robert—a gifted composer but failed performer—Clara Wieck Schumann was one of the great piano virtuosos of the nineteenth century. When she married, however, she took up the dual roles of wife to Robert and mother to the eight children she soon bore him. She, too, had tried her hand at musical composition, writing mostly art songs and character pieces for piano. But despite her unmistakable talent as a composer, Clara was ambivalent about the capacity of women, herself included, to excel as creative artists. As she wrote in her diary in 1839: "I once believed that I possessed creative talent, but I have given up this idea; a woman must not desire to compose. There has never yet been one able to do it, should I expect to be that one?"

Clara's most productive period as a composer coincided with the early years of her marriage; after the birth of several children, her pace slowed. Following Robert's death, Clara ceased composing altogether. She eventually resumed her career as a touring piano virtuoso, but never remarried. Concertizing across Europe into the 1890s, she always appeared dressed in black—the "widow's weeds" of perpetual mourning. Proving that life sometimes imitates art, Clara remained true to the pledge heard in her song "Liebst du um Schönheit": "I will love you eternally." Today Clara and Robert rest side by side in a small cemetery in Bonn, Germany, two souls exemplifying the spirit of the Romantic age.

"Liebst du um Schönheit" (1841)

"Liebst du um Schönheit" ("If You Love for Beauty") composed a year after the couple's marriage, sets to music a four-stanza love poem by German Romantic poet Joseph Eichendorff (1788–1857). In this wistful, playful text, the poet states three reasons (stanzas 1–3) why the lady should *not* be loved—not for beauty, youth, or money (all three of which Clara actually possessed)—but one (last stanza) for which she *should* be loved—for love alone.

Although the figures of melody and accompaniment presented in the first strophe prevail in the subsequent ones, Clara employs here what is called **modified strophic form;** the music changes slightly from one stanza to the next and thus can be represented as **AA'A"A'''**.

Example 11-8 shows the melody of strophe 1 and how it is modified in strophe 2. The ever-evolving music gives this art song its remarkable freshness. Did Clara sell herself short when she declared that "a woman must not desire to compose"? You be the judge.

Example 11-8 ➤

Strophe 1

Liebst du um Schön-heit, o nicht mich lie-be! Lie - be die Son-ne, sie trägt ein gold-nes Haar!_
(If you love for beauty, don't love me! Love the sun, with her golden hair!)

Strophe 2

Liebst du um Ju - gend, o nicht mich lie-be! Lie-be den Frühl-ing der jung ist je - des Jahr!
(If you love for youth, don't love me! Love the spring, which is young each year!)

Clara Schumann, "Liebst du um Schönheit" (1841)

Intro
22

Genre: Art song
Form: Modified strophic

WHAT TO LISTEN FOR: The ever-so-slight changes in the vocal line and accompaniment from one stanza to the next; the musical freshness and sparkle that can perhaps be created only by a young person in love

Listen to streaming music in an Active Listening Guide at CourseMate and in the eBook.

Romantic Piano Music

Review the evolution of the piano in the keyboard videos on the text website.

We've all banged away on a piano at one time or another. Some of us may have had piano lessons requiring endless finger exercises, accompanied by our mother's prediction: "Some day you'll thank me for this." But did you ever stop to think about how the piano came to be?

The first piano was constructed around 1700 as an alternative to the harpsichord, as a way of giving more dynamics and shading to the musical line. Mozart was the first composer to use the piano exclusively, beginning around 1770. His was a small instrument with only 61 keys, a frame made of wood, and a weight of about 120 pounds (see p. 131). A century later, spurred by the new technology of the Industrial Revolution, the piano had grown into the 88-key, cast iron–framed, 1,200-pound grand monster that we know today. Iron had replaced wood, strings had become thicker and stronger, and foot pedals had been added. On the right side was the **sustaining pedal,** which enabled strings to continue to sound after the performer had lifted his or her hand from the corresponding keys. On the left was the **soft pedal,** which softened the dynamic level by shifting the position of the hammers relative to the strings. Finally, in the 1850s, the Steinway Company of New York began **cross-stringing** the piano, overlaying the lowest-sounding strings across those of the middle register, and thereby

> A large, concert grand piano once owned by Franz Liszt and now in the Liszt Museum in Budapest, Hungary. The instrument was made by the Chickering Piano Company of Boston (the largest U.S. piano manufacturer before the appearance of the Steinway Company) and shipped overseas to Liszt as a marketing tool: "If Liszt plays a Chickering, so, young American, should you!"

© Craig Wright

producing a richer, more homogeneous sound. By the mid-nineteenth century, all the essential features of the modern piano were in place—the essential design of the piano hasn't changed in 150 years.

As the piano grew larger and more expressive, it became something of a home entertainment center. In the days before television and video games, the family could gather around the piano to while away the evening hours. Every aspiring middle-class home had to have a piano, both for family enjoyment and as a status symbol—the high-art instrument in the parlor signified to visitors that they had entered a cultured home. Parents made sure their children, especially the girls, received lessons, and publishers, eager to profit from new enthusiasm for the piano, turned out reams of sheet music for pianists of all skill levels.

Spurred by the sudden popularity of the piano, a host of virtuoso performers descended upon the concert halls of Europe with fingers blazing. What they played was often more a display of technical fireworks—rapid octaves, racing chromatic scales, thundering chords—than of musical substance. Happily, however, several of the greatest piano virtuosos of the nineteenth century were also gifted composers.

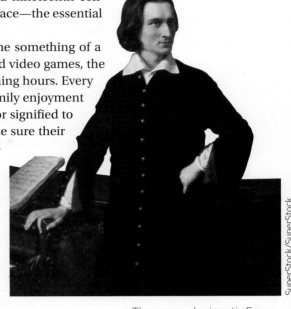

∧ The young, charismatic Franz Liszt, the preeminent pianist of the Romantic era

SuperStock/SuperStock

Franz Liszt (1811–1886)

Franz Liszt was not merely a composer and pianist—he was a phenomenon, perhaps the most flamboyant artistic personality of the entire nineteenth century. Handsome, supremely talented, and equally self-confident, he strutted across the stage as the musical sex symbol of the Romantic era. He could also play the piano like no other. Between 1839 and 1847, Liszt gave more than a thousand concerts, from Ireland to Turkey, from Sweden to Spain, from Portugal to Russia. Everywhere he went, the handsome pianist was greeted with the same sort of mass hysteria experienced by today's rock stars. Audiences of three thousand crowded into the larger halls. Women tried to rip off his silk scarf and white gloves, and fought for a lock of his hair. **Lisztomania** swept across Europe.

Despite their obvious sensationalism, Liszt's concerts in the 1840s established the format of our modern-day piano **recital.** He was the first to play entire programs from memory (not reading from music). He was the first to place the piano parallel with the line of the stage so that neither his back nor his full face, but rather his extraordinary side profile, was visible to the audience. He was the first to perform on the stage alone—up to that point, concerts traditionally had included numerous performers on the program. These solo appearances were called first "soliloquies" and then "recitals," suggesting they were like personal dramatic recitations. As Liszt modestly claimed in his adopted French, "Le concert, c'est moi!"

Judging from contemporary accounts, Liszt was the greatest pianist who ever lived, certainly with regard to technical facility. He had large hands and unusually long fingers with very little web-like connective tissue between them, which allowed him to make wide stretches with relative ease. He could

∨ Lisztomania, as depicted in 1842. A recital by Liszt was likely to create the sort of sensation that a concert by a rock star might generate today. Women fought for a lock of his hair, a broken string from his piano, or a shred of his velvet gloves.

Lebrecht Music & Arts

play a melody in octaves when others could play only the single notes of the line. If others might execute a passage in octaves, Liszt could dash it off in more impressive-sounding tenths (octave plus third). So he wrote daredevil music full of virtuosic display, as we see in Example 11-9, which goes lightning fast.

Example 11-9 ➤

The preceding example is drawn from one of Liszt's etudes. An **etude** is a short, one-movement composition designed to improve a particular aspect of a performer's technique (fast scales, more rapid note repetition, surer leaps, and so on). These works require almost superhuman technical skill. Ironically, such "study pieces" by Liszt are not useful for the average pianist—to practice them you must already be a virtuoso!

But Liszt's reputation as a supremely gifted performer and a flamboyant stage personality does not diminish his importance as a composer. His novel approach to musical form, as best heard in his Piano Sonata in B minor, and harmonic progressions (chord changes), most evident in his late works of the 1880s, foreshadow musical practices of the twentieth century. His piano piece *Nuages Gris* (*Gray Clouds*) was composed in 1881, not 1930 as it sounds.

Frédéric Chopin (1810–1849)

Frédéric Chopin was a very different sort of person than his close friend Franz Liszt. Whereas Liszt was virile and flamboyant, Chopin was physically slight and somewhat sickly. He was also introverted and hated performing in public. Like Liszt, Chopin was a composer and a piano virtuoso, but he did not create moments of technical display merely for their sensational effects. In Chopin's music the physical challenges for the pianist grow out of, but never overshadow, the composer's intrinsic musical ideas.

Chopin was born in Warsaw, Poland, to a French father and a Polish mother. The father taught French—then the universal language of the aristocracy—at an elite secondary school for the sons of Polish nobility. As a student there, Frédéric not only gained an excellent general education but also acquired aristocratic friends and tastes. Fearing that Warsaw was too small and provincial, the young composer moved first to Vienna and then, in September 1831, to Paris. That very year Poland's fight for independence was crushed by Russian troops. Although Chopin spent the rest of his life mainly in France, the expatriate composer became a voice for Polish musical nationalism (for nationalism, see Chapter 14).

Chopin was a rarity among Romantic composers—he wrote only works for solo piano or ensemble pieces (including songs) in which the piano figures prominently. His works for solo piano include those in the Polish national style (called mazurkas and polonaises), three piano sonatas, a set of twenty-four preludes (one in each of the major and minor keys), twenty-four etudes (technical studies), and twenty-one nocturnes. Far better than the other genres for piano, the dream-like nocturnes embody the essence of musical Romanticism.

Nocturne in C♯ minor, Opus 27, No. 1 (1835)

If you want to hear music that is almost painfully beautiful, download a Chopin nocturne.

A **nocturne** (night piece) is a slow, dreamy genre of piano music that came into favor in the 1820s and 1830s. It suggests moonlit nights, romantic longing, and a certain wistful melancholy, all evoked through bittersweet melodies and softly strumming harmonies. To set a nocturnal mood in his Nocturne in C♯ minor, Chopin begins with a tonic C♯ minor chord spun out as an arpeggio in the bass, like a harp or guitar played in the moonlight. The melody (**A**) enters in minor but immediately turns to major, by means of an added sharp. As the opening melody repeats again and again in the course of the work, so, too, the harmony shifts expressively, bending back and forth from minor to major (see arrows), from dark to light. This twisting of mode is one way that the composer creates the "bittersweet" feeling.

A superbly Romantic portrait of Chopin by the famous French painter Eugène Delacroix (1799–1863)

Example 11-10:  2/3 at 0:00 ➤

Soon the opening melody breaks off, and a more passionate, agitated mood takes hold. A new theme (**B**) enters and the tempo increases. The bass now begins a long, mostly chromatic ascent. Here Chopin joins a long list of composers who have employed rising chromaticism to create a feeling of anxiety and growing tension.

Example 11-11: 2:16 ➤

A climax is reached at the peak of this line, emphasized by a remarkable chord change—a chord with four sharps is immediately followed by one with four flats (see Ex. 11-2). The sudden juxtaposition of such distant chords creates bold harmonic shifts of the sort favored by Romantic composers as they strove to fashion a new, more colorful harmonic language. Now a third melody (**C**) enters, which eventually gives way to **A** by means of a descending, recitative-like passage.

The return to **A** is especially rich and satisfying, as the harp-like accompaniment and plaintive melody rise from the depths of the fading bass. Finally, in a brief coda, a piercing dissonance sounds and then resolves to consonance (5:18–5:23), as the fears of the nocturnal world dissolve into a heavenly major realm. As the German poet Heine said of Chopin, "He hails from the land of Mozart, Raphael, and Goethe. His true home is in the realm of Poetry."

Listening Cue

Frédéric Chopin, Nocturne in C♯ minor, Opus 27, No. 1 (1835)

Genre: Nocturne
Form: **ABCA**

WHAT TO LISTEN FOR: How sections **B** and **C** gradually built tension, but only to serve as a foil for the exquisitely beautiful opening and closing (**A**). The point of this kind of music is perhaps not to engage the analytical mind, but rather to shut it down in favor of a subconscious world of dreams.

 Listen to streaming music in an Active Listening Guide at CourseMate and in the eBook.

TWELVE

Romantic Orchestral Music

Technology has sometimes profoundly affected the history of music. Think, for instance, of the invention of the electrically amplified guitar, which made possible the sounds of rock virtuosos such as Jimi Hendrix and Eric Clapton. Think, too, of the more recent MP3 file, the iPod, the iPhone, and YouTube, which have made music instantly audible anywhere around the world and Western music a global musical force. Just as the digital revolution has altered our contemporary musical landscape, the technological advancements that led to the modern symphony orchestra transformed nineteenth-century music.

v A modern French horn with valves, an invention of the 1820s. The valves allow the performer to engage different lengths of tubing instantly and thereby play a fully chromatic scale.

The Romantic Orchestra

In many ways the symphony orchestra that we hear today was a product of the nineteenth-century Industrial Revolution. Around 1830, some existing orchestral instruments received mechanical enhancements. The wood of the flute, for example, was replaced by silver, and the instrument was supplied with a new fingering mechanism that added to its agility and made it easier to play in tune. Similarly, the trumpet and French horn were provided with valves that improved technical facility and accuracy of pitch in all keys. The French horn in particular became an object of special affection during the Romantic period. Its rich, dark tone and its traditional association with the hunt of the forest—and by extension, all of nature—made it the Romantic instrument par excellence.

Entirely new instruments were added to the Romantic orchestra as well. Beethoven expanded its range both high and low. In his famous Symphony No. 5 (1808; see p. 146) he called for a piccolo (a high flute), trombones, and a contrabassoon (a bass bassoon)—the first time any of these had been heard in a symphony. In 1830, Hector Berlioz went even further, requiring an early form of the tuba, a low-pitched oboe, a cornet, and two harps in his *Symphonie fantastique*.

Greater Size, Greater Volume

Berlioz, a composer who personified the Romantic spirit, had a typically grandiose notion of what the ideal symphony orchestra should contain (see chapter-opening image for a caricature of the public's impression of his vision). He wanted no fewer than 467 performers, including 120 violins, 40 violas, 45 cellos, 35 double basses, and 30 harps! Such a gigantic instrumental force was never actually assembled, but Berlioz's utopian vision indicates the direction in which Romantic composers were headed. By the second half of the nineteenth century, orchestras with nearly a hundred players were not uncommon. Compare, for example, the number and variety of instruments required for a typical eighteenth-century performance of Mozart's Symphony

Watch a video of Craig Wright's Open Yale Course class session 20, "The Colossal Symphony: Beethoven, Berlioz, Mahler, and Shostakovich," at CourseMate for this text.

in G minor (1788) with the symphony orchestra needed for Berlioz's *Symphonie fantastique* (1830) and for Gustav Mahler's Symphony No. 1 (1889). In the course of a hundred years the orchestra had tripled in size. But it went no further: The symphony orchestra that we hear today is essentially that of the late nineteenth century.

Our reaction to the Romantic orchestra today, however, is very different from the response of nineteenth-century listeners. Modern ears have been desensitized by an overexposure to electronically amplified sound. But imagine the impact of an orchestra of a hundred players before the days of amplification. Apart from the military cannon and the steam engine, the

Hear Berlioz's colossal *Grande Messe des morts*, Op. 5 (Requiem), *Dies irae*, *Tuba mirum*, in the YouTube playlist at CourseMate for this text.

The Growth of the Symphony Orchestra		
Mozart (1788) Symphony in G minor	Berlioz (1830) Symphonie fantastique	Mahler (1889) Symphony No. 1
Woodwinds		
1 flute	1 piccolo	3 piccolos
2 oboes	2 flutes	4 flutes
2 clarinets	2 oboes	4 oboes
2 bassoons	1 English horn	1 English horn
	2 B♭ clarinets	4 B♭ clarinets
	1 E♭ clarinet	2 E♭ clarinets
	4 bassoons	1 bass clarinet
		3 bassoons
		1 contrabassoon
Brasses		
2 French horns	4 French horns	7 French horns
	2 trumpets	5 trumpets
	2 cornets	4 trombones
	3 trombones	1 tuba
	2 ophicleides (tubas)	
Strings		
1st violins (8)*	1st violins (15)*	1st violins (20)*
2nd violins (8)	2nd violins (14)	2nd violins (18)
violas (4)	violas (8)	violas (14)
cellos (4)	cellos (12)	cellos (12)
double basses (3)	double basses (8)	double basses (18)
	2 harps	1 harp
Percussion		
	timpani	timpani (2 players)
	bass drum	bass drum
	snare drum	triangle, cymbals
	cymbals and bells	tam-tam
Total: 36	*Total: 89*	*Total: 129*

*Number of string players estimated according to standards of the period

nineteenth-century orchestra produced the loudest sonic level of any human contrivance. The big sound—and the big contrasts—of the nineteenth-century orchestra were new and startling, and audiences packed ever-larger concert halls to hear them, as if they were the latest form of special effects. To maximize (and sometimes minimize) this sound, Romantic composers prescribed an extravagant range of dynamics such as *pppp* (super *pianissimo*) and *ffff* (super *fortissimo*). Such sonic extremes are typical of the Romantic era, an age that indulged in wild mood swings and excesses of many kinds.

⌄ A large orchestra depicted at Covent Garden Theater, London, in 1846. The conductor stands toward the middle, baton in hand, with strings to his right and woodwinds, brass, and percussion to his left. It was typical in this period to put all or part of the orchestra on risers to allow the sound to project more fully.

Monumental and Miniature Size

It is axiomatic in music that the greater the number of performers, the greater the length of the performance. Romantic composers took advantage of the newly enriched sounds of the symphony orchestra to lay out broad, sweeping melodies and indulge in gigantic crescendos. Everything in music, it seemed, was expanding—a process that paralleled the ideas of the new scientific age. This was the period, of course, in which Charles Darwin posited that the earth was not merely seven thousand years old, as the Bible suggested, but several million. If Mozart's G minor symphony (1788) lasts twenty minutes, Berlioz's *Symphonie fantastique* (1830) takes about fifty-five minutes, and Mahler's Symphony No. 2 (1894) clocks in at nearly an hour and a half. Perhaps the longest of all was Richard Wagner's four-opera *Ring* cycle (1853–1874), which runs some *seventeen hours* over the course of four evenings.

Yet, paradoxically, Romantic composers were not interested only in the grandiose; the miniature fascinated them as well. In works of only a brief minute or two, they tried to capture the essence of a single mood, sentiment, or emotion. Such a miniature was called a **character piece.** It was usually, but not always, written for the piano and often made use of simple binary (**AB**) or ternary (**ABA**) form. In this chapter, we will explore two very different musical works, the first a monumental one by Hector Berlioz, and the second a miniature piece by Peter Tchaikovsky.

 ## Program Music

The Romantic love of literature stimulated interest not only in the art song (see Chapter 11) but also in program music. Indeed, the nineteenth century can fairly be called the "century of program music." True, there had been earlier isolated examples of program music—in Vivaldi's *The Four Seasons,* for example (see pp. 79–81). But Romantic composers believed that music could be more than pure, abstract sound—that musical sounds alone (without a text) could tell a story. Most important, they now had the power and color of the newly enlarged orchestra to help tell the tale.

Program music is instrumental music, usually written for symphony orchestra, that seeks to re-create in sound the events and emotions portrayed in some extramusical source: a story, legend, play, novel, or even historical event. The theory of program music rests on the fact that specific musical gestures can evoke particular feelings and associations. A lyrical melody may spur memories of love, harshly dissonant chords might imply conflict, or a sudden trumpet call may suggest the arrival of the hero, for example. By stringing together such musical gestures in a convincing sequence, a composer might tell a story through music. Program music is fully harmonious with the strongly literary spirit of the nineteenth century.

A few Romantic composers, notably Johannes Brahms (1833–1897), resisted the seductive lure of program music and continued to write what came to be called **absolute music**—symphonies, sonatas, quartets, and other instrumental music without extramusical or programmatic references (see Chapter 14). Most others, however, desiring to convey a clear, coherent message, took advantage of the more overtly narrative character of program music. In 1850, composer Franz Liszt got to the heart of the matter when he observed that a program "provided a means by which to protect the listener against a wrong poetical interpretation and to direct his attention to the poetical idea of the whole."

Hector Berlioz (1803–1869) and the Program Symphony

Hector Berlioz was one of the most original figures in the history of music. He was born in 1803 near the mountain city of Grenoble, France, the son of a local doctor. As a youth, Berlioz studied mainly the sciences and ancient Roman literature. Although local tutors taught him to play the flute and guitar, he had no systematic training in music theory or composition and little exposure to the music of the great masters. Among the major composers of the nineteenth century, he was the only one without fluency at the keyboard. He never studied piano and could do no more than bang out a few chords.

At the age of seventeen, Berlioz was sent off to Paris to study medicine, his father's profession. For two years he pursued a program in the physical sciences, earning a degree in 1821. But Berlioz found the reality of the dissecting table repulsive and the allure of the opera house and concert hall irresistible. After a period of soul-searching, and the inevitable falling-out with his parents over the choice of a career, he vowed to become "no doctor or apothecary but a great composer."

His dismayed father immediately cut off his living stipend, leaving young Berlioz to ponder how he might support himself while studying composition at the Paris Conservatory (the French national school of music). Other composers had relied on teaching as a means to earn a regular income, but Berlioz, with no particular skill at any instrument, was not qualified to give music lessons. Instead, he turned to music criticism, writing reviews and articles for

Scala/Art Resource, NY

▲ Hector Berlioz at the age of twenty-nine

literary journals. Berlioz was the first composer to earn a livelihood as a music critic, and it was criticism, not composition, that remained his primary source of income for the rest of his life.

Perhaps it was inevitable that Berlioz would turn to writing about music, for in his mind, there was always a connection between music and the written word. As a student, Berlioz encountered the works of Shakespeare, and the experience changed his life: "Shakespeare, coming upon me unawares, struck me like a thunderbolt. The lightning flash of that discovery revealed to me at a stroke the whole heaven of art." Berlioz devoured Shakespeare's plays and based musical compositions on four of them: *The Tempest, King Lear, Hamlet,* and *Romeo and Juliet.* The common denominator in the art of both Shakespeare and Berlioz is range of expression. Just as no dramatist before Shakespeare had portrayed the full spectrum of human emotions on the stage, so no composer before Berlioz, not even Beethoven, had undertaken to create such a wide range of moods through sound.

To depict wild swings of mood in music, Berlioz called for enormous orchestral and choral forces—hundreds and hundreds of performers (see above p. 170). He also experimented with new instruments: the **ophicleide** (an early form of the tuba), the **English horn** (a low oboe), the harp (an ancient instrument that he brought into the symphony orchestra for the first time), the **cornet** (a brass instrument with valves, borrowed from the military band), and even the newly invented saxophone. In 1843, he wrote a textbook on **orchestration**— the art of arranging a composer's music for just the right instruments—still used today in colleges and conservatories around the world. The boy who could play only guitar had become a master of the orchestra!

Berlioz's approach to musical form was equally innovative; he rarely used such standard forms as sonata–allegro or theme and variations. Instead, he preferred to create forms that flowed from the particular narrative of the story at hand. His French compatriots called his seemingly formless compositions "bizarre" and "monstrous," and thought him something of a madman. Subscribing to the adage "No man is a prophet in his own land," Berlioz took his progressive music to London, Vienna, Prague, and even Moscow, introducing such works as *Symphonie fantastique* and *Roméo et Juliette.* He died in Paris in 1869, isolated and embittered, the little recognition he received in his native France having come too late to boost his career or self-esteem.

Symphonie fantastique (1830)

Berlioz's most celebrated composition, then and now, is his *Symphonie fantastique,* perhaps the single most radical example of musical Romanticism. Over the course of five movements, Berlioz tells a story in music and thereby creates the first **program symphony**—a multimovement work for orchestra that depicts a succession of events, scenes, or ideas drawn from outside of music. The history surrounding the creation of the *Symphonie fantastique* is as fascinating, indeed fantastical, as the piece itself.

In 1827, a troupe of English actors came to Paris to present Shakespeare's *Hamlet* and *Romeo and Juliet.* Though he understood little English, Berlioz attended and was overwhelmed by the human insights, touching beauty, and sometimes brutal onstage action that characterizes Shakespearean drama. But Berlioz not only fell in love with Shakespeare's work, he was also smitten with the leading lady who played Ophelia to Hamlet and Juliet to Romeo, one Harriet Smithson. As a crazed young man might stalk a Hollywood starlet today, Berlioz wrote passionate letters and chased after Smithson. Eventually, his ardor cooled—for a time, he even became engaged to someone else. But the experience of an all-consuming love, the despair of rejection, and the vision of darkness and possible death furnished the stimulus—and story line—for an unusually imaginative symphony.

Symphonie fantastique derives its name not because it is "fantastic" in the sense of "wonderful" (though it is), but because it is a fantasy: Through the course of a symphony, Berlioz fantasizes about his relationship with Harriet Smithson. The thread that binds the five disparate movements is a single melody that personifies the beloved. Berlioz called this theme his **idée fixe** ("fixed idea" or musical fixation); the melody is always present, like Harriet, an obsession in Berlioz's tortured mind. However, as his feelings about Harriet change from movement to movement, the composer transforms the fundamental melody, altering the pitches, rhythms, and instrumental color. To make sure the listener could follow this wild progression of emotional states, Berlioz prepared a written program to be read as the music was performed. His lurid fantasy involves unrequited love, attempted suicide by drug overdose, an imaginary murder, and a hellish revenge.

∧ The actress Harriet Smithson became an obsession for Berlioz and the source of inspiration for his *Symphonie fantastique.* Eventually, Berlioz did meet and marry Smithson. Today they lie side by side in the cemetery of Montmartre in Paris.

FIRST MOVEMENT: REVERIES, PASSIONS

> Program: A young musician . . . sees for the first time a woman who embodies all the charms of the ideal being he has imagined in his dreams. . . . The subject of the first movement is the passage from this state of melancholy reverie, interrupted by a few moments of joy, to that of delirious passion, with movements of fury, jealousy, and its return to tenderness, tears, and religious consolation.

A slow introduction ("this state of melancholy reverie") prepares the way for the first vision of the beloved, who is represented by the first appearance of the main theme, the *idée fixe.*

Example 12-1 ➤

The movement unfolds in something akin to sonata–allegro form. The "recapitulation," however, does not so much repeat the *idée fixe* as transform the melody to reflect the artist's feelings of sorrow and tenderness.

SECOND MOVEMENT: A BALL

> Program: The artist finds himself . . . in the midst of the tumult of a party.

A lilting waltz now begins, but it is interrupted by the unexpected appearance of the *idée fixe* (the beloved has arrived), its rhythm changed to accommodate the triple meter of the waltz. Four harps add a graceful accompaniment when the waltz returns, and, toward the end, there is even a lovely solo for cornet. The sequence of waltz–*idée fixe*–waltz creates a ternary form.

THIRD MOVEMENT: SCENE IN THE COUNTRY

> Program: Finding himself one evening in the country, the artist hears in the distance two shepherds piping. . . . He reflects upon his isolation and hopes that soon he will no longer be alone.

The dialogue between the shepherds is presented by an English horn and an oboe, the latter played offstage to give the effect of a distant response. The unexpected appearance of the *idée fixe* in the woodwinds suggests that the artist has hopes of winning his beloved. But has she falsely encouraged him? In response to the lonely petition of an English horn, we now hear only the rumble of distant thunder in the timpani. The call for love goes unanswered.

FOURTH MOVEMENT: MARCH TO THE SCAFFOLD

> Program: Having realized that his love goes unrecognized, the artist poisons himself with opium. The dose of the narcotic, too weak to kill him, plunges him into a sleep accompanied by the most horrible visions. He dreams that he has killed the one he loved, that he is condemned, led to the scaffold, and now witnesses his own execution.

This drug-induced nightmare centers on the march to the scaffold where the artist is to be executed. The steady beat of the low strings and the muffled bass drum sound the steps of the procession. Near the end, the image of the beloved returns in the clarinet, only to be suddenly cut off by a *fortissimo* crash by the full orchestra. The guillotine has fallen and with it the lover's head.

FIFTH MOVEMENT: DREAM OF THE WITCHES' SABBATH

> Program: He sees himself at the witches' sabbath surrounded by a troop of frightful shadows, sorcerers, and monsters of all sorts, gathered for his funeral. Strange noises, groans, bursts of laughter, distant cries echoed by others. The beloved melody returns again, but it has lost its noble, modest character and is now only base, trivial, and grotesque. An outburst of joy at her arrival; she joins in the devilish orgy.

In this monstrous finale, Berlioz creates his personal vision of hell. A crowd of witches and ghouls is summoned to dance around the corpse of the artist on its way to the inferno. Eerie sounds are produced by the strings, using mutes, and by the high woodwinds and French horn, playing glissandos. A piercing clarinet enters with a horrid parody of the *idée fixe* as Harriet Smithson, now in the frightful garb of a wicked old hag, comes on stage.

∨ *Witches' Sabbath* by Francisco de Goya (1746–1828) bears the same title as the finale of Berlioz's *Symphonie fantastique*. Both create images of the bizarre and macabre so dear to the hearts of Romantic artists.

Giraudon/The Bridgeman Art Library

Example 12-2: 2/1 at 1:40 >

She is greeted by a joyous *fortissimo* outburst by the full assembly as all proceed to dance to the now perverted *idée fixe*. Suddenly the music becomes ominously quiet, and in one of the most strikingly original moments in all of classical music, great Gothic church bells are heard. Against this solemn backdrop sounds the burial hymn of the medieval Church, the **Dies irae**, played by ophicleides (tubas) and bassoons. (In more recent years, the *Dies irae* has been used to signal doom and gloom in movie thrillers including *The Nightmare Before Christmas, Sleeping with the Enemy,* and *The Shining.*)

Example 12-3: 3:23 >

[Di - es   i - rae   di - es   il - la   sol - vet   sae -   clum   in   fa - vil - la]
[Day of anger, day of wrath, on which the ages will be changed to ash]

Not only is the orchestration sensational, the musical symbolism is sacrilegious. Just as the painter Goya (see p. 176) parodies the Catholic Mass in his *Witches' Sabbath*—making babies serve as communion wafers—so Berlioz creates a mockery of one of the most venerable Gregorian chants of the Catholic Church. First, the *Dies irae* is played by the horns twice as fast (a process called rhythmic **diminution**). Then the sacred melody is transformed into a jazzed-up dance tune played by a shrill, high clarinet, the entire scene now becoming a blasphemous black Mass.

Example 12-4: 3:55 >

As the ceremony proceeds, the witches begin to dance. But they do so in a strange way: They enter one by one and create a **fugato,** a fugal passage within a symphonic movement. The successive entries of more and more voices, or dancing witches, creates the effect of a growing tumult around the corpse of the artist.

Example 12-5: 5:16 >

A climax is reached as the witches' theme, played by the strings, and the *Dies irae* melody, played by the brasses and woodwinds, sound together in different keys, a bizarre example of **double counterpoint.** Stranger still is the sound that follows, for Berlioz instructs the violins to play **col legno** (with the wood)—to strike the strings, not with the usual front of the bow, but with the wooden back, creating a noise evocative of the crackling of hellfire. Berlioz was nothing if not a novel orchestrator.

To the audience that first heard the *Symphonie fantastique* on December 5, 1830, all of this must have seemed deranged: new instruments, novel playing effects, simultaneous melodies in different keys, and a nontraditional musical form that grows out of the events in a tabloid-headline-like program. But it all works. Composer Berlioz breaks all the conventional rules of music. Yet he does so in a way that produces a wholly integrated, unified, and ultimately satisfying work of art. The separate effects may be revolutionary and momentarily shocking, but they are consistent and logical among themselves when heard within the total artistic concept. Had Berlioz never written another note of music, he would still be justly famous for this single masterpiece of Romantic genius. As the German Romantic philosopher Arthur Schopenhauer (1788–1860) said, "A person of talent hits a target no one else can hit; a genius hits a target no one else can see."

Listening Cue

Hector Berlioz, *Symphonie fantastique* (1830)

1–2

Fifth movement, "Dream of the Witches' Sabbath"

WHAT TO LISTEN FOR: The various transformations of the *idée fixe* and the *Dies irae*, and the extraordinary orchestral effects Berlioz employs to tell his bizarre tale—his fantastical vision of hell

🔊 Listen to streaming music in an Active Listening Guide at CourseMate or in the eBook.

🔊 Take online Listening Exercise 27 at CourseMate or in the eBook.

But how did Berlioz's drama really end? In truth, Berlioz did meet and marry Harriet, but the two lived miserably together ever after. He complained about her increasing weight, she about his infidelities. After Harriet died in 1854, Berlioz promptly married his longtime mistress. When the composer himself died in 1869, he was buried next to his second wife. But a century later, during the centenary commemorating his death, Romantic enthusiasts repositioned the remains of star-crossed Hector and Harriet. Today they lie side by side in the Parisian cemetery of Montmartre.

Peter Tchaikovsky (1840–1893) and Ballet Music

The Romantic mania for program music continued throughout the nineteenth century, most notably in the tone poems of Peter Tchaikovsky. A **tone poem** is a one-movement work for orchestra that captures the emotions and events of a story through music. Thus a tone poem is really no different from a program symphony, except that everything happens in just one movement. Today the best-known tone poems are Richard Strauss's *Also sprach Zarathustra* (1896; see p. 11) and Tchaikovsky's *Romeo and Juliet* (1869). Yet Tchaikovsky was unique among the major composers of the nineteenth century. He excelled in an artistic genre that others did not: ballet.

Tchaikovsky was born in 1840 into an upper-middle-class family in provincial Russia. He showed a keen ear for music in his earliest years and by the age of six could speak fluent French and German. (An excellent musical ear and a capacity to learn foreign languages often go hand in hand—both involve processing patterns of sound.) As to his career, his parents determined that law would provide the safest path to success. But, like Robert Schumann before him, Tchaikovsky eventually realized that it was music, not law, that fired his imagination, so he made his way to the Saint Petersburg Conservatory of Music. When he graduated in 1866 Tchaikovsky was immediately offered a position at the newly formed Moscow Conservatory, that of professor of harmony and musical composition.

▲ Peter Tchaikovsky

Lebrecht Music & Arts

In truth, it was not his conservatory job in Moscow that supported Tchaikovsky during most of his mature years, but rather a private arrangement with an eccentric patroness, Madame Nadezhda von Meck. This wealthy, music-loving widow furnished him with an annual income of 6,000 rubles (about $45,000 U.S. today) on the condition that she and the composer never meet—a requirement not always easily fulfilled, because the two sometimes resided at the same summer estate. In addition to this annuity, in 1881, Tsar Alexander III awarded Tchaikovsky an annual pension of 3,000 rubles in recognition of his importance to Russian cultural life. Now a man of independent means, Tchaikovsky traveled extensively in Western Europe, and even to America. He enjoyed the freedom that so many artists find necessary to creative activity.

Tchaikovsky's creative output touched every genre of nineteenth-century classical music, including opera, song, string quartet, piano sonata, concerto, and symphony. But today concertgoers know Tchaikovsky best for his program music and ballets. For example, his programmatic *The 1812 Overture* (1882), which commemorates the Russian defeat of Napoleon in 1812, is heard in the United States on the Fourth of July, with Tchaikovsky's musical pyrotechnics usually accompanied by fireworks in the night sky. By the end of the nineteenth century, Tchaikovsky was the world's most popular orchestral composer, the "big name" brought from Europe to America when star appeal was needed to add luster to the opening of Carnegie Hall in 1891. He died suddenly in 1893, at the age of fifty-three, after drinking unboiled water during an epidemic of cholera.

Tchaikovsky's Ballets

Ballet, like opera, calls to mind "high-end" culture. Indeed, the origins of ballet are tied to the history of opera, for ballet emerged from a hybrid of the two genres performed at the French royal court of Louis XIV (who reigned 1643–1715). Throughout the eighteenth century, no opera was complete without a ballet or two to provide a pleasant diversion. By the early nineteenth century, however, this dance spectacle had separated from opera and moved on stage as the independent genre we know today. A **ballet** is thus a dramatic dance in which the characters, using various stylized steps and pantomime, tell a story. While ballet first developed in France, during the nineteenth century it gained great popularity, and indeed an adopted homeland, in Russia. Even today, the terms *Russian* and *ballerina* seem inextricably linked.

Early in his career, Tchaikovsky realized that ballet required precisely the compositional skills that he possessed. Unlike Bach, Mozart, and Beethoven,

▲ Nadezhda von Meck was the widow of an engineer who made a fortune constructing the first railroads in Russia during the 1860s and 1870s. She used her money, in part, to support composers such as Tchaikovsky and, later, Claude Debussy.

Topham/The Image Works

A recent production of *The Nutcracker* by the Royal Ballet, showing a *pas de deux* in "Dance of the Sugar Plum Fairy"

Watch part of a performance of *The Nutcracker* in the YouTube playlist at CourseMate for this text.

Tchaikovsky was not a "developer"—he was not good at teasing out intricate thematic relationships over long spans of time. Instead, his gift was to create one striking melody and mood after another—to create one vivid scene and then move on to the next. And this is precisely what **ballet music** requires—not symphonic invention or contrapuntal intricacy, but short bursts of tuneful melody and captivating rhythm, all intended to capture the emotional essence of the scene. *Short* is the operative word here; because dancing in a ballet is exhausting, neither the principals nor the *corps de ballet* hold center stage for more than three minutes at a time. Tchaikovsky's "short-segment" style proved perfect for the demands of ballet. From his pen flowed *Swan Lake* (1876), *Sleeping Beauty* (1889), and *The Nutcracker* (1892), arguably the three most popular works in the entire repertoire of grand Romantic ballet.

Who doesn't know some of the ballet music from *The Nutcracker* (1892), a holiday ritual as traditional as caroling and gift giving? The story, typical of Romantic-era narratives, springs from a fairy-tale fantasy. After a Christmas Eve celebration, an exhausted young girl, Clara, falls asleep and dreams of people from exotic places and toys that come to life. Fantastical characters parade before us, not merely accompanied but literally brought to life by the music. In "Dance of the Reed Pipes," sleeping Clara imagines she sees shepherds dancing in a meadow. Because shepherds since time immemorial had played "pan pipes," Tchaikovsky orchestrates this scene in a way that features flutes. (The tableau is also called the "Dance of the Toy Flutes.") The rhythm of the music, first duple and slow, then duple and fast, propels the dancing shepherds. Indeed ballet music must not only create evocative moods through colorful orchestration, it must also project a strong, clear metrical pulse to animate—indeed, regulate—the steps of the dancers. Whether the music is ballet or hip hop, if you can't hear the beat, you can't dance.

Listening Cue

Peter Tchaikovsky, "Dance of the Reed Pipes" from *The Nutcracker* (1891)

Intro
25

Situation: In this portion of the ballet, Clara's dream takes her and the Handsome Prince to exotic places around the globe (China, Arabia, Russia, and Spain among them), and for each, Tchaikovsky creates music that sounds evocative of a foreign locale, at least to Western ears. While in China, we encounter a group of dancing shepherds playing reed pipes—hence the prominence of the flutes.

Genre: Ballet music

WHAT TO LISTEN FOR: Not only the charming sound of the flutes, but the clear-cut ternary form (**ABA**): flutes in major, followed by soft trumpets in minor (1:22), and a return (1:57) to the flutes at the end.

Listen to streaming music in an Active Listening Guide at CourseMate or in the eBook.

Finally, it is important to keep in mind that ballet music is not program music. Program music is a purely instrumental genre in which sounds alone create the narrative. In ballet music, on the other hand, music is an adjunct: the movements, facial expressions, and gestures of the dancers tell the story.

chapter THIRTEEN

Romantic Opera

Rob Moore/Lebrecht Music & Arts

Watch a video of Craig Wright's Open Yale Course class session 19, "Romantic Opera: Verdi's *La Traviata*, Bocelli, Pavarotti, and Domingo," at CourseMate for this text.

The nineteenth century is often called the "golden age of opera." It is the century of Rossini, Bellini, Verdi, Wagner, Bizet, and Puccini. Notice that four of these opera composers were Italian. The Italian language, with its evenly spaced, open vowels, is perfectly suited for singing, and the people of Italy seem to have an innate love of melody. Perhaps for this reason, opera began in Italy, around 1600 (see p. 70). Thereafter, Italian opera dominated the European stage. When Handel wrote opera for London in the 1720s and Mozart for Vienna in the 1780s, they did so using mainly the language and traditions of Italian opera. Even today, Italian remains the language most frequently heard in opera houses around the world, from La Scala in Milan to the Metropolitan Opera in New York.

In the early nineteenth century, the primacy of Italian opera was maintained almost single-handedly by Gioachino Rossini (1792–1868), the composer of *The Barber of Seville* (1816). Surprising as it may now seem, Rossini was the most celebrated musician in Europe during the 1820s, far exceeding even Beethoven in fame. Why this "Rossini fever," as it was called? Because Rossini wrote operas—not symphonies or string quartets—and opera was then the leading genre of musical entertainment. Indeed, during Rossini's lifetime, opera captured the popular imagination in much the way that films do today.

Rossini and his younger contemporaries pioneered a style of opera in which the attention was focused exclusively on the solo voice—on the art of beautiful, sometimes extravagant, singing, called **bel canto**. As one Italian newspaper of the day declared, "In the theatrical arts it is said that three things are required: action, action, action; likewise, three things are demanded for music: voice, voice, voice." Not surprisingly, by placing such importance on the voices of the leading singers, *bel canto* opera fostered a star system among the cast. Usually, it was the lyric soprano—heroine and **prima donna** (first lady)—who held the most exalted position in the operatic firmament. By the 1880s, she would also be called a **diva,** Italian for "goddess." Indeed, the diva and her beautiful voice would rule Italian *bel canto* opera throughout the nineteenth century and even up to the present day.

Giuseppe Verdi (1813–1901)

The name Giuseppe Verdi (VAIR-dee) is virtually synonymous with Italian opera. For six decades, from the time of *Nabucco* in 1842 until *Falstaff* in 1893, Verdi had almost no rival for the affections of the opera-loving public in Italy and throughout Europe. Even today the best-loved of his twenty-six operas are more readily available—in opera houses, TV productions, DVDs, and webcasts—than those of any other composer.

Verdi was born near Busseto in northern Italy in 1813, the son of a tavern keeper. He was no musical prodigy: At the age of eighteen, Verdi was rejected for admission to the Conservatory of Music in Milan because he was already too old and his piano technique faulty. Indeed, not before the age of twenty-nine did he finally achieve musical success, with the opera *Nabucco* (1842). A surprise hit when premiered at La Scala Opera House in Milan, *Nabucco* launched Verdi's career in Europe, and eventually North and South America as well.

▲ The reigning opera diva Renée Fleming of Rochester, New York, specializes in *bel canto* opera.

Kevin Mazur/WireImage/Getty Images

Today Giuseppe Verdi would be characterized variously as a political "leftist," "rebel," and/or "revolutionary." He worked for the overthrow of the Austrian government, which then ruled most of Italy. By coincidence, the name "Verdi" ("Green" in Italian) had the same letters as **V**ittorio **E**manuele **R**e **d'I**talia, the people's choice to lead a new, free, unified Italy. Verdi willing lent his name to the nationalist Green Party. During the 1840s, popular cries of "Viva, Verdi" ("Long Live the Green [Nationalist] Party") echoed in support of Italian unification. Yet it was not only Verdi's name but also his music that connected the composer to Italian nationalism. In *Nabucco,* for example, Verdi honors a suppressed people (in this case the Jews), who groan under the rule of a cruel foreign power (the Babylonians). Sensitive listeners heard Verdi's choruses as "protest music," singable tunes that intend to effect political change. In 1849, however, much to Verdi's dismay, the nationalist revolution failed, crushed by foreign troops.

v La Scala Opera House about 1830. Verdi's first four and last two operas had their premieres at La Scala, then as now the foremost opera house in Italy.

© Scala/Art Resource, NY

Disillusioned with politics, in 1850 Verdi temporarily moved to Paris and turned his attention from national to personal drama. In quick order, he composed a trio of works without which no opera house today could function: *Rigoletto* (1851), *La traviata* (1853), and *Il trovatore* (1853). Upon his return to Italy in 1857, the number, but not the quality, of Verdi's operas declined. He composed only when the subject was of special interest or the money so great that he couldn't refuse. His opera *Aida* (1871), commissioned to celebrate the opening of the Suez Canal, brought him an astonishing fee—the equivalent of about $720,000 in today's dollars. Verdi had become wealthy, so he retired to his estate in northern Italy to lead the life of a country squire—or so he thought.

v A photograph of Giuseppe Verdi, taken about 1885, on an early published score of his opera *La traviata*

But like a performer who feels he owes the audience more, or has something more to prove to himself, Verdi returned to the theater, composing the critically acclaimed *Otello* (1887) and *Falstaff* (1893), both based on plays of Shakespeare. Of all artists, musical or otherwise, late-bloomer Verdi created quality works at the most advanced age: *Falstaff* was composed in his eightieth year.

Verdi's Dramaturgy and Musical Style

When the curtain goes up on a Verdi opera, the listener will find elements of dramaturgy—construction of the drama—and musical style that are unique to this composer. For Giuseppe Verdi, conflict should inform every scene, and he expressed conflict, whether personal or national, by juxtaposing self-contained, clearly contrasting units of music. A rousing march, a patriotic chorus, a passionate recitative, and a lyrical aria might follow in quick succession. The composer aims not at musical and dramatic subtlety but rather at banner headlines of emotion. The psychic states

VERDI.
"LA TRAVIATA."

Mary Evans Picture Library/The Image Works

of the characters are so clearly depicted, sometimes exaggerated, that the drama comes perilously close to melodrama, reliant on sentimentality and sensationalism at the expense of subtle character development. But it is never dull. There is action, passion, and intensity, all the things that give an opera mass appeal. In 1854, Verdi said, "There is one thing the public will not tolerate in the theater: boredom."

How does Verdi generate this feeling of intense passion and nonstop action? He does so by creating a new kind of recitative and a new style of aria. As before, recitative still narrates the action, and the aria still expresses the character's emotional states. But Verdi replaces simple recitative, accompanied only by *basso continuo* (see p. 68), with orchestrally accompanied *recitativo accompagnato.* This allows the action to flow smoothly from orchestrally accompanied aria to orchestrally accompanied recitative and back without a jarring change of texture. As for the aria, Verdi brings to it a new intensity. Yes, he is a composer squarely in the tradition of Italian *bel canto* opera. He focuses his attention on the solo voice and on a lyrical, beautiful vocal line. Indeed, no composer had a greater gift for writing simple, memorable melodies that the audience could whistle on the way out of the theater. Yet Verdi also adds intensity and passion to these arias by pushing the singers to the upper reaches of their range. The thrilling moments in which the hero (the tenor) or the heroine (the soprano) go right to the top are literally the high points of any Verdi opera.

La traviata (1853)

We may measure the high intensity and passion in Verdi's operas by listening to a portion of his *La traviata,* written in Paris in 1853. *La traviata* means literally "The Woman Gone Astray." The wayward woman here is the sickly Violetta Valery, a courtesan, or high-class prostitute, who first resists and then succumbs to the love of young Alfredo Germont. Then, without explanation, Violetta deserts Alfredo, in truth so that her scandalous reputation will not bring disgrace on his respectable family. The hot-tempered Alfredo now publicly insults Violetta, fights a duel with her new "protector," and is banished from France. When the nature of Violetta's sacrifice is revealed, Alfredo rushes back to Paris. But it is too late! She is dying of tuberculosis—her fate dictated by an operatic convention that requires the heroine to sing one last show-stopping aria and then expire.

Verdi based the libretto of *La traviata* on a play that he had seen in Paris in 1852 called *Camille,* by Alexandre Dumas the younger. (His father, Alexandre Dumas senior, wrote *The Count of Monte Cristo* and *The Three Musketeers.*) *Camille* tells the story of the real-life figure Marie Duplessis, mistress of the playwright Dumas and, for a short time, of the composer-pianist Franz Liszt as well (see Chapter 11). Verdi renamed her Violetta and had her serve as the model for the courtesan in his opera *La traviata.* Like many in this period, Marie died young of tuberculosis, at the age of twenty-three.

As we join *La traviata* toward the end of the first act, we see Violetta and Alfredo in the midst of a gala. Violetta finds herself strangely attracted to the dashing young man and contemplates a union with him. But knowing that she is ill, and fearing the entanglements of love, our heroine rejects the whole idea as impossible. Forget love, she says in an impassioned accompanied recitative: "Folly! Folly! What sort of crazy dream is this!" As Violetta's emotional barometer

Watch two parts of *La traviata,* as well as "La donna è mobile" from Verdi's *Rigoletto,* in the YouTube playlist at CourseMate for this text.

v Marie Duplessis. The end of her brief, scandalous life is the subject of Giuseppe Verdi's opera *La traviata.* So notorious had she become by the time of her death at the age of twenty-three that Charles Dickens said, "You would have thought her passing was a question of the death of a hero or a Joan of Arc."

Lebrecht Music & Arts

rises, so does her music, climaxing at the end of the recitative with an extraordinary outburst on the word "Gioir" ("Enjoy"). Through this high-flying music, Verdi defines the dangerous "live-for the moment" side of Violetta's character. Indeed, there is something about the height and intensity of the pitch (piercing enough to shatter a glass!) that suggests Violetta is out of control. Recitative yields to aria, and the scene concludes with "Sempre libera" ("Always Free"), one of the great show arias for soprano voice. Here the soprano must project an emotional state bordering on hysteria, yet maintain absolute control over the pitch in her singing. Violetta's declaration of independence is briefly broken by the offstage voice of Alfredo, who reminds her of the seductive power of love. This, too, Violetta brushes aside as she emphatically repeats her pledge always to be free.

Everett Collection

▲ As writer Mark Evan Bonds has pointed out, the romantic comedy *Pretty Woman* (1990), starring Richard Gere and Julia Roberts, is a cinematic "remake" of the story of *La traviata*—respectable businessman meets call girl. An important difference, however, is that in Verdi's treatment, as often happens in opera, there is no Hollywood ending: The tragic heroine dies at the end. It is not a coincidence—but, instead, a Romantic convention—that all four operas discussed in this chapter conclude with the tragic death of the heroine.

Listening Cue

Giuseppe Verdi, *La traviata* (1853), Act I, Scene 6

2
4–6

Characters: Violetta and Alfredo (outside her window)
Situation: Violetta, having at first thought Alfredo might be "Mr. Right," rejects this notion, vowing emphatically to remain free. This she accomplishes, but only briefly.

WHAT TO LISTEN FOR: An accompanied recitative climaxing with "Enjoy" that then yields to a two-strophe aria (track 5), the second strophe of which (track 6) is even more brilliant and showy (more *bel canto*) than the first

🔊 Listen to streaming music in an Active Listening Guide at CourseMate or in the eBook.

🔊 Take online Listening Exercise 28 at CourseMate or in the eBook.

 Germany

Historical periods often seem to look back to other historical periods for inspiration. The Renaissance and the Classical era, for example, embraced elements of Greek and Roman antiquity. The Romantic imagination, however, chose to model itself on the Middle Ages. A nostalgic fondness for a dimly understood "dark ages" developed early in the nineteenth century, especially north of the Alps. In these years philologists (scholars of language) began to rediscover and publish "lost" medieval sagas and epic poems: the Anglo-Saxon *Beowulf* (1815), the German *Song of the Nibelungs* (1820), and the Finnish *Kalevala* (1835) among them. These were not medieval historical records, but rather flights of fancy in which a bard told of dark castles, fair maidens, heroic

The Bard, Martin, John/Yale Center for British Art, Paul Mellon Collection, USA/Paul Mellon Collection/The Bridgeman Art Library

⌃ In his epic painting *The Bard* (1817), Englishman John Martin sets the image of a poet against the backdrop of a medieval landscape replete with castle above and knights below. The force of untamed Nature, another theme important to the Romantics, is also depicted here.

princes, and fire-breathing dragons. Inspired by these stories, Romantic artists such as John Martin (1789–1854) envisioned neo-medieval landscapes in paint, novelists such as Alfred Tennyson (1809–1892) fantasized in prose, and composers, most notably Richard Wagner, constructed operas with mythical backdrops. The popularity of "fantasy literature" continues today. Think of the success of C. S. Lewis's *The Chronicles of Narnia,* J. R. R. Tolkien's *The Hobbit* and *The Lord of the Rings,* and J. K. Rowling's Gothic *Harry Potter* series. These are wonderful authors in the literal sense, yet they all owe a debt of gratitude to the past master of the epic fantasy series: Richard Wagner.

Richard Wagner (1813–1883)

The discovery of a deeply rooted German literature went hand in hand with the development of a national tradition of German opera, one led by Richard Wagner (REEK-hard VAHG-ner). Before Wagner, German composers rarely wrote operas in their native language. Wagner, on the other hand, not only set German librettos exclusively; he also wrote them himself. Indeed, Wagner was a poet, philosopher, politician, propagandist, and visionary who believed that operas—his operas—would revolutionize society. Naturally, many of his contemporaries were skeptical, and even today opinion about Wagner is strongly divided. Some people are left cold, believing Wagner's music to be long-winded and his operatic plots devoid of realistic human drama. (In this camp was Mark Twain, who quipped famously: "Wagner's music is not nearly as bad as it sounds!") Some, knowing of Wagner's rabid anti-Semitism and Adolf Hitler's adoration of Wagner, refuse to listen at all. (Wagner's music is still unofficially banned in Israel.) But others are converted into adoring Wagnerites at the first sound of the composer's heroic themes and powerful orchestral climaxes.

Who was this controversial artist who has stirred such mixed feelings within the musical public for more than a century? A native of Leipzig, Germany, who studied a bit of music at the church where Bach had worked (see Chapter 6), Wagner was largely self-taught in musical matters. After a succession of jobs as opera director in several small German towns, he moved to Paris in 1839 in hopes of seeing his first opera produced there. But instead of meeting acclaim in Paris, as had Liszt and Chopin before him, Wagner was greeted with thundering indifference. No one would produce his work. Reduced to poverty, he spent a brief stint in debtor's prison.

When Wagner's big break came, it was not in Paris but back in his native Germany, in the city of Dresden. His opera *Rienzi* was given a hearing there in 1842, and Wagner was soon offered the post of director of the Dresden Opera. During the next six years, he created three additional German Romantic operas for the Dresden stage: *Der fliegende Holländer* (*The Flying Dutchman,* 1844), *Tannhäuser* (1845), and *Lohengrin* (1848). All three involve plots situated in some ill-defined "Middle Ages." In the aftermath of the political revolution that swept much of Europe in 1848, Wagner was forced to flee Dresden, though in truth he took flight as much to avoid his creditors as to escape any repressive government.

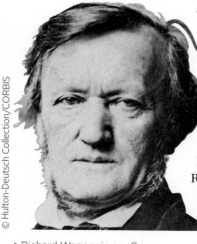

© Hulton-Deutsch Collection/CORBIS

⌃ Richard Wagner in an 1871 photograph

Wagner found a safe haven in Switzerland, which was to be his home, on and off, for the next dozen years. Having read the recently published edition of the Germanic epic entitled *Niebelungenlied* (*Song of the Nibelungs*), Wagner began to imagine a complex of music dramas on a vast and unprecedented scale. What he ultimately created was *Der Ring des Nibelungen (The Ring of the Nibelungs),* a set of four operas, now called the **Ring cycle,** intended to be performed during the course of four successive evenings. As with Tolkien's trilogy *The Lord of the Rings,* Wagner's Ring cycle involves wizards, goblins, giants, dragons, and sword-wielding heroes. Both sagas also revolve around a much-coveted ring, which offers its possessor unparalleled power, but also carries a sinister curse. And as with Tolkien's tale, Wagner's story is of epic length. *Das Rheingold,* the first opera, lasts two and a half hours; *Die Walküre* and *Siegfried* each runs nearly four and a half hours; the finale, *Götterdämmerung (Twilight of the Gods),* goes on for no less than five and a half hours. Wagner began the project in 1853 and did not finish until 1874, perhaps the longest-running project by a single creator in the history of art.

Not surprisingly, producers were reluctant to mount the operas of Wagner's Ring, given their massive scope and fantastical subject matter. So with typical tenacity, Wagner solicited the money to build his own opera house at Bayreuth, Germany. Here the first **Bayreuth Festival** took place in August 1876 with three performances of the Ring cycle, the first time any of these operas had been performed. Following Wagner's death in 1883, his remains were interred on the grounds of the Wagner villa in Bayreuth. Still controlled by the descendants of Wagner today, the Bayreuth Festival continues to stage the music dramas of Wagner—and only Wagner. Each summer thousands of opera lovers make the pilgrimage to this theatrical shrine to one of art's most determined, and ruthless, visionaries.

Wagner's "Music Dramas"

With few exceptions, Wagner composed only opera, ignoring such concert hall genres as the symphony and the concerto. But he wanted his opera to be radically different, so he gave it a new name: "**music drama.**" Wagner's music drama differs from conventional Italian opera in several ways. First, Wagner did away with the traditional "numbers" opera—a string of separate units such as aria, recitative, duet, and the like; no longer would the dramatic action grind to a halt in order to spotlight the vocal flourishes of a soloist. Instead, he wrote a seamless flow of undifferentiated solo singing and declamation, what is called "endless melody." Second, Wagner removed ensemble singing almost entirely; duets, trios, choruses, and full-cast finales became extremely rare. Finally, Wagner banished the tuneful aria to the wings. He avoids melodic repetition, symmetry, and regular cadences—all things that can make a tune "catchy"; his "melodies" are long-flowing, nonrepetitive, and not particularly song-like. As the tuneful aria decreases in importance, the role of the orchestra increases.

With Wagner, the orchestra is everything. It sounds forth the main musical themes, develops and exploits them, and thereby plays out the drama through purely instrumental music. As had Beethoven and Berlioz before him, Wagner

Hear music from Wagner's Götterdämmerung in the iTunes playlist at CourseMate for this text.

Watch a performance of Wotan's Farewell from *Die Walküre*, in the YouTube playlist at CourseMate for this text.

▾ Bayreuth Festival Theater, an opera house built especially to produce the music dramas of Richard Wagner—and only Wagner

Interfoto/Alamy

continued to expand the size of the orchestra. The orchestra he requires for the Ring cycle, for example, is massive, especially with regard to the brasses: four trumpets, four trombones, eight horns (four doubling on tuba), and a contrabass (very low) tuba. If Wagner's music sounds powerful, it is the heavy artillery of the brasses that make it so.

A bigger orchestra demanded, in turn, more forceful singers. To be heard above an orchestra of nearly a hundred players, large, specially trained voices were needed: the so-called Wagnerian tenor and Wagnerian soprano. The voice types that typically dominate the operatic stage today—with their powerful sound and wide vibrato—first developed in Wagner's music dramas.

Tristan und Isolde (1865)

Wagner took twenty-one years (1853–1874) to complete the Ring cycle, and no opera in the set was performed during this period. To pay the bills during this interval, Wagner composed two other operas: *Tristan und Isolde* (1865) and *Die Meistersinger von Nürnberg* (*The Mastersingers of Nuremberg,* 1868). Like the Ring cycle, *Tristan* is built on a medieval legend—a tale that depicts the love between Isolde, an Irish princess, and Tristan, a knight in the service of King Mark of Cornwall (England). Their love, however, is both illicit and ill-fated. They have mistakenly drunk a magical love potion; Isolde forgets her lawful husband (King Mark), and Tristan forgets his royal duty. Despairing of any happy union with Isolde in this world, Tristan allows himself to be mortally wounded in combat and sails off to his native Brittany to die. Isolde pursues him but arrives just in time to have him expire in her arms. Knowing that their union will only be consummated through death, Isolde sings her **Liebestod** ("Love-Death"), an ecstatic vision of their love beyond the grave, and then she, too, expires next to her lover's body. This was the sort of all-consuming, sacrificial love so dear to the hearts of Romantic artists.

Although the plot of *Tristan* suggests an action drama, in truth very little action occurs on stage. Instead, Wagner offers a "psychodrama," in which the thoughts, both conscious and unconscious, of the principal characters are projected through short, suggestive musical motives. Wagner's disciples called each a **leitmotif** (signature tune), a distinctive unit of music designed to represent a character, object, or idea. Usually the leitmotifs are not sung by the singers, but rather played by the orchestra. In this way, an element of the subconscious can be introduced into the drama: The orchestra can give a sense of what a character is thinking even when he or she is singing about something else. By developing, extending, varying, contrasting, and resolving these representational leitmotifs, Wagner is able to play out the essence of the drama almost without recourse to his singers.

The leitmotifs in *Tristan* are associated mainly with feelings rather than concrete objects or persons. Typical are those representing "Longing," "Desire," and "Ecstasy."

▼ Cosima Wagner (daughter of Franz Liszt and Marie d'Agoult), Richard Wagner, and Liszt at Wagner's villa in Bayreuth in 1880. At the right is a young admirer of Wagner, Hans von Wolzogen, who first coined the term *leitmotif.*

Mary Evans Picture Library/The Image Works

Example 13-1 ➤

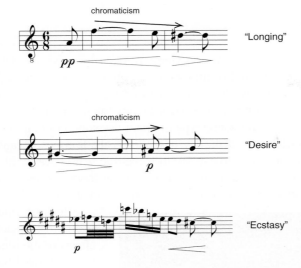

"Longing"

"Desire"

"Ecstasy"

Notice how both the "Longing" and "Desire" motifs involve chromatic lines, the first descending, the second ascending (see arrows). This sort of linear chromatic motion made it easy for the composer to wind continually through many different keys, not stopping long enough to establish any one as a home base, or tonic. This type of twisting chromatic harmony (discussed on p. 156) suggests the extreme pain felt by the ill-fated lovers.

As you listen to the final scene of *Tristan,* you can feel Wagner trying to draw you into his all-enveloping world of love, longing, desire, and death. Here Isolde cradles the body of the dead Tristan and prepares to share his fate. As she sings her justly famous *Liebestod,* the leitmotifs sound forth, usually in rising melodic sequences so as to convey a sense of continual longing and rising desire. Cadences are avoided, thereby increasing the endlessly restless mood. Dissonances are placed at points of climax to heighten the feeling of pain and anguish. At the end, the music reaches one last, ecstatic climax (/8 at 0:50), and thereafter all is consonance and reduced movement—Isolde has joined Tristan in the world beyond.

Listening Cue

Richard Wagner, *Liebestod,* from *Tristan und Isolde* (1865)

2
7–8

Characters: The lovers Tristan and Isolde
Situation: Tristan's castle in Brittany; Isolde cradles Tristan in her arms as she prepares to join him in death.

WHAT TO LISTEN FOR: Pick out the leitmotifs, but more importantly, listen to the growing waves of sound, rising and falling, at approximately thirty-second intervals, each starting on a higher pitch, until an ecstatic conclusion is reached (track 8 at 0:50).

🔊) Listen to streaming music in an Active Listening Guide at CourseMate or in the eBook.

🔊) Take online Listening Exercise 29 at CourseMate or in the eBook.

Nineteenth-Century Realistic Opera

Romantic opera, both Italian and German, typically concludes with the lovers eternally united, if not in life, then in death. Moreover, the stage is populated by larger-than-life characters or by the well-to-do, people of leisure untroubled by mundane concerns or financial worries. During the second half of the nineteenth century, however, a contrasting type of opera developed in Europe, one more in tune with the social truths of the day. It is called **realistic opera,** because the subject matter treats issues of everyday life in a realistic way. Poverty, physical abuse, industrial exploitation, and crime—afflictions of the lower classes in particular—are presented on stage for all to see. In realistic opera, rarely is there a happy ending.

Realistic opera was part of an artistic reaction to the ill effects of the nineteenth-century Industrial Revolution, an economic transformation that brought with it great prosperity for some, but oppressive factory conditions and social disintegration for others. Science played a role here, too, for the nineteenth century witnessed the emergence of the theory of evolution. First popularized in Charles Darwin's *On the Origin of Species* (1859), evolutionary theory suggests a dog-eat-dog world in which only the fittest survive. Painters such as J.-F. Millet (1814–1875) and the young Vincent van Gogh (1853–1890) captured on canvas the life of the downtrodden. Writer Charles Dickens (1812–1870) did the same in his realistic novels such as *Oliver Twist* (1838) and *Bleak House* (1852). The aim of these artists was to transform the mundane and the commonplace into art, to find the poetic and heroic in even the most ordinary aspects of human experience.

Must art imitate life? Composers of realistic opera thought so and thus embraced even the gritty and unsavory aspects of nineteenth-century existence. The plots of their operas could read like tabloid headlines: "Knife-Wielding Gypsy Girl Arrested in Cigarette Factory" (Bizet's *Carmen*, 1875); "Jealous Clown Stabs Wife to Death" (Leoncavallo's *Pagliacci*, 1892); "Abused Singer Murders Chief of Police" (Puccini's *Tosca*, 1892). If traditional Romantic opera is usually sentimental, nineteenth-century realistic opera is sensational.

v Vincent van Gogh, *The Potato Eaters* (1885). During his youth, van Gogh chose to live and work in the coal-mining region of eastern Belgium. This grim painting records his impressions of life within a mining family and the evening meal of potatoes and tea.

Art Resource, NY

Hear Luciano Pavarotti sing "E lucevan le stele" from Puccini's *Tosca*, in the iTunes playlist at CourseMate for this text.

Georges Bizet's *Carmen* (1875)

The first important realistic opera is *Carmen* (1875) by Georges Bizet (bee-SAY). Bizet (1838–1875), who spent his short life entirely in Paris, was primarily an opera composer, and *Carmen* is his masterpiece. Set in nineteenth-century

Spain, *Carmen* centers on a sensual young gypsy woman known only as Carmen. This sexually assertive, willful woman holds the populace in her sway. By means of her alluring dance and song, she seduces a naïve army corporal, Don José. Falling hopelessly in love, Don José deserts his military post, "marries" Carmen, and takes up with her gypsy bandit friends. But Carmen, who refuses to belong to any man, soon abandons Don José to give herself to the handsome bullfighter Escamillo. Having lost all for nothing, the humiliated Don José stabs Carmen to death in a bloody ending.

This violent conclusion highlights the stark realism of *Carmen*. The heroine is a woman of easy virtue available to every man, albeit on her own terms. She lives for the moment, surrounded by social outcasts (gypsies), prostitutes, and thieves. All this was shocking stuff for the refined Parisian audiences of Bizet's day. During the first rehearsals in 1875, the women of the chorus threatened to strike because they were asked to smoke and fight on stage. Critics called the libretto "obscene." Bizet's producers asked him to tone down the more lurid aspects of the drama (especially the bloody ending)—to make it more acceptable as family entertainment—but he refused.

Carmen is full of alluring melodies including the well-known Toreador Song and the even more beloved Habanera. In fashioning these tunes, Bizet borrowed phrases from several Spanish popular songs, folk songs, and **flamenco** melodies (songs of southern Spain infused with gypsy elements). The Habanera, which introduces the character Carmen, makes use of a then-popular Spanish song.

Literally, **habanera** means "the thing from Havana." Musically, it is a type of dance-song that developed in Spanish-controlled Cuba during the early nineteenth century. African and Latin influences on its musical style can perhaps be seen in the descending chromatic scale, and certainly in the static harmony (the downbeat of every measure is a D in the bass), as well as in the insistent, repetitious rhythm (). The infectious rhythm of the habanera gives it its irresistible quality—we all want to get up and join the dance. But the habanera is a sensual dance, like its descendant the tango, and this sensual quality contributes greatly to Carmen's seductive aura.

▲ Beyoncé poses with the appropriately seductive red dress that she wore in *Carmen: A Hip Hopera.*

See a video of the Muppets' Habanera performance, in the YouTube playlist at CourseMate for this text.

Example 13-2 ➤

(Love is like an elusive bird that cannot be tamed. You call it in vain if it decides to refuse.)

The structure of Bizet's Habanera is straightforward (Ex. 13-2). At first, Carmen sings a descending chromatic line of four 4-bar phrases ("Love is like an elusive bird"). By their nature, highly chromatic melodies often seem to have no tonal center. This one, too, is musically noncommittal and slippery, just as Carmen herself is both ambiguous and evasive. The chorus immediately repeats the chromatic melody, but now Carmen voluptuously glides above it, singing the single word "*L'amour*" ("Love"). As her voice soars, like the elusive bird of love, the tonality brightens from minor to major. To this is then added a refrain ("Love is like a gypsy child") in which the melody alternates between a major triad and a minor one. Against this refrain, the chorus shouts, "Watch out!" warning of Carmen's destructive qualities. This same structure—a chromatically descending melody, followed by a triadic refrain with choral shouts—then repeats. Bizet wanted his Habanera to establish the character of Carmen as a sensual enchantress. In every way, the music *is* Carmen. And like Carmen, once this seductive melody has us in its spell, it will never let go.

Listening Cue

Georges Bizet, Habanera, from *Carmen* (1875)

2
9

Situation: The scantily clad gypsy woman Carmen, exuding an almost primeval sexuality, dances before Don José, soldiers, and other gypsies.

WHAT TO LISTEN FOR: The sultry habanera rhythm, then Carmen's sensuous melody, and finally her soaring voice on the word "L'amour" ("Love") as the chorus accompanies. A second strophe (2:21) follows the same formal plan.

🔊)) Listen to streaming music in an Active Listening Guide at CourseMate or in the eBook.

🔊)) Take online Listening Exercise 30 at CourseMate or in the eBook.

Giacomo Puccini's *La bohème* (1896)

Italian realistic opera of the late nineteenth century goes by its own special name, **verismo opera** (*verismo* is Italian for "realism"). Yet while it enjoys a separate name, *verismo* opera in Italy was little different than realistic opera elsewhere. Although many Italian composers wrote *verismo* operas, by far the best known today is Giacomo Puccini.

Giacomo Puccini (1858–1924) was the scion of four generations of musicians from the northern Italian town of Lucca. His father and his grandfather had both written operas, and his forebears before them had composed religious music for the local cathedral. But Puccini, like Verdi, was no child prodigy. For a decade following his graduation from the Milan Conservatory, he lived in poverty as he struggled to develop a distinctive operatic style. Not until the age of thirty-five did he score his first triumph, the *verismo* opera *Manon Lescaut* (1893). Thereafter, successes came in quick order: *La bohème* (1896), *Tosca* (1900), and *Madama Butterfly* (1904). Growing famous, wealthy, and a bit complacent, Puccini worked less and less frequently. His last, and many believe his best, opera, *Turandot,* was left unfinished at the time of his death from throat cancer in 1924.

Watch "Nessun dorma" from *Turandot*, in the YouTube playlist at CourseMate for this text.

Puccini's best-known opera—indeed the most famous of all *verismo* operas—is *La bohème* (*Bohemian Life,* 1896). The realism of *La bohème* rests in the setting and characters: the principals are bohemians—unconventional artists living in abject poverty. The hero, Rodolfo (a poet), and his pals Schaunard (a musician), Colline (a philosopher), and Marcello (a painter), inhabit an unheated attic on the Left Bank of Paris. The heroine, Mimi, their neighbor, is a poor seamstress with tuberculosis. Rodolfo and Mimi meet and fall in love. He grows obsessively jealous while she becomes progressively more ill. They separate for a time, only to return to each other's arms immediately before Mimi's death. If this sounds familiar, there may be a reason: The Pulitzer Prize–winning musical *Rent* (1996, produced as a motion picture in 2005) is a modern adaptation of this bohemian tale, but there the protagonist dies of AIDS in Greenwich Village, rather than of tuberculosis in Paris.

▲ Giacomo Puccini

In truth, there isn't much of a plot to *La bohème,* nor is there much character development. Instead, the glorious sound of the human voice (*bel canto* singing) carries the day. Puccini continues the nineteenth-century tendency to lessen the distinction between recitative and aria. His solos typically start syllabically (no more than one note per syllable), as if the character is beginning a conversation. As the speaker's ardor grows, the voice gains intensity and becomes more expansive, with the strings doubling the melody to add warmth and expression. When Rodolfo, for example, sings of Mimi's frozen little hand in the aria "Che gelida manina" ("Ah, What a Frozen Little Hand"), we move imperceptibly from recitative to aria, gradually transcending the squalor of the Left Bank garret and soaring to a better world far beyond. The contrast between the dreary stage setting and the transcendental beauty of the music is the great paradox of realistic opera.

Listening Cue

Giacomo Puccini, *La bohème* (1896)

Intro
10

Aria, "Che gelida manina," *La bohème*

Characters: The poor poet Rodolfo and the equally impoverished seamstress Mimi
Situation: Mimi has knocked on Rodolfo's door to ask for a light for her candle. Charmed by the lovely stranger, he naturally obliges. The wind again blows out Mimi's candle, and amidst the confusion, she drops her key. As the two search for it in the darkness, Rodolfo by chance touches her hand and, then holding it, seizes the moment to tell her about himself and his hopes.
Performer: Renowned tenor Plácido Domingo

WHAT TO LISTEN FOR: The gradual trajectory of the voice moving low to high, speech to song, over the course of an increasingly passionate and ever-more-beautiful four-minute work

🔊)) Listen to streaming music in an Active Listening Guide at CourseMate or in the eBook.

chapter **FOURTEEN**

Late Romantic Orchestral Music

The late nineteenth century was the heyday of the symphony orchestra. Think about how sound was made in those days—there were no iPods or computers and no amplified surround sound, indeed, no electronically amplified sound at all. To enjoy a thrilling sonic experience, listeners had to attend a concert of a large symphony orchestra. Today, of course, we don't have to do that: Digital downloads are only a click away. But progress comes at a price; the recent revolution in electronically disseminated music has been accompanied by a decline in the quality of sound that we hear. Listening to Beethoven or Wagner via compressed MP3 or M4A files gives only a vague approximation of the nineteenth-century original. To experience the real thing, we must go to a large concert hall preserving the architecture, acoustics, and ambience of the Romantic period.

Romantic Values and Today's Concert Hall

The late Romantic era was a golden age for the construction of large concert halls, not only in Europe but also in the United States. During this period, "music-only" auditoriums were built in Vienna (Musikverein, 1870), New York (Carnegie Hall, 1891), and Boston (Symphony Hall, 1900), which were and remain among the best ever constructed, especially in terms of their excellent acoustics. The new Walt Disney Concert Hall in Los Angeles (2003) and the Schermerhorn Symphony Center in Nashville (2006) continue this tradition. Indeed the Schermerhorn Center copies many of the architectural features of Vienna's nineteenth-century Musikverein (compare p. 9 with the image below). All of these centers were built to be large concert halls, seating 2,000 to 2,700 listeners, devoted primarily to classical music.

Classical music in many ways is a conservative art. What today's symphony-goer experiences does not differ much from what listeners of the late Romantic

◄ The Musikverein (Music Center) of Vienna, initiated by admirers of Beethoven and often performed in by Brahms. It set the standard throughout the Western world for a "music-only" environment and for quality acoustics.

JazzSign/Lebrecht Music & Arts

era experienced. The concert hall is about the same size (average 2,500), and the symphony orchestra that performs there includes about the same number of musicians (90 to 100 players at full strength). So, too, has the music on the program remained largely unchanged since the end of the nineteenth century.

Prior to 1800, almost all music was disposable music—popular music, in a sense. It was composed as entertainment for the moment and was then forgotten. But the nineteenth century looked back on Beethoven, Mozart, and Haydn, and began to see them as geniuses whose great symphonies were worthy of preservation and repeated performance (see p. 109). These and the best works of succeeding generations came to form a **canon,** indeed a *museum* of classical music, and still today they form the core of the concert repertoire.

How we experience concert hall music today reflects the reverential view of music that developed during the Romantic era. Prior to 1800, a concert was as much a social event as a musical one. People talked, drank, ate, played cards, flirted, and wandered about during the performance. Dogs ran freely on the ground floor, and armed guards roamed the hall to maintain a least some order. When people turned to the music, they were loud and demonstrative. They hummed along with the melody and tapped the beat to the music they liked. If a performance went well, people applauded, not only at the ends of pieces but also between movements.

Around 1840, however, a sudden hush descended upon the concert hall—it became more like a church or temple. With the revered figure of the Romantic artist-composer now before them, members of the audience sat in respectful silence. They expected not merely to be entertained, but to be educated, or even morally uplifted, by the music performed. In sum, the attitudes about concert music that arose in the nineteenth century still govern our thinking today. Where we go for a concert, whom we see on stage, what we hear, and how we dress and behave are not eternal ideals, with us since time immemorial, but are instead values created during the Romantic period.

v Silhouette of composer Carl Maria von Weber conducting with a rolled sheet of music so as to highlight the movement of his hand and thereby show the beat

Lebrecht Music & Arts

The Conductor

As the streets of London became more congested with wagons in the mid-nineteenth century, traffic cops appeared, waving red and green flags and then lanterns at night. So, too, as the Romantic symphony orchestra became larger and more complex, a musical "traffic cop" was needed: the conductor waving a baton. In Mozart's day the leader of the orchestra was one of the performers, either a keyboardist or the first violinist, who led by moving his head and body. Beethoven, however, at least at the end of his life, stood before the orchestra with his back to the audience and waved his hands, gesturing how the music should go. Thereafter, conductors might lead with a rolled-up piece of paper, a violin bow, a handkerchief, or a wooden baton, each object intending to clarify the meter and the speed of the beat. Sometimes the leader merely banged the beat on a music stand. Gradually during the nineteenth century, however, this director evolved from a mere time-beater into an interpreter, and sometimes a dictator, of the musical score. The modern conductor had arrived, and what he conducted was usually a symphony or a concerto.

The Late Romantic Symphony and Concerto

The symphony orchestra is so called because it most often performs a type, or genre, of music called the symphony. Symphonic composers in the Romantic period generally continued to follow the four-movement format inherited from their Classical forebears—(1) fast, (2) slow, (3) minuet or scherzo, and (4) fast. Yet throughout the nineteenth century, the movements got progressively longer. Perhaps as a consequence, composers wrote fewer symphonies. Schumann and Brahms composed only 4; Mendelssohn, 5; Tchaikovsky, 6; and Dvořák, Bruckner, and Mahler, 9 each. No one approached the 40-odd symphonies of Mozart, to say nothing of the 106 of Haydn.

Similarly for the concerto, with expanded length came a reduction in number. A Classical concerto may last twenty minutes, a Romantic one forty; Mozart gave us twenty-three piano concertos, but Beethoven only five. Beethoven, Mendelssohn, Brahms, and Tchaikovsky penned just a single violin concerto apiece, yet each is a substantial showpiece for the soloist. Despite its growing length, the Romantic concerto retained the three-movement plan established during the Classical period—fast, slow, fast.

Appropriate for an era that glorified the individual, the nineteenth century was the age of the solo concerto. Vivaldi and Bach had written concertos for several soloists at a time (a genre called the concerto grosso; see p. 78), and both Bach and Mozart had composed a concerto for three keyboardists at once. But during the Romantic era the solo **virtuoso,** the star instrumentalist on whom the spotlight shone, took center stage. Virtuosos such as pianist Franz Liszt (see p. 165) and violinist Niccolò Paginini (1782–1840) mesmerized audiences with their personal charisma and technical razzle-dazzle. They spent long hours practicing mechanical exercises—arpeggios, tremolos, trills, and scales played in thirds, sixths, and octaves—to develop wizard-like hand speed on their instruments. Naturally, some of what they played for the public was lacking in musical substance—flashy showpieces designed to appeal immediately to the audiences that packed the ever-larger concert halls. Liszt sometimes played at the keyboard with a lighted cigar between his fingers. Paganini secretly tuned the four strings of his violin in ways that would allow him to negotiate extraordinarily difficult passages with ease. So great was his fame that Paganini's likeness appeared on napkins, ties, pipes, billiard cues, and powder boxes. Like the superstar athlete of today, the virtuoso musician of the nineteenth century had become a celebrity and marketing tool.

In the concert hall of the Romantic era, the virtuoso captivated the audience with his magical powers. In the composing room, however, another figure loomed large over the desk of every composer about to write a symphony or concerto: Beethoven (see p. 199). Beethoven had set new standards for length, power, and virtuosic bravura. Wagner asked why anyone after Beethoven bothered to write symphonies at all, given the dramatic impact of Beethoven's

Watch a video of Craig Wright's Open Yale Course class session 20, "The Colossal Symphony: Beethoven, Berlioz, Mahler, and Shostakovich," at CourseMate for this text.

▲ Niccolò Paganini

CORBIS

Third, Fifth, and Ninth. Wagner himself wrote only one, and Verdi none. Some composers, notably Berlioz and Liszt, turned to a completely different sort of symphony, the program symphony (see pp. 173–174), in which an external scenario determined the musical events; others wrote tone poems (see p. 178) that were never longer than a single movement. Not until the late Romantic period, nearly fifty years after Beethoven's death, did someone emerge as his successor in the genres of the symphony and concerto. That figure was Johannes Brahms.

Johannes Brahms (1833–1897)

The Art Archive

∧ Johannes Brahms in his early thirties. Said an observer of the time, "The broad chest, the Herculean shoulders, the powerful head, which he threw back energetically when playing—all betrayed an artistic personality replete with the spirit of true genius."

Brahms was born in the north German port city of Hamburg in 1833. He was given the Latin name Johannes to distinguish him from his father Johann, a street musician and beer-hall fiddler. Although Johannes's formal education never went beyond primary school, his father saw to it that he received the best training on the piano and in music theory, with the works of Bach and Beethoven given pride of place. While he studied these masters by day, by night Brahms earned money playing out-of-tune pianos in "stimulation bars" on the Hamburg waterfront. (Between 1960 and 1962, The Beatles went to Hamburg to play in the descendants of these strip joints.) To get his hands on better instruments, Brahms sometimes practiced in the showrooms of local piano stores.

Brahms first caught the public's attention in 1853, when Robert Schumann published a highly laudatory article proclaiming him to be a musical messiah, the heir apparent to Haydn, Mozart, and Beethoven. Brahms, in turn, embraced Robert and his wife, Clara (see pp. 162–164), as his musical mentors. After Robert was confined to a mental institution, Brahms became Clara's confidant, and his respect and affection for her ripened into love, despite the fact that she was fourteen years his senior. Whether owing to his unconsummated love for Clara or his intense focus on his music, Brahms remained a bachelor all his life.

Disappointed first in love and then in his attempt to gain a conducting position in his native Hamburg, Brahms moved to Vienna in 1862. He supported his modest lifestyle—very "un-Wagnerian," he called it—by performing and conducting. His fame as a composer increased dramatically in 1868 with performances of his *German Requiem,* which was soon sold to amateur choruses around the world. In this same year, he composed what is today perhaps his best-known piece, the simple yet beautiful art song known among English speakers as "Brahms's Lullaby" (see pp. 42–43 and (Intro)/21). Honorary degrees from Cambridge University (1876) and Breslau University (1879) attested to his growing stature. After Wagner's death in 1883, Brahms was generally considered the greatest living German composer. His own death, from liver cancer, came in the spring of 1897. He was buried in the central cemetery of Vienna, thirty feet from the graves of Beethoven and Schubert.

Vienna was (and remains) a very conservative city, fiercely protective of its rich musical heritage. That Brahms should choose it as his place of residence is not surprising—Vienna had been the home of Haydn, Mozart, Beethoven, and Schubert, and the conservative Brahms found inspiration in the music of these past masters. Again and again, he returned to traditional genres, such as

Listen to Brahms's *Academic Festival Overture* in the iTunes playlist at CourseMate for this text.

the symphony and concerto, and to conventional forms, such as sonata–allegro and theme and variations. Most telling, Brahms composed no program music. Instead, he chose to write what is called **absolute music:** chamber sonatas, symphonies, and concertos without narrative or "storytelling" intent. The music of Brahms unfolds as patterns of pure, abstract sound within the tight confines of traditional forms. Although Brahms could write lovely Romantic melodies, he was at heart a contrapuntalist, a "developer" in the tradition of Bach and Beethoven. Indeed, he was to be dubbed the last of classical music's "three Bs": Bach, Beethoven, and Brahms.

Violin Concerto in D major (1878)

In 1870, Brahms wrote, "I shall never compose a symphony! You have no idea how the likes of us feel when we hear the tramp of a giant like him behind us." "That giant," of course, was Beethoven, and Brahms, like other nineteenth-century composers, was terrified by the prospect of competing with his revered predecessor. But Brahms did go on to write a symphony—indeed, four of them, first performed, in turn, in 1876, 1877, 1883, and 1885. In the midst of this symphonic activity, Brahms also wrote his only violin concerto, which rivals the earlier violin concerto of Beethoven.

How do you write a concerto for an instrument that you can't play? How do you know how to make the instrument sound good and what to avoid? Brahms, who was trained as a pianist and not a violinist, did as composers before and after him: He turned to a virtuoso on the instrument—in this case, his friend Joseph Joachim (1831–1907). When the concerto was premiered in 1878, Joachim played the solo part while Brahms conducted the orchestra. One technical "trick" that Joachim surely insisted that Brahms employ is the art of playing **double stops.** Usually, we think of the violin as a monophonic instrument,

The Art Archive/Museum der Stadt Wien/Collection Dagli Orti/The Picture Desk

◄ Brahms's composing room in Vienna. On the wall, looking down on the piano, is a bust of Beethoven. The spirit of Beethoven loomed large over the entire nineteenth century (see also the painting on p. 140) and over Brahms in particular.

capable of executing only one line of music. But a good violinist can hold (stop) two and sometimes more strings simultaneously and sweep across them with the bow. This imparts a richer, more chordal sound to the soloist's part. Example 14-1 shows how Brahms incorporates double stops (here, two or four pitches played simultaneously) into the melody of the last movement of his concerto.

Example 14-1 ➤

▲ American-born violinist virtuosa Hilary Hahn, whose spirited and beautifully clear performance is heard on ② / 12–14, made this recording at the age of twenty-two.

When he arrived at the finale of his Violin Concerto, Brahms the conservative turned to a form traditionally used in the last movement of a concerto: the rondo. Recall that a rondo centers on a single theme that serves as a musical refrain (see p. 45). Here the refrain has the flavor of a gypsy tune, like the Hungarian dances Brahms often heard in Viennese cafés as he sipped beer and chatted with friends. What marks this refrain is its lively rhythm:

Above this foot-tapping motive, the violin sometimes soars with difficult passage work (scales, arpeggios, and double stops). The makers of the Academy Award–winning *There Will Be Blood* (2007) featured this movement by Brahms in the soundtrack of the film, perhaps to represent the tug of war (concerto) between the greedy oil man and the landowners. Indeed, the nineteenth-century solo concerto was not only a "concerted" effort by all participants, but also a contest between soloist and orchestra. Sometimes the orchestra supports the soloist, and sometimes it competes with it, running away with the rondo theme. Listen to this exciting movement and declare a winner: soloist, orchestra, or listener.

Listening Cue

Johannes Brahms, Violin Concerto in D major (1878)

12–14

Third movement, *Allegro giocoso, ma non tropo vivace* **(fast and playful, but not too lively)**

Genre: Concerto
Form: Rondo

WHAT TO LISTEN FOR: The exchanges between the soloist and the orchestra, and the "anything you can do, I can do better" spirit that develops. The constantly returning rondo theme (Ex. 14-1) is easy to recognize, no matter who performs it.

🔊)) Listen to streaming music in an Active Listening Guide at CourseMate or in the eBook.

🔊)) Take online Listening Exercise 31 at CourseMate or in the eBook.

More Great Late Romantic Symphonies and Concertos

The nineteenth century was a period in which the view of time and the concept of the universe changed dramatically—the earth was seen as millions of years old, not just thousands, and the distance to the moon calculated at 250,000 miles, not just 100,000, as formerly believed. So, too, in music time slowed down and distances between sections expanded. The enlarged symphony orchestra and more powerful piano allowed for sound itself to carry, or fill, the moment. The composer (and listener) could sit with a chord, perhaps wallow in it, and the sound of the instruments would be so beautiful that nothing else was needed, at least for a long time. Consequently, movements of symphonies and sonatas became progressively longer, sometimes *very* long (see p. 172). (This was a great development for music lovers, but not for writers of textbooks. Just four or five long movements might consume an entire CD, and space here doesn't allow for more than one.) But these symphonies and concertos of the late Romantic era are more than worthy of a hearing, and here's where to start.

Peter Tchaikovsky is known today primarily for his tone poems, such as *Romeo and Juliet* and *The 1812 Overture,* and ballets, such as *Swan Lake* and *The Nutcracker* (see p. 180). But Tchaikovsky also wrote six symphonies and three large-scale concertos (one each for piano, violin, and cello). Of these perhaps the best are the Symphony No. 6 in B minor (1893) and the Violin Concerto in D (1878).

Two other symphonists also loomed large: Antonín Dvořák (1841–1904) and Gustav Mahler (1860–1911). Both wrote nine symphonies, and Dvořák composed one important concerto for cello as well. Dvořák was one of several significant nineteenth-century artists and intellectuals born in the Czech Republic. The composer spent most of his productive life in Prague, but he also lived in the United States for nearly three years, summering in Spillville, Iowa, in 1892. His beloved Symphony No. 9 in E minor "From the New World" (1893) was written during this period.

Gustav Mahler, too, was born in a region of the Czech Republic (in Moravia). Like his countryman Sigmund Freud (1856–1939), however, he moved to Vienna for his professional training and there he spent the better part of his career. Mahler also traveled to the United States (1909–1911), conducting the New York Philharmonic and touring American cities with that group. His 1910 concert in New Haven, Connecticut, was even reviewed by a college newspaper (the *Yale Daily News*). There are many spellbinding symphonic movements by Mahler, several of which reach colossal size and monumental length with the addition of solo voice and chorus.

Listen to Tchaikovsky's Violin Concerto in D, third movement, in the YouTube playlist at CourseMate for this text.

Listen to Dvořák's Symphony No. 9, second movement, with its famous "going home" theme, in the YouTube playlist at CourseMate for this text.

Listen to Mahler's Symphony No. 4, fourth movement, in the YouTube playlist at CourseMate for this text.

Music and Nationalism

Today we are witnessing a globalization of music, and of culture generally. Internet sites such as Google and Facebook covertly encourage the adoption of English as a universal language and overtly promote economic ties that jump across borders. The various nations of Europe have formed a European

Listen to a familiar example of Smetana's Czech nationalistic music from *Má vlast—The Moldau*—in the iTunes playlist at CourseMate for this text.

Community, and we in the United States belong to the North America Free Trade Zone (NAFTA). University students are encouraged to spend a semester studying abroad. Everyone, it seems, is looking outward.

In the nineteenth century, however, things were very different. People were looking inward, often for a force that would liberate them from political oppression. At a time when people of one language were frequently ruled by foreigners who spoke another, Europe's ethnic groups came to realize that their ethnicity might be an agent of liberation. Driven by the unifying force of group identity, the Greeks threw off the Turks and formed their own country (1820s), the French-speaking Belgians rebelled from the Dutch (1830s), and the Finns from the Russians (1860s). Similarly, the Italian city-states expelled their Austrian rulers to form a unified nation in 1861, and a decade later a hodgepodge of German-speaking principalities united into what we now call Germany. Prior to the nineteenth century French, German, and Russian were the dominant languages of Europe; thereafter literary works published in Czech, Hungarian, Norwegian, and Finnish, among other languages, were not uncommon.

Music played an important part in this ethnic awakening, sounding out cultural differences and providing a rallying point in a process called **musical nationalism.** National anthems, native dances, protest songs, and victory symphonies all evoked through music the rising tide of national identity. *The Star-Spangled Banner,* the *Marseillaise* (French national anthem), and *Italian Brothers, Italy Has Arisen* (Italian national anthem), for example, were all products of this patriotic zeal. But how did a composer create music that sounded ethnic or national? He did so by incorporating indigenous folk songs, native scales, dance rhythms, and local instrumental sounds. Ethnic sentiments could also be conveyed by the use of national subjects—the life of a national hero, for example—as the basis of an opera or a tone poem. Among Romantic compositions with overtly nationalistic titles are Liszt's *Hungarian Rhapsodies*, Rimsky-Korsakov's *Russian Easter Overture*, Dvořák's *Slavonic Dances*, Smetana's *Má vlast (My Fatherland)*, and Sibelius's *Finlandia*. For all these composers, a musical signifier (a folk song, for example) served as a badge of both personal identity and national pride.

Russian Nationalism: Modest Musorgsky (1839–1881)

Russia was one of the first countries to develop its own national style of art music, one distinct and separate from the traditions of German orchestral music and Italian opera. An early use of Russian subject matter can be found in Mikhail Glinka's opera *A Life for the Tsar* (1836). As a review of the first performance reported: "All were enthralled with the sounds of the native, Russian national music. Everyone showed complete accord in the expression of enthusiasm that the patriotic content of the opera aroused." Glinka's nationalist spirit was passed to a group of young composers whom contemporaries dubbed "The Mighty Handful" or, less grandiosely, the **Russian Five:** Alexander Borodin (1833–1887), César Cui (1835–1918), Mily Balakirev (1837–1910), Nikolai Rimsky-Korsakov (1844–1908), and Modest Musorgsky (1839–1881). Like Glinka, they created a national art by taking the sophisticated traditions of Western classical music and incorporating therein simple elements of Russian folk and religious music. Of the "Russian Five," the most original and least Western in musical style was Modest Musorgsky.

As with most members of the "Russian Five," Musorgsky (pronounced "moo-SORG-ski") did not at first seem destined for a career in music. He was trained to be a military officer and for a period of four years was commissioned in the Russian army. He resigned his appointment in 1858 in favor of a minor post as a civil servant and more free time to indulge his avocation, musical composition. The next year he said, "I have been a cosmopolitan [Western classical composer], but now there's been some sort of regeneration. Everything Russian is becoming dear to me." Unfortunately, his brief, chaotic life was marked by increasing poverty, depression, and alcoholism, a development evident in the one surviving portrait of him. During his few periods of creative productivity, Musorgsky managed to compile a small body of work which includes a boldly inventive tone poem, *Night on Bald Mountain* (1867, used prominently in Walt Disney's *Fantasia*); an imaginative set of miniatures (character pieces) called *Pictures at an Exhibition* (1874); and an operatic masterpiece, *Boris Godunov* (1874), based on the life of a popular sixteenth-century Russian tsar. Many of Musorgsky's works were left unfinished at the time of his death in 1881.

▲ Modest Musorgsky

PICTURES AT AN EXHIBITION (1874)

The genesis of *Pictures at an Exhibition* can be traced to the death of Musorgsky's close friend, the Russian painter and architect Victor Hartmann, who had died suddenly of a heart attack in 1873. As a memorial to Hartmann, friends mounted an exhibition of his paintings and drawings in Moscow the next year. Musorgsky was inspired to capture the spirit of Hartmann's works in a series of ten short pieces for piano. To provide unity within the sequence of musical pictures, the composer hit on the idea of incorporating a recurring interlude, which he called *Promenade.* This gave listeners the impression of enjoying a leisurely stroll into and through a gallery, moving from one of Hartmann's images to the next each time the *Promenade* music was heard.

Today *Pictures at an Exhibition* is best known in the brilliantly orchestrated version by Maurice Ravel (1875–1937), completed in 1922. (Perhaps by coincidence, the first attempts at making color motion pictures occurred about this same time.) Whether fulfilling Musorgsky's original intent or going beyond it, Ravel's version greatly enhances the impact of the music by replacing the "black-and-white" sounds of the piano with the radiant color of the full late-Romantic orchestra.

With the *Promenade* we enter not any gallery but one filled with purely Russian art. The tempo is marked "Fast but resolute, in the Russian manner"; the meter is irregular, as in a folk dance, with alternating five- and six-beat measures; and the melody is built on a **pentatonic scale,** which uses only five notes instead of the usual Western scale of seven—here B♭ C, D, F, and G. Throughout the world, indigenous folk cultures use the pentatonic (five-note) scale. To Western ears, then, *Promenade,* like Russia itself, seems both familiar and strange.

To appreciate the power of the pentatonic scale around the globe, watch "World Science Fair 2009: Bobby McFerrin Demonstrates" in the YouTube playlist at CourseMate for this text.

Example 14-2 ➤

Modest Musorgsky, *Promenade* **from** *Pictures at an Exhibition* **(1874)**
Orchestrated by Maurice Ravel (1922)

WHAT TO LISTEN FOR: The alternation of texture between monophony (brilliant trumpet) and homophony (full brasses). Also try conducting with the music and you'll notice how the meter continually shifts—a characteristic of folk music.

 Listen to streaming music in an Active Listening Guide at CourseMate or in the eBook.

> Victor Hartmann's vision *The Great Gate of Kiev*, which inspired the last of the musical paintings in Musorgsky's *Pictures at an Exhibition*. Note the bells in the tower, a motif that is featured prominently at the very end of Musorgsky's musical evocation of this design.

© RIA Novosti/The Bridgeman Art Library

Having entered the musical picture gallery, the visitor now focuses in turn on a musical evocation of each of ten paintings: first a depiction of an elf-like gnome, then an old castle, and so on. As we walk from image to image, the *Promenade* theme accompanies us. Finally, we arrive at the tenth and last picture, Musorgsky's musical rendering of a grand and glorious gate. This final scene is based on Hartmann's *The Great Gate of Kiev,* the painter's vision of a triumphant gate to the city of Kiev (then part of Russia), something like a Russian version of the *Arc de Triomphe* in Paris. Using rondo form (here **ABABCA**), Musorgsky arranges his thematic material to give the impression of a parade passing beneath the giant gate. Its majesty is first evoked through the grand sound of the full brasses (theme **A**). Suddenly the music shifts to solemn woodwinds quietly playing a harmonized chant from the liturgy of the Russian Orthodox Church (**B**), thereby suggesting a procession of Russian pilgrims. Even the composer-viewer seems to walk beneath the gate as the *Promenade* theme (**C**) appears, before a final return to a panoramic view of the gate (**A**), now with Hartmann's bells ringing triumphantly.

Modest Musorgsky, *The Great Gate of Kiev* **from** *Pictures at an Exhibition* **(1874)**
Orchestrated by Maurice Ravel (1922)

Form: Rondo (**ABABCA**)

WHAT TO LISTEN FOR: Three distinctively different kinds of music: **A** (brasses and full orchestra at 0:00), **B** (woodwinds at 0:57), and **C** (*Promenade* theme at 3:01). **A** sounds Western; **B** and **C** more Russian. Most important, listen to how Musorgsky makes the gate theme (**A**) appear more and more grand with each appearance.

 Listen to streaming music in an Active Listening Guide at CourseMate or in the eBook.

Take online Listening Exercise 32 at CourseMate or in the eBook.

European Impressionism and Modernism

"A PIANO.

If the speed is open, if the color is careless, if the selection of a strong scent is not awkward, if the button holder is held by all the waving color and there is no color, not any color." —Gertrude Stein, *Tender Buttons*

This verse about a piano was written by American poet Gertrude Stein (1874–1946) in 1914, while she was living in Paris. Can you make sense of it? Stein, a mentor to painter Pablo Picasso (1881–1973), poet Ezra Pound (1885–1972), and novelist Ernest Hemingway (1899–1961), was an early promoter of Modernism, a style that prevailed in all the arts between 1900 and 1945. Today Modernist art is no longer "modern" in a chronological sense; some of it is now more than a hundred years old. But if "modern" means a radical departure from traditional values, then this description remains apt. It still shocks us more than the more recent art of the Postmodernist period (1945–present). Modernism took the usual expectations for a poem, for example—that it make sense as narrative or image, and possess proper grammar and syntax—and turned them upside down. So, too, with Modernist music, the concertgoer's expectations for what makes a good melody, pleasing harmony, and regular meter were confounded. Listeners of the early twentieth century were just as baffled by the Modernist sounds of Stravinsky and Schoenberg as they were by the poetry of Gertrude Stein that opens this chapter.

Modernism: An Anti-Romantic Movement

But why did such a radically different kind of expression emerge shortly after 1900? In part because of a violent social disruption that shook Europe and (to a far lesser degree) North America: the run-up to, and outbreak of, World War I. For the Western world, the first two decades of the twentieth century constituted a social earthquake of the highest magnitude. World War I (1914–1918) left 9 million soldiers dead on the battlefields. Shocked by the carnage, intellectuals turned away from the predominantly idealistic, sentimental aesthetics of Romanticism—how could one think of love and beauty in the face of wholesale destruction? For writers, painters, and composers alike, disjunction, anxiety, and even hysteria became valid artistic sentiments that reflected the realities of the day. The epicenter of this upheaval was France and Germany.

As early as 1870 the two countries fought what we now call the Franco-Prussian War, and tensions simmered ominously throughout the decades that followed. Developments in the arts mirrored the unsettled times, and composers across Europe began to turn against conventional musical expression. In *fin-de-siècle* (end-of-nineteenth-century) Paris, the Impressionists, led by Claude Debussy, mounted a quiet protest against the excesses of German Romanticism. Shortly thereafter, Modernism—in the hands of the revolutionary Russian expatriate Igor Stravinsky—arrived in Paris with full force. In the German-speaking lands, the Expressionists, including Arnold Schoenberg, staged the most upsetting revolt of all against tonality and tradition, conveying their anxiety through radical dissonance. Shock began to replace beauty as the defining component of musical art.

Not all listeners were pleased with this change. Schoenberg's early experiments with dissonance were received at first with hoots from a hostile public in Vienna in 1913; that same year Stravinsky's *Le Sacre du printemps (The Rite of Spring)* caused a riot at its Parisian premiere. Such avant-garde composers sought to shake their listeners out of a state of complacency, to yank them out of a Romantic idealism and back to harsh reality.

Impressionism

But let's back up to Impressionism, a musical style in some ways midway between the lush sounds of Romanticism and the bombshells of Modernism. As we have seen, Romantic music reached its peak during the late nineteenth century in the grandiose works of Wagner, Tchaikovsky, Brahms, and Mahler, all of whom were German speaking or composed in a Germanic style. By 1900, however, this German-dominated musical empire had started to weaken. Not surprisingly, the strongest challenge to the hegemony of the Germans came from their enemies, the French. French composers began to ridicule the sentimentality of Romanticism in general and the grandiose structures of the German style in particular. German music was said to be too heavy, too pretentious, and too bombastic, like one of Wagner's Nordic giants. Meaningful expression, it was believed, might be communicated in more subtle ways, in something other than sheer volume of sound and epic length.

Impressionism in Painting and Music

The movement that arose in France in opposition to German Romantic music has been given the name **Impressionism.** We are, of course, more familiar with this term as a designation for a school of late-nineteenth-century painters working in and around Paris, including Claude Monet (1840–1926), Auguste Renoir (1841–1919), Edgar Degas (1834–1917), Camille Pissarro (1830–1903), and the American Mary Cassatt (1844–1926). You can see the painting that gave its name to the epoch, Monet's *Impression: Sunrise* (1873), on the first page of this chapter. There, the ships, rowboats, and other elements in the early morning light are more suggested than fully rendered. In 1874, Claude Monet submitted this painting to be exhibited at the Salon of the French Academy of Fine Arts, but it was rejected. One critic, Louis Leroy, derisively said: "Wallpaper in its most embryonic state is more finished than that seascape." In the uproar that followed, Monet and his fellow artists were disparagingly called "impressionists" for the seemingly imprecise quality of their art. The painters accepted the name, partly as an act of defiance against the establishment, and soon the term was universally adopted.

▼ Claude Monet, *Woman with Umbrella* (1886). The Impressionist canvas is not a finished surface in the traditional sense. Rather, the painter breaks down light into separate dabs of color and juxtaposes them for the viewer's eye to reassemble. Here bold brushstrokes convey an astonishing sense of movement, freshness, and sparkling light.

Woman with Parasol turned to the Left, 1886 (oil on canvas), Monet, Claude (1840–1926)/ Musée d'Orsay, Paris, France/Giraudon/The Bridgeman Art Library

It is ironic that French Impressionism, which once generated such controversy, is now the most popular of all artistic styles. Indeed, judging by museum attendance and reproductions sold, there is an almost limitless enthusiasm for the art of Monet, Degas, Renoir, and their associates—precisely the paintings that the artists' contemporaries mocked and jeered. But what is it about the Impressionist style that initially caused such a furor?

The Impressionists saw the world as awash in vibrant rays of light and sought to capture the aura that sun-dappled objects created in the eyes of the beholder. To accomplish this, they covered their canvases with small, dab-like brushstrokes in which light was broken down into spots of color, thereby creating a sense of movement and fluidity. Shapes are not clearly defined but blurred, more suggested than delineated. Minor details disappear. Sunlight is everywhere and everything shimmer.

For their part, musicians found inspiration in the Impressionist art of the day. They, too, began to work with dabs of color. Claude Debussy, whose compositions most consistently displayed the Impressionist style in music, was delighted to be grouped with the Impressionist painters. "You do me great honor by calling me a pupil of Claude Monet," he told a friend in 1916. Debussy gave various collections of his compositions such artistic titles as *Sketches, Images,* and *Prints.* Rare are the moments in history when the aesthetic aims of painters and musicians were as closely allied.

Claude Debussy (1862–1918)

Watch a video of Craig Wright's Open Yale Course class session 21, "Musical Impressionism and Exoticism: Debussy, Ravel, and Monet," at CourseMate for this text.

Debussy was born in 1862 into a modest family living in a small town outside Paris. As neither of his parents was musical, it came as a surprise when their son demonstrated talent at the keyboard. At the age of ten, he was sent to the Paris Conservatory for lessons in piano, composition, and music theory. Owing to his skill as a performer, he was soon engaged for summer work in the household of Nadezhda von Meck, a wealthy patroness of the arts and the principal supporter of Tchaikovsky (see p. 179). This employment took him, in turn, to Italy, Russia, and Vienna. In 1884, he won the Prix de Rome, an official prize in composition funded by the French government, one that required a three-year stay in Rome. But Debussy was not happy in the Eternal City. He preferred Paris with its bistros, cafés, and bohemian ambience.

Returning to Paris more or less permanently in 1887, the young Frenchman continued to study his craft and to search for his own independent voice as a composer. He had some minor successes, and yet, as he said in 1893, "There are still things that I am not able to do—create masterpieces, for example." But the next year, in 1894, he did just that. With the completion of *Prélude à l'Après-midi d'un faune (Prelude to The Afternoon of a Faun),* he gave to the public what has become his most enduring orchestral work. Debussy's later compositions, including his opera *Pelléas et Mélisande* (1902), the symphonic poem *La mer* (*The Sea,* 1905), and his two books of *Préludes* for piano, met with less popular favor. Critics complained that Debussy's works were lacking in traditional form, melody, and forward motion—in other words, they had characteristics of Modernism. Illness and the outbreak of World War I in 1914 brought Debussy's innovations to a halt. He died of cancer in the spring of 1918 while the guns of the German army were shelling Paris from the north.

▲ Claude Debussy at the age of twenty-four

Claude Debussy (1862–1918) 1886 (oil on canvas), Pinta, Henri Ludovic Marius (b. 1856)/Villa Medici, Rome, Italy/Giraudon/The Bridgeman Art Library

Prelude to The Afternoon of a Faun (1894)

Debussy spent more of his time in the company of poets and painters than musicians. His orchestral *Prelude to The Afternoon of a Faun,* in fact, was written to precede a stage reading of the poem *The Afternoon of a Faun* by his friend and mentor Stéphane Mallarmé. The faun of Mallarmé's poem is not a young deer but a satyr (a mythological beast that is half man, half goat), who spends his days in lustful pursuit of the nymphs of the forest. On this afternoon, we see the faun, exhausted from the morning's escapades, reclining on the forest floor in the still air of the midday heat. He contemplates future conquests while blowing listlessly on his panpipes. The following passage from Mallarmé's poem suggests the dream-like mood, vague and elusive, that Debussy sought to re-create in his musical setting:

> No murmur of water in the woodland scene,
> Bathed only in the sounds of my flute.
> And the only breeze, except for my two pipes,
> Blows itself empty long before
> It can scatter the sound in an arid rain.
> On a horizon unmoved by a ripple
> This sound, visible and serene,
> Mounts to the heavens, an inspired wisp.

Not wishing to compose narrative programmatic music in the tradition of Berlioz or Tchaikovsky, Debussy made no effort to follow closely the events in Mallarmé's poem. As he said at the time of the first performance in December 1894, "My *Prelude* is really a sequence of mood paintings, throughout which the desire and dreams of the Faun move in the heat of the midday sun." When Mallarmé heard the music, he, in turn, said the following about Debussy's musical response to the poem: "I never expected anything like it. The music prolongs the emotion of my poem and paints its scenery more passionately than colors could."

Note that both musician and poet refer to *Prelude to The Afternoon of a Faun* in terms of painting. But how does one create a painting in music? Here a musical tableau is depicted by using the distinctive colors of the instruments, especially the woodwinds, to evoke vibrant moods and sensations. The flute has one timbre, the oboe another, and the clarinet yet a third. Debussy has said, in effect: "Let us focus on the sound-producing capacity of the instruments, let us see what new shades can be elicited from them, let us try new registers, let us try new combinations." Thus a solo flute begins in its lowest register (the pipes of the faun), followed by a harp glissando, then dabs of color from the French horn. These tonal impressions swirl, dissolve, and form again, but seem not to progress. There are no repeating rhythms or clear-cut meters to push the music forward; instead of a singable melody as we know it, we hear a twisting, undulating swirl of sound (Ex. 15-1). All is languid beauty, a music that is utterly original and shockingly sensual.

v Mallarmé's *The Afternoon of a Faun* created something of a sensation among late-nineteenth-century artists. This painting by Pal Szinyei Merse (1845–1920) is just one of several such representations of the faun and woodland nymphs. Notice that he holds classical panpipes, which Debussy transformed into the sound of the flute.

Example 15-1 ➤

Listening Cue

Claude Debussy, *Prelude to The Afternooon of a Faun* (1894)

Genre: Symphonic poem (tone poem)
Form: Ternary **(ABA)**

WHAT TO LISTEN FOR: First, the hazy undulating flute and then the kaleidoscope of instrumental colors that continually dissolve one into the next. Within the ternary form, sections **A** (track 15) and **A'** (track 17) sound modern because of the wisp-like melodies, and the prominence of the woodwinds. **B** (track 16), with its long, lush string melody (2:19), seems to return to the sentimentality of the Romanic period.

 Listen to streaming music in an Active Listening Guide at CourseMate or in the eBook.

 Take online Listening Exercise 33 at CourseMate or in the eBook.

Impressionism and Modernism

Impressionism was not the mother of Modernism—more like its aunt. It possessed some, but by no means all of the musical characteristics of the later, more radical modern style. Most innovative was Debussy's turn away from what he called the German "developmental agenda." The composer believed that music need not progress and evolve to be pleasing to the listener. Rather, Debussy created repetitive, *ostinato*-like melodies and harmonies that meander without a well-defined goal. He demonstrated that music did not have to march along with a strong meter—it could just relax and enjoy the moment. Most important, Debussy rejected the clearly delineated themes of the German Romantics—preferring momentary splashes of sound color instead of arching melodies and motivic development. For him, color and texture might exist independent of melody and, perhaps, overshadow it.

Later in the twentieth century, Debussy's approach was taken up by important American Modernists such as Charles Ives (1874–1954), Edgard Varèse (1883–1965), and John Cage (1912–1992), as we shall see in Chapter 16. These revolutionary composers rely not on recognizable melodies and harmonic progressions to structure their music; rather, following the path of the Impressionist painters and musicians that preceded them, they explore the emotive power of pure color.

Watch a video of Craig Wright's Open Yale Course class session 22, "Modernism and Mahler," at CourseMate for this text.

Modernist Painting and Music: The Rejection of Representational Art

Photography was invented in France around 1830 and by the end of the nineteenth century, photographic images had become commonplace. Perhaps there was a connection between the appearance of a machine that could duplicate the visual world exactly and the sudden disinclination of painters to do so. Whatever the cause, representational art began to disappear, pushed aside first by Impressionism and then by a more radical new style emanating from Paris in the early 1900s called **Cubism.** In a Cubist painting, the artist fractures and dislocates formal reality into geometrical blocks and planes, as in the famous *Les Demoiselles d'Avignon*, created in 1907 by Pablo Picasso (1881–1973), where the female form has been recast into angular, interlocking shapes. In Germany, Austria, and Scandinavia, a different, yet equally radical style of art— **Expressionism**—developed around this time. The aim of Expressionism was not to depict objects as they are seen but to express the strong emotion that these objects generated in the artist. An iconic example is Edvard Munch's *The Scream* (below), which features in clashing colors and distorted shapes a subject crying out to an unsympathetic world.

One can see clear parallels between visual art and emerging currents of Modernist music during this period. It is not surprising, then, that the two most influential composers of the early twentieth century—Igor Stravinsky and Arnold Schoenberg—had close ties with artists in other media. On the one hand, Stravinsky might be seen as a musical counterpart to Picasso—the two friends admired each other's works and occasionally collaborated artistically. And Schoenberg, a talented painter himself (see p. 219) found artistic camaraderie in the works of the German Expressionist painters, who so distorted formal reality that objects in their paintings were sometimes barely recognizable.

ʌ One of the first statements of Cubist art, Picasso's *Les Demoiselles d'Avignon* (1907). The ladies of the evening are depicted by means of geometric shapes on a flat, two-dimensional plane. Like much avant-garde music of the time, Cubist paintings reject the emotionalism and decorative appeal of nineteenth-century art.

Melody: More Angularity and Chromaticism

Just as the conventional figure vanished from avant-garde painting (see Picasso and Munch), so, too, the traditional (singable) melody disappeared from early Modernist music. Indeed, there are very few themes in twentieth-century music that the listener goes away humming. If Romantic melody is generally smooth, diatonic, and conjunct in motion (moving more by steps than by leaps), early-twentieth-century melody tends to be fragmented and angular, like a Cubist painting. The

ʌ *The Scream* (1893), by Edvard Munch

Watch a film on Cubism as four-dimensional art in the YouTube playlist at CourseMate for this text.

Listen to an example of Schoenberg's music, Concerto for Piano, in the iTunes playlist at CourseMate for this text.

young avant-garde composers went to great lengths to *avoid* writing conjunct, stepwise lines. Rather than moving up a half-step from C to D♭, for example, they were inclined to jump down a major seventh to the D♭ an octave below. Avoiding a simple interval for a more distant one an octave above or below is called **octave displacement;** it is a feature of modern music. So, too, is the heavy use of chromaticism. In the following example by Arnold Schoenberg, notice how the melody makes large leaps where it might more easily move by steps and also how several sharps and flats are introduced to produce a highly chromatic line.

Example 15-2 ➤

Harmony: The "Emancipation of Dissonance," New Chords, New Systems

Ever since the late Middle Ages, the basic building block of Western music had been the triad—a consonant, three-note chord (see p. 25). A composer might introduce dissonance (a nontriad tone) for variety and tension, yet the rules of consonant harmony required that a dissonant pitch move (resolve) immediately to a consonant one (a member of the triad). Dissonance was subordinate to, and controlled by, the triad. By the first decade of the twentieth century, however, composers such as Arnold Schoenberg were using so much dissonance that the triad lost its adhesive force. Schoenberg famously referred to this development as "the emancipation of dissonance," meaning that dissonance was now liberated from the requirement that it resolve into a consonant triad.

At first, audiences rebelled when they heard Schoenberg's dissonance-filled scores, but the composer ultimately succeeded in "raising the bar" for what the ear might stand, thereby preparing listeners for a much higher level of dissonance in both classical and popular music. Indeed, the work of Schoenberg and like-minded composers paved the way, albeit indirectly, for the heavy dissonances of today's progressive jazz and the dissonant "metal" styles of Metallica, Slipknot, and others.

Early-twentieth-century composers created dissonance not only by obscuring or distorting the traditional triad but also by introducing new chords. One technique for creating new chords was the superimposition of more thirds above the consonant triad. In this way were produced not only the **seventh chord** (a seventh chord spans seven letters of the scale, from A to G, for example) but also the **ninth chord** and the **eleventh chord.** The more thirds that were added on top of the basic triad, the more dissonant the sound of the chord.

Example 15-3 ➤

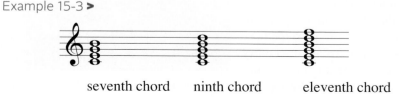

seventh chord   ninth chord   eleventh chord

The ultimate new chord was the **tone cluster,** the simultaneous sounding of a number of pitches only a whole step or a half step apart. Example 15-4 shows a tone cluster created by the American Modernist Charles Ives (1874–1954). But you, too, can create this high-dissonance chord simply by striking a group of adjacent keys on the piano with your fist or forearm. Try it.

Example 15-4 ➤

∧ Despite his studious looks, Igor Stravinsky enjoyed life among the fashionable in the fast lane of twentieth-century art and culture. The film *Coco and Igor* (2009) links him romantically with French fashion designer Coco Chanel, founder of the House of Chanel.

Chromatic dissonance, new chords, and tone clusters all weakened the force of tonality, the "cohesive glue" of traditional music. As a substitute, Igor Stravinsky used long ostinatos to set a tonal foundation, whereas Arnold Schoenberg invented an entirely new type of musical structure called twelve-tone music (see p. 221).

Igor Stravinsky (1882–1971)

For three-quarters of the twentieth century, Igor Stravinsky personified the cultural pluralism and stylistic diversity of cutting-edge art music. He created masterpieces in many different genres: opera, ballet, symphony, concerto, church Mass, and cantata. His versatility was such that he could set to music a classical Greek drama (*Oedipus Rex,* 1927) one day and write a ballet for baby elephants (*Circus Polka,* 1942) the next. Throughout his long life, he traveled with the fashionable set of high art. Although reared in St. Petersburg, Russia, he later lived in Paris, Venice, Lausanne, New York, and Hollywood. Forced to become an expatriate by the Russian Revolution (1917), he took French citizenship in 1934, and then, having moved to the United States at the outbreak of World War II, he became an American citizen in 1945. He counted among his friends painter Pablo Picasso (1881–1973), novelist Aldous Huxley (1894–1963), and poet T. S. Eliot (1888–1965). On his eightieth birthday, in 1962, he was honored by President John F. Kennedy at the White House and, later in the same year, by Russian Premier Nikita Khrushchev in the Kremlin. He died in New York in 1971 at the age of eighty-eight.

Stravinsky rose to international fame as a composer of ballet music. In 1908, his early scores caught the attention of Sergei Diaghilev (1872–1929), the legendary **impresario** (producer) of Russian opera and ballet. Diaghilev wanted to bring modern Russian ballet to Paris, at that time the artistic capital of the world. So he formed a dance company, called the *Ballets russes* (Russian Ballets), and hired, over the course of time, the most progressive artists he could find: Pablo Picasso and Henri Matisse for scenic designs, and Claude Debussy and Stravinsky, among others, as composers. Stravinsky soon became the principal composer of the company, and the *Ballets russes* became the focus of his musical activity for the next ten years. Accordingly, the decade 1910–1920 has become known as Stravinsky's Russian ballet period.

∧ Sergei Diaghilev in New York in 1916. Diaghilev's creation, the modern dance company he called *Ballets russes*, has been immortalized by the award-winning film *Ballets Russes* (2005).

Although Stravinsky's style continually evolved over the course of nearly seventy years, a recognizable "Stravinsky sound" is always evident. In simple terms, his music is lean, clean, and cool. Stravinsky's instrumental colors are not rich, "homogenized" sounds, as when the winds and strings together join on a single line, but rather lean, distinctly separate colors. Taking a cue from the music of his friend Claude Debussy, Stravinsky downplays the warm strings, preferring instead the tones of piercing winds and brittle percussion. Thus, although his orchestral scores are often opulent, they are rarely lush or sentimental. Most important, rhythm propels Stravinsky's music. His beat is strong, but often metrically irregular, and he builds complexity by requiring independent meters and rhythms to sound simultaneously (see below). Many of these stylistic traits can be heard in his most celebrated work, *The Rite of Spring*, a watershed of musical Modernism.

Le Sacre du printemps (The Rite of Spring, 1913)

Igor Stravinsky composed three important early ballet scores for Diaghilev's dance company: *The Firebird* (1910), *Petrushka* (1911), and *The Rite of Spring* (1913). All are built on Russian folk tales—a legacy of musical nationalism (see Chapter 14)—and all make use of the large, colorful orchestra of the late nineteenth century. Yet the choreography for these Russian ballets is not the refined, graceful ballet in the Romantic tradition, the sort that we associate with Tchaikovsky's *Swan Lake* and *The Nutcracker* (see p. 180). These are modern dances with angular poses and abrupt, jerky motions, as in the Matisses shown here. To inspire this dance in the modern style, Stravinsky composed rhythms and chords that explode with a primordial force.

Although *The Rite of Spring* has been called *the* great masterpiece of modern music, at its premiere it provoked not admiration but a riot of dissent. This premiere, the most notorious in the history of Western music, took place on an unusually hot evening, May 29, 1913, at the newly built Théâtre Champs-Élysées in Paris. With the very first sounds of the orchestra, many in the packed theater voiced, shouted, and hissed their displeasure. Some, feigning auditory pain, yelled for a doctor, others for two. There were arguments and flying fists as opponents and partisans warred over this Russian brand of modern art. To restore calm, the curtain was lowered momentarily and the house lights were turned on and off. All in vain. The musicians still could not be heard, and consequently, the dancers had difficulty coordinating their movements with the music.

v (top) In 1909, Henri Matisse painted the first of two canvases titled *Dance*. Here he achieves a raw primitive power by exaggerating a few basic lines and employing a few cool tones. Two years later, he created an even more intense vision of the same scene. (bottom) In *Dance* (1911), Matisse uses greater angularity and more intense colors, and thereby inspires a more intense reaction to this later version of a primitive dance scene.

©2010 Succession H. Matisse/Artists Rights Society (ARS), New York//Digital Image © The Museum of Modern Art/Licensed by SCALA/Art Resource, NY

©2010 Succession H. Matisse/Artists Rights Society (ARS), New York//Photo: Archives Henri Matisse

The disorder was experienced firsthand by a visiting critic of the *New York Press,* who reported as follows:

> I was sitting in a box in which I had rented one seat. Three ladies sat in front of me and a young man occupied the place behind me. He stood up during the course of the ballet to enable himself to see more clearly. The intense excitement under which he was laboring, thanks to the potent force of the music, betrayed itself presently when he began to beat rhythmically on the top of my head with his fists. My emotion was so great that I did not feel the blows for some time. They were perfectly synchronized with the beat of the music!

In truth, the violent reaction to *The Rite of Spring* was in part a response to the Modernist choreography, which sought to obliterate any trace of classical ballet: The dance was just as "primitive" as Stravinsky's Modernist score. But what aspects of Stravinsky's music shocked so many in the audience that night?

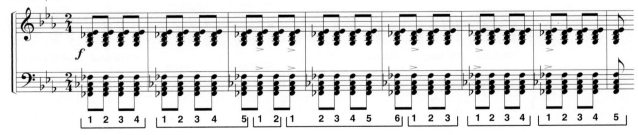

See what the riotous premiere of *The Rite of Spring* must have been like, in the YouTube playlist at CourseMate for this text.

PERCUSSIVE ORCHESTRA

First, there is a new percussive—one might say "heavy metal"—approach to the orchestra. The percussion section is enlarged to include four timpani, a triangle, a tambourine, a guiro, cymbals, antique cymbals, a bass drum, and a tam-tam. Even the string family, the traditional provider of warmth and richness in the symphony orchestra, is required to play percussively, attacking the strings with repeated down-bows at seemingly random moments of accent. Instead of warm, lush sounds, we hear bright, brittle, almost brutal ones pounded out by scraping strings, percussion, heavy woodwinds, and brasses.

IRREGULAR ACCENTS

Stravinsky intensifies the effect of his harsh, metallic sounds by placing them where they are not expected, on unaccented beats, thereby creating explosive syncopations. Notice in the following example, the famous beginning of "Augurs of Spring," how the strings accent (>) the second, fourth, and then first pulses of subsequent four-pulse measures. In this way, Stravinsky destroys ordinary 1-2-3-4 meter and forces us to hear, in succession, groups of 4, 5, 2, 6, 3, 4, and 5 pulses—a conductor's nightmare, and a dancer's as well!

Example 15-5 >

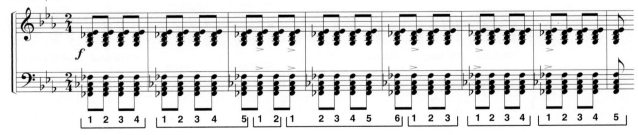

POLYMETER

The rhythm of *The Rite of Spring* is complex because Stravinsky often superimposes two or more different meters simultaneously. Notice in Example 15-6 that the oboe plays in $\frac{6}{8}$ time, the E♭ clarinet plays in $\frac{7}{8}$, while the B♭ clarinet is in $\frac{5}{8}$. This is an example of **polymeter**—two or more meters sounding simultaneously.

Example 15-6 >

oboe

Eb clarinet

Bb clarinet

To see a demonstration of how various meters can be combined, watch "Extreme Polymetric Ostinato Demonstration" in the YouTube playlist at CourseMate for this text.

POLYRHYTHM

Not only do individual parts often play separate meters, but they also sometimes project two or more independent rhythms simultaneously. Look at the reduced score given in Example 15-7. Every instrument seems to be doing its own thing! In fact, six distinct rhythms can be heard, offering a good example of **polyrhythm**—the simultaneous sounding of two or more rhythms.

Example 15-7 >

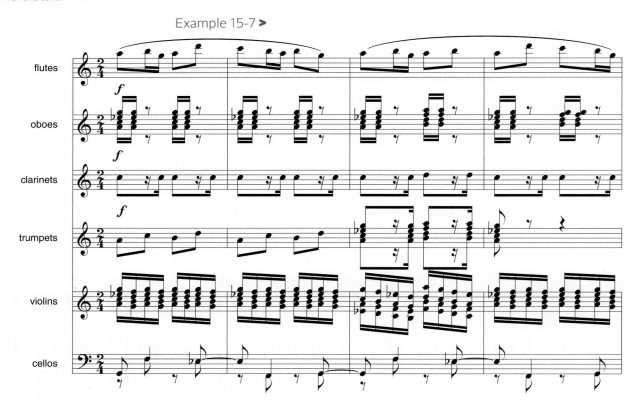

flutes

oboes

clarinets

trumpets

violins

cellos

OSTINATO FIGURES

Notice also in Example 15-7 that most of the instruments play the same motive over and over at the same pitch level. Such a repeating figure, as we have seen, is called an ostinato. In this instance we hear multiple ostinatos. Stravinsky was not the first twentieth-century composer to use ostinatos extensively—Debussy had done so earlier in his Impressionist scores. But Stravinsky employs them more often and for longer spans than did his predecessors. In *The Rite of Spring,* ostinatos give the music its incessant, driving quality, especially in the sections with fast tempos.

DISSONANT POLYCHORDS

The harsh, biting sound that is heard throughout much of *The Rite of Spring* is often created by two triads, or a triad and a seventh chord sounding at once. What results is a **polychord**—the simultaneous sounding of one triad or seventh chord with another (Fig. 15-1). When the individual chords of a polychord are only a whole step or a half step apart, the result is especially dissonant. In Example 15-8, the passage from the beginning of "Augurs of Spring," a seventh chord built on E♭ is played simultaneously with a major triad built on F♭.

See the Joffrey Ballet's re-creation of the original choreography and costuming for *The Rite of Spring*, in the YouTube playlist at CourseMate for this text.

Example 15-8 ➤

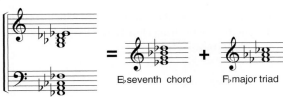

THE PLOT

The plot of *The Rite of Spring* is suggested by its subtitle, *Pictures of Pagan Russia.* Part 1, "The Kiss of the Earth," depicts the springtime rituals of primitive Slavic tribes. In Part 2, "The Sacrifice," a virgin dances herself to death as an offering to the god of spring. Before the curtain rises on Part 1, the orchestra plays an Introduction. This music sounds "creepy-crawly"—writhing motives move from soft to loud, and from one line to many, suggesting the flora and fauna of

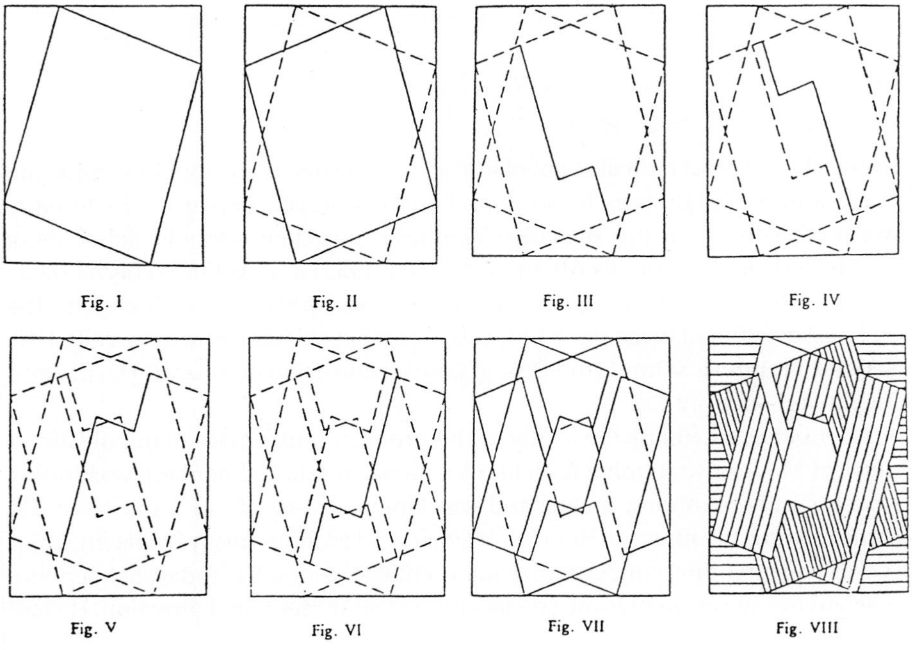

Fig. I   Fig. II   Fig. III   Fig. IV

Fig. V   Fig. VI   Fig. VII   Fig. VIII

FIGURE 15-1

In his *Schemes of Painting* (1922), the artist Albert Gleizes demonstrates that a Cubist work can be created by rotating a figure or line against itself, and then again and again until visual dissonance results. Similarly, a polychord is created by placing two or more triads or seventh chords off center and against one another, thereby creating musical dissonance.

the earth coming to life with the beginning of spring. The first scene, "Augurs of Spring," features jarring, almost brutal accents (see Ex. 15-5 on p. 215) and pounding dissonance (see Ex. 15-8). Yet there are also lyrical, almost sensuous moments in the score, especially when Stravinsky incorporates folk songs, whether quoting authentic Russian songs or (more commonly) composing his own melodies within this folk idiom. Despite the folkloric element, the bulk of the composition came from within. As Stravinsky declared, "I had only my ears to guide me. I heard and I wrote what I heard. I am the vessel through which *The Rite of Spring* passed."

Listening Cue

Igor Stravinsky, *Le Sacre du printemps* **(1913), Introduction and Scene 1**

18–19

Genre: Ballet music

WHAT TO LISTEN FOR: In the introduction, a growing cacophony of writhing woodwinds, which seem to be crawling out of the earth. In Scene 1 (track 19), an elemental pounding of dissonant string chords (see Ex. 15-5) punctuated by blasts from French horns and trumpets—"primitive Modernism" at its best.

 Listen to streaming music in an Active Listening Guide at CourseMate or in the eBook.

 Take online Listening Exercise 34 at CourseMate or in the eBook.

Following the scandalous success that attended the premiere of *The Rite of Spring,* Stravinsky extracted the music from the ballet itself and presented it as a multi-movement work for orchestra alone. The music itself was now recognized as an important, if controversial, statement of the musical avant-garde. Later, in 1940, the score of *The Rite of Spring* furnished the music for an important segment of Walt Disney's early full-length animated film *Fantasia.* Disney made Modernism mainstream.

Arnold Schoenberg (1874–1951) and the Second Viennese School

Ironically, the most radical shoot of musical Modernism took root in Vienna, the city of Mozart and Brahms, long known for its cultural conservatism. In the early twentieth century, a trio of native Viennese musicians—Arnold Schoenberg (1874–1951) and his pupils Alban Berg (1885–1935) and Anton Webern (1883–1945)—ventured to take high-art music in a completely new direction. The close association of these three innovative composers has come to be called the **Second Viennese School** (the first, of course, consisted of Mozart, Haydn, and Beethoven—see p. 103).

Arnold Schoenberg, the leader of this group, almost single-handedly thrust musical Modernism upon a reluctant Viennese public. Schoenberg was from a Jewish family of modest means and was largely self-taught as a musician. He came to know the music of Brahms, Wagner, and Mahler mostly by playing their scores and attending concerts. Like many college students of today, Schoenberg reached the age of twenty-one still lacking a clear professional direction. He had a "day job" as a bank teller, but at night he satisfied his curiosity through the study of literature, philosophy, painting, and musical composition. Eventually, his musical scores began to be heard in Vienna, though they were usually not well received.

Schoenberg's earliest compositions are written in the late Romantic style, with rich harmonies, chromatic melodies, and programmatic content. But by 1908, his music had begun to evolve in unexpected directions. Strongly influenced by Wagner's chromatic harmonies, Schoenberg started to compose works with no tonal center. If Wagner could write winding chromatic passages that temporarily obscured the tonality, why not go one step further and create fully chromatic pieces in which there is no tonality? This Schoenberg did, and in so doing created what is called **atonal music**—music without tonality, without a key center.

Schoenberg's contemporaries found his atonal music difficult. Not only was there no tonal center, but the melodies were highly disjunct, and the harmony exceedingly dissonant (see p. 212). Some performers refused to play his music, and when others did, audience reaction was occasionally violent. At one concert on March 31, 1913, the police had to be called in to restore order. Fortunately for Schoenberg, he possessed a characteristic typical of innovative geniuses throughout history: self-confidence. As he said, "One must be convinced of the infallibility of one's own fantasy; one must believe in one's own creative spirit."

Pierrot lunaire (Moonstruck Pierrot, 1912)

Pierrot lunaire (Moonstruck Pierrot), Schoenberg's best-known composition, is an exemplary work of Expressionist art (see p. 211). It is a setting for chamber ensemble and female voice of twenty-one poems by Albert Giraud. Here we meet Pierrot, a white-faced clown from the world of traditional Italian pantomime and puppet shows. Yet in this Expressionist poetry, the clown has fallen under the sway of the moon and changed into an alienated modern artist. Pierrot projects his inner anxiety by means of **Sprechstimme** ("speech-voice"; indicated by an "x" in Ex. 15-9), a technique that requires the vocalist to declaim the text more than to sing it. The voice must execute the rhythmic values exactly; but once it hits a pitch, it should quit the tone immediately, sliding away in either a downward or an upward direction. This creates exaggerated declamation of the sort one might hear from a lunatic, which is appropriate for Pierrot, given the lunar spell cast upon him.

Example 15-9 ➤

Poem 6 of *Pierrot lunaire* depicts the clown's tormented, hallucinatory vision of the suffering Madonna (Mother of Christ) at the cross. Note that the poet builds a refrain (boldface) into the text: *O Mutter aller Schmerzen* ("O Mother of all sorrows").

Steig, O Mutter aller Schmerzen **** Auf den Altar meiner Verse!	Arise, O Mother of all sorrows **** On the altar of my verse!
Blut aus deinen magern Brüsten **** Hat des Schwertes Wut vergossen. **** Deine ewig frischen Wunden **** Gleichen Augen, rot und offen,	Blood from your thin breast **** Has spilled the rage of the sword. **** Your eternally fresh wounds **** Like eyes, red and open,
Steig, O Mutter aller Schmerzen **** **Auf den Altar meiner Verse!**	**Arise, O Mother of all sorrows** **** **On the altar of my verse!**
(1:15) In den abgezehrten Händen **** Hältst du deines Sohnes Leiche **** Ihn zu zeigen aller Menschheit, **** Doch der Blick der Menschen meidet **** Dich, **O Mutter aller Schmerzen.**	In your thin and wasted hands **** You hold the body of your Son **** To show him to all mankind, **** Yet the look of men avoids **** You, **O Mother of all sorrows.**

Traditionally, composers had taken the appearance of a textual refrain as a cue to repeat the melody as well, thereby creating musical unity over the course of the work. However, Schoenberg, ever the iconoclast, avoids any and all repetition. Instead, his music unfolds in a continuum of ever-new sounds. For the listener, this creates a difficulty: The human psyche finds an unending series of new things—sounds or otherwise—very unsettling. Thus your first reaction to the dissonant continuum of pitches in *Pierrot lunaire* may be decidedly negative. Yet with repeated hearings, the force of the jarring elements of the atonal style begins to lessen, and a bizarre, eerie sort of beauty emerges, especially if you are sensitive to the meaning of the text. As every artist, Schoenberg was a creature of this time, and the twentieth century, with two world wars and many genocides, was often horrific. Schoenberg's music is important because it shows that art, like life, cannot always be "pretty."

> Notice line six of the poem *Madonna* as set by Schoenberg in *Pierrot lunaire*: "Gleichen Augen, rot und offen" ("Like eyes, red and open"). This was the emotion that Schoenberg felt when he painted the Expressionist work *Red Gaze* in 1910. As a young man, Schoenberg was uncertain whether his future in the arts lay in music or painting.

© Peter Willi/SuperStock/2011 Belmont Music Publisher, Los Angeles/ARS, New York/VBK, Vienna

Listening Cue

Arnold Schoenberg, *Pierrot lunaire* (1912), Number 6, *Madonna*

2
20

Genre: Art song

WHAT TO LISTEN FOR: The dissonant harmonies and disjunct vocal melody delivered in an almost-hysterical style called *Sprechstimme*. The accompanying chamber ensemble includes flute, clarinet, cello, and piano. Try to sing the tonic (home) pitch—impossible. This is atonal music!

 Listen to streaming music in an Active Listening Guide at CourseMate or in the eBook.

Twelve-Tone Music

When Schoenberg had created atonal music, as heard in *Pierrot lunaire,* he also created a serious artistic problem. Having removed the traditional building blocks of music (triads, tonal chord progressions, and tonal centers), what musical structures might replace them? If all twelve notes of the chromatic scale are equally important, as is true in atonal music, why choose any one pitch or another at a given moment?

By 1923, Schoenberg had solved the problem of "formal anarchy" with the creation of a process he called "composing with twelve tones." In **twelve-tone composition** the composer sets out each of the twelve notes of the chromatic scale in a fixed, predetermined order. The resulting "tone row" may start on any pitch, and, although the pitches of the row must always come in the same order, segments of it may sound together as chords. Music in which elements such as pitch, timbre, or dynamics come in a fixed series is called **serial music.** To give just one example, here is the tone row from the Trio of Schoenberg's *Suite for Piano* (1924), along with its three serial permutations:

To see a biting satire of Schoenberg's and Berg's twelve-tone music, watch "Twelve Tone Commercial" in the YouTube playlist at CourseMate for this text.

Row													Retrograde											
E	F	G	Db	Gb	Eb	Ab	D	B	C	A	Bb		Bb	A	C	B	D	Ab	Eb	Gb	Db	G	F	E
1	2	3	4	5	6	7	8	9	10	11	12		12	11	10	9	8	7	6	5	4	3	2	1

Inversion													Retrograde-inversion											
E	Eb	Db	G	D	F	C	F#	A	G#	B	Bb		Bb	B	G#	A	F#	C	F	D	G	Db	Eb	E
1	2	3	4	5	6	7	8	9	10	11	12		12	11	10	9	8	7	6	5	4	3	2	1

Watch a presentation on twelve-tone serialism in the YouTube playlist at CourseMate for this text.

Although the twelve-tone process became the rage among Modernist composers—even Stravinsky came under its sway—the listening public never fully embraced it. The twelve-tone style seemed as inaccessible and irrational as Schoenberg's earlier atonal music. Oddly, here the listening public ultimately won out, for twelve-tone composition disappeared with the Modernist movement. Indeed, the twelve-tone system has been called one of the two great failed experiments of the twentieth century, the other being Communism. Schoenberg was philosophical about the public's general dislike of his music: "If it is art, it is not for all, and if it is for all, it is not art."

American Modernism and Postmodernism

The United States is a highly pluralistic society, home to recent and not-so-recent immigrants, as well as Native Americans. This cultural and ethnic diversity is reflected in the country's many popular musical traditions, including jazz, blues, rock 'n' roll, hip hop, traditional Appalachian, bluegrass, and country and western. American art music of the past hundred years has been equally variegated, ranging from high-art European Modernism with a distinctly American flavor to, most recently, Postmodernist music. Offering both a "free market" for the exchange of artistic ideas and a safe homeland for ethnic groups from around the globe, the United States has come to enjoy the most diverse and vibrant musical culture in the world. In this chapter, we explore how several composers of high-art music added their very different voices to the diverse chorus of American music.

Aaron Copland (1900–1990)

Until the twentieth century, the United States was a cultural backwater of a European tide. European symphonic scores, for example, dominated the repertoire of symphony orchestras in New York, Boston, Cincinnati, and Chicago, among other places, in post–Civil War America. During the twentieth century, however, as the presence of the United States loomed increasingly large in the world arena, American composers provided this emerging nation with its own distinctive musical identity—one not only attuned to the Modernist style then prevalent in Europe, but one that also sounded truly American. The composer who best captured the spirit of the American heartland was Aaron Copland, who, ironically, spent much of his life within the confines of New York City.

Copland was born in Brooklyn to Jewish immigrant parents. After a rudimentary musical education in New York, he set sail for Paris to broaden his artistic horizons. In this he was not alone, for the City of Light at this time attracted young writers, painters, and musicians from around the world, including Igor Stravinsky (1882–1974), Pablo Picasso (1881–1973), James Joyce (1882–1941), Gertrude Stein (1874–1946), Ernest Hemingway (1898–1961), and F. Scott Fitzgerald (1896–1940). After three years of study, Copland returned to the United States, determined to compose in a distinctly American style. Like other young expatriate artists during the 1920s, Copland had to leave his homeland to learn what made it unique: "In greater or lesser degree," he remarked, "all of us discovered America in Europe."

During the late 1920s and early 1930s, Copland sought to forge an

▾ Aaron Copland

AP Images/Martell

American style by incorporating into his music elements of jazz, recognized the world over as a uniquely American creation. Copland then turned his attention to a series of projects with rural and western American subjects. The ballet scores *Billy the Kid* (1938) and *Rodeo* (1942) are set in the West and make use of classic cowboy songs like "Goodbye, Old Paint" and "The Old Chisholm Trail." Another ballet, *Appalachian Spring* (1944), re-creates the ambience of the Pennsylvania farm country, and his only opera, *The Tender Land* (1954), is set in the cornbelt of the Midwest. In 2009 Ken Burns featured Copland's music prominently in the soundtrack of his TV miniseries *The National Parks: America's Best Idea.* What could be more American than the wide-open sounds of Aaron Copland?

Copland's Music

Copland evokes a sense of space in his music by means of a distinctive kind of orchestration called "open scoring." He typically creates a solid bass, a very thin middle, and a top of one or two high, clear tones, such as those of the clarinet or flute. This separation and careful spacing of the instruments create the fresh, uncluttered sound so pleasing in Copland's music. Another characteristic element of Copland's style is the use of Americana; he incorporates American folk and popular songs to soften the dissonant harmonies and disjunct melodies of European Modernism. Copland's melodies tend to be more stepwise and diatonic than those of other twentieth-century composers, perhaps because Western folk and popular tunes are fundamentally conjunct and nonchromatic. His harmonies are almost always tonal and often change slowly in a way that can evoke the vastness and grandeur of the American landscape. The triad, too, is still important to Copland, perhaps for its stability and simplicity; dissonance unfolds slowly, rather than in a jarringly abrupt, Modernist fashion. Spatial clarity, folk songs, and a conservative approach to dissonance, then, mark Copland's most popular scores.

The direct clarity of Aaron Copland's music is not accidental. During the Great Depression of the 1930s, he became convinced that the gulf between modern music and the ordinary citizen had become too great—that dissonance and atonality had little to say to most music lovers. "It made no sense to ignore them [ordinary listeners] and to continue writing as if they did not exist. I felt that it was worth the effort to see if I couldn't say what I had to say in the simplest possible terms." Thus he not only wrote appealing new tonal works like *Fanfare for the Common Man* (1942) but also incorporated simple, traditional tunes such as "The Gift to Be Simple," which he uses in *Appalachian Spring.*

Appalachian Spring (1944)

Appalachian Spring is a one-act ballet that tells the story of "a pioneer celebration of spring in a newly built farmhouse in the State of Pennsylvania in the early 1800s." A new bride and her farmer husband express through dance the anxieties and joys of life in pioneer America. The work was composed in 1944 for the great American

∨ A scene from Martha Graham's ballet *Appalachian Spring*, with music by Aaron Copland. Here Katherine Crockett dances the role of the Bride (New York, 1999).

©Julie Lemberger/CORBIS

choreographer Martha Graham (1893–1991), and it won Copland a Pulitzer Prize the following year. The score is divided into eight connected sections that differ in tempo and mood. Copland provided a brief description of each of these orchestral scenes.

SECTION 1

"Introduction of the characters one by one, in a suffused light." The quiet beauty of the land at daybreak is revealed, as the orchestra slowly presents, one by one, the notes of the tonic and dominant triads.

Example 16-1 ➤

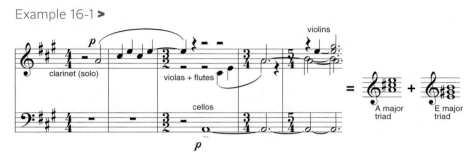

While this overlapping presentation of two triads constitutes a polychord of the sort created by Stravinsky (see p. 217), the effect is only mildly dissonant because of the slow, quiet way in which the notes of the two chords are introduced. The serene simplicity of the introduction sets the tone for the entire work.

SECTION 2

"A sentiment both elated and religious gives the keynote of this scene." The early calm is suddenly broken by a lively dance with a salient rhythm played aggressively in the strings (Ex. 16-2). The dance has all the modern rhythmic vigor of Stravinsky's music, but none of the extreme polymeter (see p. 215). As the dance proceeds, a more restrained hymn-like melody emerges in the trumpet (Ex. 16-3). The juxtaposition of these contrasting themes could not better illustrate the sonic difference between European Modernism and American folk simplicity.

Example 16-2: 2 /22 at 0:17 ➤

Example 16-3: 2 /22 at 0:43 ➤

SECTIONS 3–6

Section 3 is a dance for the two principals, a *pas de deux* in ballet parlance, accompanied by lyrical writing for strings and winds. Sections 4 and 5 are musical depictions of the livelier aspects of country life, with Section 4 including a toe-tapping hoedown, while Section 6 recalls the quiet calm of the opening of the ballet.

SECTION 7

"Calm and flowing. Scenes of daily activity for the Bride and her Farmer-husband." For this section, Copland chose to make use of a traditional tune of the Shakers, an extreme religious sect that prospered in the Appalachian region in the early nineteenth century and whose members expressed their spiritual intensity in frenzied singing, dancing, and shaking. Today this tune is famous, having been featured, among other places, in a John Williams piece for Barack Obama's inauguration in 2009. But the melody has become well known only because Copland featured it in *Appalachian Spring*. In fact, the composer plucked it from an obscure book of folk songs in 1944 because he thought the simple, diatonic tune (Ex. 16-4) fit well with the American character of the ballet, and because the text of the Shaker song is harmonious with what occurs on stage: "scenes of daily activity."

Example 16-4 ➤

'Tis the gift to be simple,
'Tis the gift to be free,
'Tis the gift to come down where we ought to be,
And when we find ourselves in the place just right,
'Twill be in the valley of love and delight.

In the five variations that follow, *The Gift to Be Simple* is not so much varied as it is clothed in different instrumental attire.

SECTION 8

"The Bride takes her place among her neighbors." Serenity returns to the scene as the strings play a slow, mostly stepwise descent, as Copland says, "like a prayer." The hymn-like melody from Section 2 is heard again in the flute, followed by the quiet "landscape music" from the beginning of the ballet. Darkness has again descended on the valley, leaving the young pioneer couple "strong in their new house" and secure in their community.

Listening Cue

Aaron Copland, *Appalachian Spring* **(1944)**

Sections 1, 2, and 7

(2)
21–23

Genre: Ballet music

WHAT TO LISTEN FOR: Section 1: The distinctly Copland sound caused by an orchestration that clearly separates low supporting strings from high solo woodwinds. Section 2 (track 22): Percussive, dissonant Modernism soon made to contrast with a lyrical hymn-like tune in the trumpet. Section 7 (track 23): The inventive use of theme-and-variations form in which the composer changes the feeling associated with the theme from irrepressibly cheerful to, at the end, triumphant.

🔊 Listen to streaming music in an Active Listening Guide at CourseMate or in the eBook.

Ellen Taaffe Zwilich (b. 1939)

By the end of the Second World War, American composers such as Charles Ives (1874–1954), Roy Harris (1898–1979), and Aaron Copland had taken European Modernism and given it a distinctly American voice. Consequently, American composers thereafter no longer felt obliged to forge a national style. Paraphrasing what Ellen Taaffe Zwilich said in 2007 about the "mindset" of American composers during the last century: "There was a time, in the 1920s with the music of Copland, for example, when we were searching for an American voice. Then we went beyond that stage. Our musical interests are now really quite all over the map."

The daughter of an airline pilot, Zwilich was born in Miami and educated at The Florida State University. She then moved to New York City where she played violin in the American Symphony Orchestra, studied composition at the Juilliard School, and worked for a time as an usher at Carnegie Hall. Zwilich's big "break" came in 1983, when she became the first woman to win the Pulitzer Prize in music. During 1995–1998, she was the first person of either gender to occupy the newly created Composer's Chair at Carnegie Hall—usher had become director. Today Zwilich enjoys a status to which all modern composers aspire: She is free to devote herself almost exclusively to writing music, sustained mainly by her royalties and commissions. Recently, the New York Philharmonic and the Chicago Symphony Orchestra each paid five-figure sums for a single new composition.

▲ Ellen Taaffe Zwilich

Concerto Grosso 1985 (1985)

Just how far ranging, forward and backward, Zwilich's musical vision extends, can be heard in her *Concerto Grosso 1985*. Commissioned by the Washington Friends of Handel, this work honors the composer George Frideric Handel (see Chapter 6), a leading exponent of the concerto grosso. Here Zwilich follows a twentieth-century musical procedure generally called **Neoclassicism**—the use of the genres, forms, and aesthetics of the Baroque (1600–1750) or Classical (1750–1820) periods to inform a new, Modernist composition. In *Concerto Grosso 1985* Zwilich embraces several elements of Baroque musical style: a regular rhythmic pulse, a repeating bass pedal point, a walking bass, terraced dynamics, and a harpsichord. Most directly, she incorporates a Baroque melody—borrowed from Handel's Violin Sonata in D major (Ex. 16-5A)—at the opening of each movement of her concerto. Yet, Zwilich throws in a modern touch, adding twisting chromaticism (Ex. 16-5B) and a biting, dissonant harmony to Handel's original theme. Further, she demands an insistent, pounding style of playing that would have shocked the eighteenth-century master. Is this music Baroque or Modernist? Mostly the latter—here music of the past inspires the present.

Example 16-5A ➤

mp

Handel's original melody

Example 16-5B ➤

mp

Zwilich's modernization of it

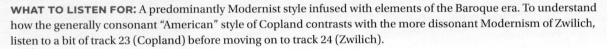

Listening Cue

Ellen Taaffe Zwilich, *Concerto Grosso 1985* **(1985)**

Third movement, *Largo* **(slow and broad)**

2
24

Genre: Concerto grosso

WHAT TO LISTEN FOR: A predominantly Modernist style infused with elements of the Baroque era. To understand how the generally consonant "American" style of Copland contrasts with the more dissonant Modernism of Zwilich, listen to a bit of track 23 (Copland) before moving on to track 24 (Zwilich).

 Listen to streaming music in an Active Listening Guide at CourseMate or in the eBook.

 Take online Listening Exercise 35 at CourseMate or in the eBook.

 ## Jazz

Just as Ellen Zwilich sometimes borrows the idioms of the Baroque or Classical eras for her Modernist music, so, too, her scores sometimes incorporate elements of a uniquely American kind of music: jazz. That Debussy, Stravinsky, and Copland also did suggests the importance of jazz to both European and American Modernism.

Jazz is a lively, energetic music with pulsating rhythms and scintillating syncopations, usually played by either a small instrumental ensemble (a combo) or a larger group (a big band). Jazz originated as, and maintains elements of, popular music; it is passed along mainly by oral tradition (not written notation), involves spontaneous improvisation, and was traditionally performed in entertainment spots. But during the twentieth century, jazz also came to demand great technical virtuosity and developed its own body of music theory and historical criticism—both hallmarks of an art in a mature "classical stage." For this reason jazz is often called "America's classical music." Today jazz is just as likely to be heard uptown at New York's Lincoln Center (a traditional bastion of classical music) as it is downtown at the Blue Note Café. What began around 1910 as alternative-culture music by minority outsiders has, a century later, solidified into a mainstream cultural tradition, albeit with conventions all its own.

The roots of jazz are found in the rhythms and vocal practices of sub-Saharan Africa, and these traditions accompanied African slaves to America. By the turn of the twentieth century, the descendants of slaves had come to express themselves in a plaintive, wailing style of singing called the **blues,** and in a highly syncopated kind of piano playing called **ragtime,** popularized by Scott Joplin (1868–1917). The first jazz bands, made up of Creoles and African Americans, were centered in New Orleans where **New Orleans jazz** (sometimes called "Dixieland jazz") arose. Disseminated by the newly invented radio during the 1920s, the seemingly risqué sounds of African-American jazz bands were embraced by middle-class whites as music

Bettmann/CORBIS

Ⅴ Duke Ellington (seated at the piano) and his big band in 1943. Unlike other band leaders of this time, Ellington was as much a composer and arranger as he was a performer.

suitable for social dancing. So popular did jazz become that the decade of the 1920s came to be dubbed "the Jazz Age." In these years George Gershwin created his *Rhapsody in Blue* (1924) in a style called **symphonic jazz,** a fusion of jazz and classical idioms meant for listening. But during the Great Depression (1929–1941) and World War II (1929–1945) "**swing** bands" and "**big bands**" with leaders such as Benny Goodman and Duke Ellington continued to make music for dancing. With the second half of the twentieth century, however, came a succession of more esoteric, less danceable jazz styles—**bebop, cool jazz,** and **free jazz;** in these the beat is not always clearly defined and the changing harmonies are difficult to follow. The advent rock 'n' roll in the 1950s—with its pounding beat and backbeat—ended jazz's preeminent status as America's favorite dance music.

To be sure, jazz is not one style but many, ranging from blues and ragtime to free jazz. The essence of jazz, however, can be heard in the **cool jazz** style of Miles Davis. "Cool" arose as a reaction to the "hot," high-pitched, hard-driving music of earlier **bebop** jazz. By contrast, cool jazz emphasizes lyricism, lower instrumental registers, moderate tempos, and quieter dynamic levels. Trumpeter Miles Davis (1926–1991) popularized the term *cool* when he issued his iconic album *Birth of the Cool* (1949–1950). Davis was a seminal force in his day—every "jazzer" wanted to play like Miles Davis—and still today his style is often imitated by trumpeters such as Wynton Marsalis (b. 1961) and Chris Botti (b. 1962). For his album *Birth of the Cool*, Davis assembled nine players. To the core of the usual jazz combo (trumpet, saxophone, piano, drums, and bass) Davis added orchestral instruments, including tuba and French horn, so as to lend greater body to the sound. Although the tempo of the track "Jeru" is moderately fast, solo instrumentalists Gerry Mulligan (saxophone) and Miles Davis (trumpet) play with a smooth, mellow sound: hence the name "cool."

Ⅴ Miles Davis at a recording session for his influential album *Birth of the Cool*

Hulton-Deutsch Collection/CORBIS

Written and arranged by Gerry Mulligan

"Jeru"

Performed by Miles Davis and His Orchestra (recorded 1949)

WHAT TO LISTEN FOR: A bouncy tune played by the band a total of three times; at the end of statement one and two, first Davis and then Mulligan play solos. The solos are not blaring or "in your face," but reserved and in the middle range of the instruments.

) Listen to streaming music in an Active Listening Guide at the CourseMate or eBook.

 # Postmodernism

▲ Jeff Koons's figure of a bare-backed blonde hugging a toy Pink Panther provokes, as does much Postmodern art, an argument: What is art? What makes a work of genius? While some may say that Koons's porcelain figure *Pink Panther* (1988) is not art, it sold at auction on May 10, 2011, for $16.8 million. But does artistic value equate with money? To think further about what makes art—and great art in particular—consider another sculpture shown in this book, Michaelangelo's *David* (p. 56).

In the course of this book, we have discussed the music and culture of many different eras: from the Medieval to the Baroque, and from the Renaissance to the Romantic. But how can we describe the music being composed today? We are modern people, so we might first assume that our art belongs to the Modernist age. But Modernism, it turns out, is no longer cutting edge. In the years since World War II it has been superseded by a new style, aptly called Postmodernism. While Modernism was a reaction to, and a playing off against, the genres, forms, and procedures of previous Western historical periods, Postmodern artists do not labor under the "anxiety of influence" of any previous era.

Instead, Postmodernism is an all-inclusive, "anything goes" age. For Postmodernists, art is for everyone, not just an elite few, and all art is of equal potential. Andy Warhol's famous paintings of Campbell's Soup cans or Marilyn Monroe (chapter opener), for example, are just as meaningful as Picasso's creations. Consequently, there is no "high" or "low" art, only art (and maybe not even that). As to the proper subject for art, the acceptable boundaries have exploded in the Postmodern period. In 1952 Francis Bacon, whose paintings now sell for $20 million and more, attached slabs of beef to his torso and photographed himself; in 2010 Lady Gaga shocked the crowds at the Video Music Awards in a dress made entirely of raw meat. These adventurous artists aim to show that any object can be transformed into a bold creative statement. Finally, Postmodernism holds that we live in a pluralistic world in which one culture is as important as the next. Indeed, cultural distinctions are seen to be gradually disappearing because of globalization, a process of homogenization made inevitable by instant mass-media communication. Postmodernism is thus refreshingly egalitarian when it comes to sex and gender, affirming a belief that the creations of, say, gay living black women are just as important as those of straight dead white men.

Postmodernist principles apply to music as well as art and fashion. If all art holds equal potential, then it is no longer necessary to separate classical from popular music—the two styles can even coexist within one and the same composition, as they do, for example, in recent works of

Paul McCartney and Wynton Marsalis. No longer, according to Postmodernism, need there be such distinctions between "highbrow" and "lowbrow" music; all music—classical, country, hip hop, folk, rock, and all the rest—is to be prized in equal measure. John Williams's film music is as important as Igor Stravinsky's ballet scores; Eminem is as worthy of our attention as Mozart.

Finally, Postmodernism brings with it a new agenda as to how to create music. Classical formal models, such as sonata–allegro and theme and variations, are no longer operative. Each musical composition must fashion its own unique form according to the demands and creative urges of the moment. Music no longer need be "goal oriented"; a particular piece does not have to work progressively to a defined point of arrival or climax. In today's musical culture, amplified instruments and electronic music are commonplace in symphony hall and rock arena alike. Traditional acoustic instruments must share the spotlight with newer electric and electronic ones. While Yo-Yo Ma's Stradivarius cello is a cultural treasure, so, too, is Jimi Hendrix's electric guitar. Postmodernism embraces an egalitarian, pluralistic musical world in which technology plays an important role. Today, unlike in the past, when a listener attends a concert of new "art" music, it is impossible to predict what he or she will hear.

Electronic Music: From Thomas Edison to Radiohead

The application of modern technology to music began in 1877 when Thomas Edison patented the phonograph. Around 1920, sounds of the phonograph became harnessed to electromagnetic wave diffusion via the radio; the principal content of the radio broadcast was music, some live, but most played from phonograph records. The magnetic tape recorder appeared in 1936 as a means of recording and hearing music, but during the 1990s that technology was replaced by the CD and it, in turn, by downloaded MP3 and M4A files of today. Thus the means of dissemination of music has changed radically during the last hundred years. To hear music, it is no longer necessary to learn to play an instrument or go to a concert; just buy a digital download.

Technology has revolutionized not merely the dissemination of music, but also how it is created. Most traditional music around the world was and is played on acoustic instruments (ones made of natural materials). But shortly after World War II, new technology led to the development of **electronic music** produced by a **synthesizer**—a machine that can create, transform, and combine (synthesize) sounds by means of electronic circuitry. Edgard Varèse (1883–1965), working in both New York and Paris, was one of the earliest practitioners of electronic music. Varèse's experimental compositions—including the landmark *Poème électronique* (1958)—combine music generated by a synthesizer with bits of *musique concrète,* or "found sound." **Musique concrète** is so called because the composer works, not with sounds written for voice or musical instruments, but with those found naturally in the everyday world. A car horn, a person speaking in a room, or a dog's barking may be captured by recorder and doctored in some way—reassembled and repeated (mixed, and looped) to form an unexpected montage of sound.

The technological advancements that so altered the classical music landscape were soon appropriated by pop artists—and with remarkable success. The Beatles' John Lennon used "tape looping" to create a novel background ambience for his song "Revolution 9" (1968). As Lennon recounted, "We were cutting up [tapes of] classical music and making different size loops, and then I got an engineer tape on which an engineer was saying, 'Number nine, number nine, number nine.' All those different bits of sound and noises were all compiled. . . . I fed them all in and mixed them live." Lennon also added *musique concrète* (found sound) to a few Beatles songs. "Strawberry Fields Forever," for example, has a piano crash followed by a dog's whistle played at 15,000 vibrations per second. Not to be outdone, the rock band Pink Floyd incorporated the sounds of a clanging cash register into their song, appropriately titled, "Money" (1973). And filmmakers, too, jumped on the electronic bandwagon. George Lucas used banging chains to create the sound of the Imperial Walkers for his *Star Wars* epics. To be specific, he recorded, and then modified and layered, the noise of a bicycle chain falling on a concrete floor—a literal example of the principle of *musique concrète*.

What began as esoteric experiments by a few avant-garde scientists and high-art composers thus transformed the world of popular entertainment. The technological development that made this possible was miniaturization. During the 1960s, the large-console tape machine was reduced to the portable tape recorder, and then, during the 1980s, microprocessors became small enough to power keyboard synthesizers. In more recent years, the increasing power, versatility, and availability of the personal computer has facilitated revolutionary changes in the way music is composed, produced, and recorded. Almost any aspiring composer or rock band can now own the hardware required to produce and manipulate their own sounds. Today's computer-driven synthesizer can generate sounds that are almost indistinguishable from those of a ninety-piece orchestra. Consequently, **computer music** has revolutionized the world of commercial music. The computer-equipped recording studio now generates much of the music we hear on radio and television. For example, the opening theme of the perennially popular *Desperate Housewives,* written by Danny Elfman (b. 1953), is electronically based computer music, but makes use of interpolated acoustic string sounds as well.

v Composer Danny Elfman (right), seen here in an electronic recording studio, blends electronic music and traditional, acoustical sounds in his film scores, among them *Good Will Hunting, Milk, Terminator Salvation, Alice in Wonderland, Batman, Beetlejuice,* and *Men in Black* (*I, II,* and *III*).

TOUCHSTONE PICTURES/Album/Newscom

Technology has also facilitated new processes for the production of pop music. In the 1980s, rap and hip hop artists began using a technique called **sampling** whereby the rapper or producer extracts a small portion of prerecorded music and then mechanically repeats it over and over as a musical backdrop to the text that he or she raps. And in **scratching,** another technique popular in rap and hip hop, a creative DJ with one or more turntables manipulates the needles, scratching on the vinyl of the record while other prerecorded sounds loop continually in the background.

Perhaps no contemporary rock group has blended songwriting with the manipulation of electronic audio more extensively than Radiohead. For their albums and concert tours, they use not only analog and digital synthesizers but also special-effects pedals and distortion filters to re-form the audio of their voices and instruments. All these electronic devices and computer processes help give the music of Radiohead a disembodied, other-worldly quality.

John Cage (1912–1992) and Chance Music

If everything is more or less of equal value, as the Postmodernists say, why not just leave art to chance? This is essentially what American composer John Cage decided to do. Cage was born in Los Angeles, the son of an inventor. He graduated as valedictorian of Los Angeles High School and spent two years at nearby Pomona College before going to Europe to learn more about art, architecture, and music. Arriving in New York City in 1942, he worked variously as a wall washer at the YWCA, teacher of music and mycology (the science of mushrooms) at the New School for Social Research, and music director of a modern dance company.

From his earliest days as a musician, Cage had a special affection for percussion instruments and the unusual sounds they could create. His *First Construction (in Metal)* (1939) has six percussionists play piano, metal thunder-sheets, ox bells, cowbells, sleigh bells, water gongs, and brake drums, among other things. By 1941, he had collected three hundred percussion objects of this kind—anything that might make an unusual noise when struck or shaken. Cage's tinkering with percussive sounds led him to invent the **prepared piano**—a grand piano outfitted with screws, bolts, washers, erasers, and bits of felt and plastic all inserted between the strings. This transformed the piano into a one-person percussion band that could produce a great variety of sounds and noises—twangs, zaps, rattles, thuds, and the like—no two of which were exactly the same in pitch or color. In creating the prepared piano, Cage was merely continuing along the experimental trail blazed by his spiritual mentor, Edgard Varèse: "Years ago, after I decided to devote my life to music, I noticed that people distinguished between noises and sounds. I decided to follow Varèse and fight for noises, to be on the side of the underdog."

Cage's glorification of everyday noise began in earnest during the 1950s. Rather than engage in a titanic struggle to shape the elements of music, as had Beethoven, he decided to sit back, relax, and simply allow noises to occur

Frank Micelotta/Getty Images

▲ Musician Thom Yorke surrounded by some of the electronic equipment that gives his band Radiohead its distinctive "electronic" sound

To hear the sounds of a prepared piano, listen to "John Cage Sonata V" in the YouTube playlist at CourseMate for this text.

New York Times Co./Getty Images

◄ John Cage "preparing" a piano. By putting spoons, forks, screws, paper clips, and other sundry objects into the strings of the piano, the composer changes the instrument from one producing melodic tones to one generating percussive impacts.

See and hear a random performance of Cage's chance music *O'00"* in the YouTube playlist at CourseMate for this text.

around him. In creating this sort of intentionally purposeless, undirected music, Cage invented what has come to be called chance music, the ultimate Postmodernist experimentation. In **chance music,** musical events are not carefully predetermined by the composer, but come instead in an unpredictable sequence as the result of nonmusical decisions such as following astrological charts, tossing coins, throwing dice, or shuffling randomly the pages of music to be played. The musical "happening" that results is the sort of spontaneous group experience that was to flower during the 1960s. For example, in Cage's work *0'00'* (1962), performed by the composer himself that year, he sliced and prepared vegetables at a table on a stage, put them through a food processor, and then drank the juice, all the while amplifying and broadcasting the sound of these activities throughout the hall. Cage's declaration that the ordinary noise made by food processing can be "art" is virtually identical in intent to Andy Warhol's glorification of the Campbell's Soup can: Both typify the kind of radical art fashioned during the 1960s in New York City, the epicenter of Postmodernism.

Naturally, music critics called Cage a joker and a charlatan. Most would agree that his "compositions," in and of themselves, are not of great musical value in traditional terms. Nevertheless, by raising profound questions regarding the relationships between human activity, sound, and music, his compositions eloquently articulate his own musical philosophy. By focusing on the chance appearance of ordinary noise, Cage aggressively asks us to ponder the basic principles that underlie most Western music: Why must sounds of similar range and color come one after the other? Why must music have form and unity? Why must it have "meaning"? Why must it express anything? Why must it develop and climax in some organized way? Why must it be goal-oriented, as is so much of human activity in the West?

4'33" (1952)

Cage's "composition" that causes us to focus on these questions most intently is his *4'33"*. Here one or more performers carrying any sort of instrument come on stage, seat themselves, open the "score," and play nothing. For each of the three carefully timed movements, there is no notated music, only the indication *tacet* (it is silent). But as the audience soon realizes, "absolute" silence is virtually impossible to attain. With no organized sound to be heard during the four minutes and thirty-three seconds that follow, the listener gradually becomes aware of the background noise in the hall—a creaking floor, a passing car, a dropped paper clip, an electrical hum. Cage asks us to embrace these random everyday noises—to tune our ears in innocent sonic wonder. Are these sounds not of artistic value, too? What is music? What is noise? What is art?

Needless to say, we have not filled your CDs with four minutes and thirty-three seconds of background noise. You can create your own, and John Cage would have liked that. Sit in a "quiet" room for four minutes and thirty-three seconds, and notice what you hear. Perhaps this experiment will make you more aware of how important willful organization is to the art we call music. If nothing else, Cage makes us realize that music, above all, is a form of organized communication from one person to the next and that random background noise can do nothing to express or communicate ideas and feelings.

John Cage, *4'33"* **(1952)**

Genre: Chance music

WHAT TO LISTEN FOR: Nothing, except the ambient background noise of the room and whatever external noise may intrude by chance

John Adams (b. 1947) and Minimalism

Western classical music—the music of Bach, Beethoven, and Brahms—is typically constructed of large, carefully placed units. A movement of a symphony, for example, has themes, which come in a hierarchy of importance, and sections (development and coda, for example), which must be heard in a particular order. A compelling sequence of events leads to a desired end and conveys a message from composer to listener. But what would happen if composers reduced the music to just one or two simple motives and repeated these again and again? What would happen if they focused on what things *are*, rather than on what these things might *become*? Such is the approach taken by a group of American Postmodernist composers called the Minimalists.

Minimalism is a style of postmodern music, originating in the early 1960s, that takes a very small musical unit and repeats it over and over to form a composition. A three-note melodic cell, a single arpeggio, two alternating chords—these are the sort of "minimal" elements a composer might introduce, reiterate again and again, modify or expand, and then begin to repeat once more. The basic material is usually simple, tonal, and consonant. By repeating these minimal figures incessantly at a steady pulse, the composer creates a hypnotic effect—"trance music" is the name sometimes given this music. The trance-like quality of Minimalist music has influenced rock musicians (The Velvet Underground, Talking Heads, and Radiohead) and led to a new genre of pop music called "techno," or "rave," music. Minimalism, in both art and music, has been mainly an American movement. Its most successful musical practitioners are Steve Reich (b. 1936), Philip Glass (b. 1937), and John Adams (b. 1947).

John Adams (no relation to the presidents) was born in Worcester, Massachusetts, in 1947 and educated at Harvard. As a student there, he was encouraged to compose in the twelve-tone style of Arnold Schoenberg (see p. 220–221). But if Adams counted twelve-tone rows by day, he listened to The Beatles in his

ᵛ John Adams. In 2003, New York's Lincoln Center held an eight-week "Absolutely Adams" festival to go along with its annual "Mostly Mozart" program.

Ron Scherl/Redferns/Getty Images

Watch an expansive example of John Adams's minimalist style—from his opera *Nixon in China*—in the YouTube playlist at CourseMate for this text.

dorm room at night. Moving to San Francisco after graduation, Adams developed his own eclectic musical style that blended the learned with the popular and added increasing amounts of Minimalism, which was then gaining popularity in California. Some of Adams's early scores of the 1980s are strict Minimalist works, but later ones become more all-embracing; from time to time, an operatic melody or a funk bass line, for example, will creep into his constantly repeating, minimal sonorities. In 2003, Adams received the Pulitzer Prize in music for his *On the Transmigration of Souls,* which commemorated those killed in the World Trade Center terrorist attacks of 2001. Ironically, although Adams is a Minimalist composer, he has been able to extend his ever-repeating blocks of sound into lengthy operas. The best known of these are *Nixon in China* (1987) and *Doctor Atomic* (2005)—Minimalist operas that achieve maximum effect. As a creature of the Postmodernist age, Adams feels squeezed between the classical tradition and the all-powerful world of pop culture:

> I have bad days when I really feel that I'm working in an art form [classical music] that's just not relevant anymore, that had its peak in the years from Vivaldi to Bartók, and now we are just fighting over the crumbs. A really good recording of mine might sell 50,000 copies; that's very rare in classical music. For a rock group, 50,000 CDs sold would be a disaster. (*Harvard Magazine,* 24 July 2007)

Short Ride in a Fast Machine (1986)

To experience postmodern Minimalism quickly, we turn to an early work by Adams, one commissioned in 1986 by the Pittsburgh Symphony. *Short Ride in a Fast Machine* is scored for full orchestra and two electronic keyboard synthesizers. Example 16-6 shows how the music is composed of short (mostly four-note) motives that continually repeat. There are five sections to this work (we'll call them laps). In each lap, the machine seems to accelerate, not because the tempo gets faster but because more and more repeating motives are added. The effect created is that of a powerful, twentieth-century engine firing on all cylinders. As Adams has said about his Minimalist work, "You know how it is when someone asks you to ride in a terrific sports car, and then you wish you hadn't?"

Example 16-6 ➤

Listening Cue

John Adams, *Short Ride in a Fast Machine* (1986)

Delirando (with exhilaration)

WHAT TO LISTEN FOR: Lap 1: Woodblocks, woodwinds, and keyboard synthesizers; Lap 2: Bass drum "backfires"; Lap 3: Starts quietly with sinister repeating motive in bass; Lap 4: Two-note falling motive in bass; Lap 5: Trumpets play fanfare-like motives as in a "victory lap"

 Listen to streaming music in an Active Listening Guide at CourseMate or in the eBook.

Watch a video of Craig Wright's Open Yale Course class session 23, "Review of Musical Style," at CourseMate.

A complete Checklist of Musical Style for the Modern and Postmodern eras can be found at CourseMate.

The Enduring Power of Western Classical Music

We began this book by stressing the emotive power of music. Music is a form of personal expression in which a creator (the composer) sends his vision of the human experience to another human being, the listener. That vision comes not in the form of a painting, a story, or a poem, but rather as a carefully organized aggregate of sound produced by musical instruments of one sort or another. Music, like language, is an organized form of discourse that speaks to us. Once musical sound reaches the auditory receptors of our brain, it is processed more or less like linguistic sound. In the brain, sound is sound, and we react positively or negatively to the music, just as we react to good or bad news.

The emotive power of music as language was recently exemplified in the Academy Award–winning film *The King's Speech* (2010). The climax of the film comes toward the end and centers on a speech that the reigning king of England, George VI (father of the present Queen Elizabeth II), delivered on September 3, 1939. In this radio broadcast, the king must rally the English-speaking world as England declares war on Nazi Germany at the beginning of World War II, a conflagration that will result in the deaths of tens of millions of people. To be effective, King George must overcome his speech impediment: severe stuttering. The reenactment of the speech in the film is accompanied by the beginning of the second movement of Beethoven's Symphony No. 7. The movement is in theme and variations form with the theme initially sounding four times. The music starts quietly but grows in volume and emotional force with each successive statement of the theme. In the film, the voice of the king (actor Colin Firth) starts haltingly but grows progressively more forceful and secure, thereby synching with the music of Beethoven. But at the end of the speech, the makers of the film—perhaps knowing that the power of music is potentially *greater* than that of speech—do something remarkable: The volume for the king's voice is turned down, and the audience hears primarily Beethoven's music. Here Beethoven, not the king, speaks to us. The film says, in effect, words can do no more, only the power of music can carry the human spirit to this higher realm of intense feeling.

Watch this scene from *The King's Speech* in the YouTube playlist at CourseMate for this text.

Most viewers do not realize the important but subliminal role played by classical music in this film. Nor do most people realize that classical music continues to play an important part in Western culture every day. Even in times of economic recession, symphony orchestras, opera productions, chamber music festivals, and regular concert series continue to draw eager audiences. Films, TV commercials, and video games are accompanied by classical music or newly created music in the classical style. Classical music sounds among the chatter of the coffeehouse, shopping mall, and hotel lobby. Around the world the importance of Western classical music continues to grow. While some things Western are considered "decadent," our classical music is increasingly held in high esteem by other cultures. This development is part of the globalization of music.

At the moment the United States runs an annual trade deficit of nearly half a trillion dollars; we export to, far less than we import from, nations such as China, Korea, and Japan. But one commodity that has taken hold around the world, and especially in the Far East, is Western classical and popular music. Take China, for example. Walk around the new Beijing international airport and what do you hear? Background music including Mozart's serenade *Eine kleine Nachtmusik,* Beethoven's character piece *Für Elise,* and Chopin's Nocturne in E♭

major—all representing genres of music that we have studied in this book. Take a cab into the city and what blares on the radio? American-style pop music with a heavy guitar bass line and pulsating beat, with the lyrics sung in Chinese. Drive past Tiananmen Square and the tomb of Mao Zedong (1893–1976), the founder of the Chinese Communist party, and to the next building; here sits a colossal new (2007) concert hall for the performance of Western-style symphonies and operas. Continue half a mile farther to the Central Conservatory of Music and its music shop; the main items for sale are violins and pianos (both Western instruments), scores of Western classical music, and reproductions of portraits of Mozart, Beethoven, and Bach.

The global hegemony of Western music has been made possible by one thing: the instant delivery of sound by means of MP3 files. Instead of waiting to hear a visiting Western orchestra, a college student in Seoul or Singapore can now download a classical piece from iTunes or view Yo-Yo Ma (see chapter-opening image) or Lang Lang play a Beethoven sonata on YouTube just as quickly as can an American or Canadian student. Asian students, too, walk through the streets wearing earbuds and listening to music on an iPhone (created and designed in the United States but manufactured in China). Technology has made the expressive power of music speak to millions more than Beethoven, or anyone else for that matter, ever imagined.

Throughout this book, your author has tried to relate how, since the Middle Ages, Western classical music has come to acquire its distinctive genres, structures, and sound colors—how it came to be the moving force that it is today, around the world. Indeed, classical music is one of the crown jewels of Western culture. Along with democracy, freedom of religion and speech, equality of the genders, and due process under the law, the high arts of the West, not least its music, constitute the cultural traditions of which Westerners can be most proud. Classical music is something worth supporting and preserving. You, attentive listener, are now equipped to do so.

Glossary

absolute music instrumental music free of a text or any pre-existing program

a cappella a term applied to unaccompanied vocal music, originated in the expression "a cappella Sistina" ("in the Sistine Chapel" of the pope), where instruments were forbidden to accompany the singers

accent emphasis or stress placed on musical tone or chord

acoustic instrument instruments that produce sounds naturally when strings are bowed or plucked, a tube has air passed through it, or percussion instruments are struck

Alberti bass instead of having the pitches of a chord sound all together, the notes are played in succession to provide a continual stream of sound

alto the lower of the two female voice parts

antecedent phrase the opening, incomplete-sounding phrase of a melody that cadences on a note other than tonic; often followed by a consequent phrase that brings the melody to closure

aria an elaborate lyrical song for solo voice

arpeggio the notes of a triad or seventh chord played in direct succession and in a direct line up or down

art song an accompanied song or ayre with artistic aspirations

atonal music music without tonality, music without a key center; most often associated with the twentieth-century avant-garde style of Arnold Schoenberg

ballad narrative song in strophic form that told a (usually sad) tale in an unemotional way

ballet an art form that uses dance and music, along with costumes and scenery, to tell a story and display emotions through expressive gestures and movement

ballet music music composed to accompany a ballet, with short bursts of tuneful melody and captivating rhythm, all intended to capture the emotional essence of the scene

Ballets russes a Russian ballet company of the early twentieth century led by Sergei Diaghilev

baritone a male voice part of a middle range, between the higher tenor and the lower bass

bar lines vertical lines in a musical score that group beats into sets of two, three, four, or more, and thereby indicate the meter of the music

Baroque term used to describe the arts generally during the period 1600–1750 and signifying excess and extravagance

bass the lowest male vocal range

bass clef a sign placed on a staff to indicate the notes below middle C

bass drum a large, low-sounding drum struck with a soft-headed stick

basso continuo a small ensemble of at least two instrumentalists who provide a foundation for the melody or melodies above, heard almost exclusively in Baroque music

bassoon a low, double-reed instrument of the woodwind family

basso ostinato a motive or phrase in the bass that is repeated again and again

Bayreuth Festival an opera house in the town of Bayreuth, Germany, constructed exclusively for the music dramas of Richard Wagner

beat an even pulse in music that divides the passing of time into equal segments

bebop a complex, hard-driving style of jazz that emerged shortly after World War II; it is played without musical notation by a small ensemble

bel canto a style of singing and a type of Italian opera developed in the nineteenth century that features the beautiful tone and brilliant technique of the human voice

big band a mid-to large-size dance band that emerged in the 1930s to play the style of jazz called swing

binary form a musical form consisting of two units (**A** and **B**) constructed to balance and complement each other

blues an expressive, soulful style of singing that emerged from the African-American spiritual and work song at the end of the nineteenth century; its texts are strophic, its harmonies simple and repetitive

brass family a group of musical instruments traditionally made of brass and played with a mouthpiece; includes the trumpet, trombone, French horn, and tuba

bridge (*see*** transition)**

cadence the portion of a musical phrase that leads to its last chord

cadenza a showy passage for the soloist appearing near the end of the movement in a concerto; it incorporates rapid runs, arpeggios, and snippets of previously heard themes into a fantasy-like improvisation

canon (1) standard repertoire; (2) a contrapuntal form in which the individual voices enter and each in turn duplicates exactly the melody that the first voice played or sang

cantata a term originally meaning "something sung"; in its mature state it consists of several movements, including one or more arias, ariosos, and recitatives; cantatas can be on secular subjects, but those of J. S. Bach are primarily sacred in content

castrato a boy or adult singer who had been castrated to keep his voice from changing so that it would remain in the soprano register

cello (violoncello) an instrument of the violin family but more than twice the violin's size; it is played between the legs and produces a rich, lyrical tone

chamber cantata a genre that emphasized accompanied solo singing, it is usually divided into contrasting sections that alternate between recitative and aria; performed before a select group of listeners in a private residence

chamber music music for soloists performed in the home or small auditorium

chance music music that involves an element of chance (rolling dice, choosing cards, etc.) or whimsy on the part of the performers, especially popular with avant-garde composers

chanson a song sung by two, three, or four voices in French, most typically concerning the topic of love

character piece a brief instrumental work seeking to capture a single mood; a genre much favored by composers of the Romantic era

chorale the German word for the hymn of the Lutheran church; hence a simple religious melody to be sung by the congregation

chord two or more simultaneously sounding pitches

chord progression a succession of chords moving forward in a purposeful fashion

chorus textual refrain that repeats

chromatic harmony constructing chords on the five additional notes within the twelve-note scale, giving more color to the harmony

chromatic scale scale that makes use of all twelve pitches, equally divided, within the octave

church cantata a multi-movement sacred work including arias, ariosos, and recitatives performed by vocal soloists, and chorus, and a small accompanying orchestra; became the musical core of the Sunday service of the Lutheran church

clarinet a single-reed instrument of the woodwind family with a large range and a wide variety of timbres within it

classical music music that has endured the test of time and requires a particular set of skills to perform or appreciate it; it relies chiefly on acoustic instruments, preset musical notation, tends to be lengthy, and involves a variety of moods

clef a sign used to indicate the register, or range of pitches, in which an instrument is to play or a singer is to sing

coda (Italian for "tail") a final and concluding section of a musical composition

col legno (Italian for "with the wood") an instruction to string players to strike the strings of the instrument not with the horsehair of the bow, but with the wood of it

color (timbre) the character or quality of a musical tone as determined by its harmonics and its attack and decay

comic opera a genre of opera that originated in the eighteenth century, portraying everyday characters and situations, and using spoken dialogue and simple songs

computer music the most recent development in electronic music, it couples the computer with the electronic synthesizer to imitate the sounds of acoustical instruments as well as produce new sounds

concertino the group of instruments that function as soloists in a concerto grosso

concerto an instrumental genre in which one or more soloists play with and against a larger orchestra

concerto grosso a three-movement concerto of the Baroque era that pits the sound of a small group of soloists (the concertino) against that of the full orchestra (the tutti)

conductor leader of an orchestra, chorus, or band

consequent phrase the answering, second phrase of a two-part melodic unit that brings a melody to a point of repose and closure

consonance pitches sounding agreeable and stable

contrabassoon a larger, lower-sounding version of the bassoon

contrast process employed by a composer to introduce different melodies, rhythms, textures, or moods in order to provide variety

cool jazz a style of jazz that emerged in the 1950s that is softer, more relaxed, and less frenzied than bebop

cornet a brass instrument that looks like a short trumpet; it has a more mellow tone than the trumpet and is most often used in military bands

Council of Trent two-decade-long (1545–1563) conference at which leading cardinals and bishops undertook reform of the Roman Catholic Church, including its music

counterpoint the harmonious opposition of two or more independent musical lines

Counter-Reformation movement that fostered reform in the Roman Catholic Church in response to the challenge of the Protestant Reformation and led to a conservative, austere approach to art

crescendo a gradual increase in the volume of sound

cross-stringing overlaying the lowest-sounding strings across those of the middle register thereby producing a richer, more homogenous sound

Cubism Early-twentieth-century artistic style in which the artist fractures and dislocates formal reality into geometrical blocks and planes

cymbals a percussion instrument of two metal discs; they are made to crash together to create emphasis and articulation in music

decrescendo (diminuendo) gradual decrease in the intensity of sound

development the center-most portion of sonata–allegro form, in which the thematic material of the exposition is developed and extended, transformed, or reduced to its essence; it is often the most confrontational and unstable section of the movement

Dies irae a Gregorian chant composed in the thirteenth century and used as the central portion of the Requiem Mass of the Catholic Church

diminished chord a triad or seventh chord made up entirely of minor thirds and producing a tense, unstable sound

diminuendo (*see* **decrescendo**)

diminution a reduction, usually by half, of all the rhythmic durations in a melody

dissonance a discordant mingling of sounds, resulting in harmonic tension that ultimately seeks resolution

diva Italian for "goddess," she is a celebrated female opera singer

Doctrine of Affections early-seventeenth-century aesthetic theory that held that different musical moods could and should be used to influence the emotions, or affections, of the listener

dominant the chord built on the fifth degree of the scale; tends to move to tonic triads at the ends of musical phrases

doo-wop type of soul music that emerged in the 1950s as an outgrowth of the gospel hymns sung in African-American churches in urban Detroit, Chicago, and New York; its lyrics made use of repeating phrases sung in a cappella (unaccompanied) harmony below the tune

double bass the largest and lowest-pitched instrument of the string family

double counterpoint counterpoint with two themes that can reverse position, the top theme moving to the bottom and the bottom to the top (also called invertible counterpoint)

double stops technique in which a violinist holds (stops) two and sometimes more strings simultaneously, and sweeps across them with the bow

downbeat the first beat of each measure; it is indicated by a downward motion of the conductor's hand and is usually stressed

duple meter gathering of beats into two beats per measure, with every other beat stressed

dynamics the various levels of volume, loud and soft, at which sounds are produced in a musical composition

electronic music sounds produced and manipulated by magnetic tape machines, synthesizers, and/or computers

eleventh chord a chord comprised of five intervals of a third and spanning eleven different letter names of pitches

encore French word meaning "again"; the repeat of a piece demanded by an appreciative audience; an extra piece added at the end of a concert

English horn an alto oboe, pitched at the interval a fifth below the oboe, much favored by composers of the Romantic era

Enlightenment eighteenth-century period in philosophy and letters during which thinkers gave free rein to the pursuit of truth and the discovery of natural laws

episode a passage of free, non-imitative counterpoint found in a fugue

"Eroica" ("Heroic") Symphony Beethoven's third symphony, it was originally composed to honor Napoleon Bonaparte; more than any other single orchestral work, it changed the historical direction of the symphony

Esterházy family the richest and most influential among the German-speaking aristocrats of eighteenth-century Hungary, with extensive landholdings southeast of Vienna and a passionate interest in music

etude a short one-movement composition designed to improve one aspect of a performer's technique

exposition in a fugue, the opening section, in which each voice in turn has the opportunity to present the subject; in sonata–allegro form, the principal section, in which all thematic material is presented

Expressionism powerful movement in the early-twentieth-century arts, initially a German-Austrian development that arose in Berlin, Munich, and Vienna; its aim was not to depict objects as they are seen but to express the strong emotion that the object generates in the artist

falsetto a high, soprano-like voice produced by adult male singers when they sing in head voice and not in full chest voice

figured bass in musical notation, a numerical shorthand that tells the player which unwritten notes to fill in above the written bass note

finale the last movement of any multimovement genre of classical music; e.g., the final movement of a symphony

flamenco a genre of Spanish song and dance, with guitar accompaniment, that originated in southern-most Spain and exhibits non-Western, possibly Arab-influenced, scales

flat musical symbol that lowers a pitch by a half step

flute a high-sounding member of the woodwind family; initially made of wood, but more recently, beginning in the nineteenth century, of silver or even platinum

form the purposeful organization of the artist's materials; in music, the general shape of a composition as perceived by the listener

forte in musical notation, a dynamic mark indicating "loud"

fortissimo term indicating a dynamic level of "very loud"

free jazz a style of jazz perfected during the 1960s in which a soloist indulges in flights of creative fancy without concern for the rhythm, melody, or harmony of the other performers

Freemasons fraternity of the Enlightenment who believed in tolerance and universal brotherhood

French horn a brass instrument that plays in the middle range of the brass family; developed from the medieval hunting horn

fugato a short fugue set in some other musical form like sonata-allegro or theme and variations

fugue a composition for three, four, or five parts played or sung by voices or instruments, which begins with a presentation of a subject in imitation in each part and continues with modulating passages of free counterpoint and further appearances of the subject

galliard fast, leaping Renaissance dance in triple meter

genre type or class of music

glissando a device of sliding up or down the scale very rapidly

great (grand) staff a large musical staff that combines both the treble and the bass clefs

Gregorian chant a large body of unaccompanied monophonic vocal music, set to Latin texts, composed for the Western (Roman Catholic) Church over the course of fifteen centuries.

ground bass the English term for *basso ostinato*

habanera an Afro-Cuban dance-song that came to prominence in the nineteenth century, marked by a repeating bass and a repeating, syncopated rhythm

harmony sounds that provide the support and enrichment—an accompaniment—for melody

harp an ancient, plucked-string instrument with a triangular shape

harpsichord a keyboard instrument, especially popular during the Baroque era, that produces sound by depressing a key that drives a lever upward and forces a pick to pluck a string

Heiligenstadt Testament something akin to Beethoven's last will and testament, written in despair when he recognized that he would ultimately suffer a total loss of hearing; named after the Viennese suburb in which he penned it

"heroic" period (middle period) time during which Beethoven's compositions became longer, more assertive, and full of grand gestures

homophony musical texture in which the voices, or lines, all move together to new pitches at roughly the same time

humanism Renaissance belief that people have the capacity to create many things good and beautiful; it rejoiced in the human form in all its fullness, looked outward, and indulged a passion for invention and discovery

idée fixe literally a "fixed idea," but more specifically an obsessive musical theme as first used in Hector Berlioz's *Symphonie fantastique*

idiomatic writing musical composition that exploits the strengths and avoids the weaknesses of particular voices and instruments

imitation the process by which one or more musical voices, or parts, enter and duplicate exactly for a period of time the music presented by the previous voice

impresario renowned producer

Impressionism late-nineteenth-century movement that arose in France; the Impressionists were the first to reject photographic realism in painting, instead trying to re-create the impression that an object produces upon the senses in a single, fleeting moment

interval the distance between any two pitches on a musical scale

jazz a lively, energetic music with pulsating rhythms, and scintillating syncopations, usually played by a small instrumental ensemble

kettle drums (see timpani)

key a tonal center built on a tonic note and making use of a scale; also, on a keyboard instrument, one of a series of levers that can be depressed to generate sound

Köchel (K) number the numbering system that arranges Mozart's compositions in approximate chronological order

leitmotif a brief, distinctive unit of music designed to represent a character, object, or idea; a term applied to the motives in the music dramas of Richard Wagner

libretto the text of an opera

Liebestod the famous aria sung by the expiring Isolde at the end of Richard Wagner's opera *Tristan und Isolde*

Lied (pl. *Lieder*) the genre of art song, for voice and piano accompaniment, that originated in Germany around 1800

Liederabend German word indicating an informal evening gathering during which *Lieder* (art songs) are performed

Lisztomania the sort of mass hysteria, today reserved for pop music stars, that surrounded touring Romantic-era pianist Franz Liszt

London Symphonies a set of twelve compositions Haydn wrote during the latter part of his career

lyrics Text that accompanies music

madrigal a popular genre of secular vocal music that originated in Italy during the Renaissance, in which usually four or five voices sing love poems

madrigalism a device, originating in the madrigal, by which key words in a text spark a particularly expressive musical setting

major scale a seven-note scale that ascends in the following order of whole and half steps: 1-1-$\frac{1}{2}$-1-1-1-$\frac{1}{2}$

Mass the central religious service of the Roman Catholic church

measure (bar) a group of beats, or musical pulses; usually the number of beats is fixed and constant so that the measure serves as a continual unit of measurement in music

melismatic singing many notes sung to just one syllable

melodic sequence the repetition of a musical motive at successively higher or lower degrees of the scale

melody a series of notes arranged in order to form a distinctive, recognizable musical unit; it is most often placed in the highest line or voice of the music

mensural notation the earliest form of rhythmic notation, as emerged in France during the thirteenth century; from these notational symbols developed our modern signs indicating duration, such as the quarter note

meter the gathering of beats into regular groups

meter signature (time signature) two numbers, one on top of the other, usually placed at the beginning of the music to tell the performer what note value is carrying the beat and how the beats are to be grouped

mezzo-soprano a female vocal range between the alto and soprano

Minimalism a style of modern music that takes a very small amount of musical material and repeats it over and over to form a composition

minor scale a seven-note scale that ascends in the following order of whole and half steps: 1-$\frac{1}{2}$-1-1-$\frac{1}{2}$-1-1

minuet a moderate dance in triple meter, though actually danced in patterns of six steps, with no upbeat but with highly symmetrical phrasing

minuet and trio a pair of separate but related dances in triple meter, the trio having a lighter, contrasting texture; in works from the Classical era, the two dances usually come in the sequence minuet-trio-minuet and together form the third movement of a four-movement symphony or a string quartet

mode a pattern of pitches forming a scale; the two primary modes in Western music are major and minor

modified strophic form strophic form in which the music is modified briefly to accommodate a particularly expressive word or phrase in the text

modulation the process in music whereby the tonal center changes from one key to another, from G major to C major, for example

monody a general term connoting solo singing accompanied by a *basso continuo* in the early Baroque period; early Baroque genre in which a few instruments accompanied a solo singer performing a song based on a highly charged, emotional text

monophony a musical texture involving only a single line of music with no accompaniment

motet a composition for choir or larger chorus setting a religious, devotional, or solemn text, often sung a cappella

motive a short, distinctive melodic figure that stands by itself

mouthpiece a detachable portion of a brass instrument into which the player blows

movement a large, independent section of a major instrumental work, such as a sonata, dance suite, symphony, quartet, or concerto

music the rational organization of sounds and silences passing through time

music drama a term used for the mature operas of Richard Wagner

musical nationalism the musical expression of ethnic and linguistic distinctions through the use of such indigenous folk elements as folk songs, native scales, dance rhythms, and local instrumental sounds as well as through the use of national subjects for program music or opera

musique concrète music in which the composer works directly with sounds recorded on magnetic tape, not with musical notation and performers

mute any device that muffles the sound of a musical instrument; on a trumpet, for example, it is a cup that is placed inside the bell of the instrument

Neo-classicism early-twentieth-century style which emphasized classical forms and smaller ensembles of the sort that had existed in the Baroque and Classical periods

New Orleans jazz an early style of jazz that emphasized improvisation by a small group of soloists (cornet, clarinet, and trombone) and a rhythm section

ninth chord a chord spanning nine letters of the scale and constructed by superimposing four intervals of a third

nocturne a slow, introspective type of music, usually for piano, with rich harmonies and poignant dissonances intending to convey the mysteries of the night

oboe an instrument of the woodwind family; the highest-pitched of the double-reed instruments

octave the interval comprising the first and eighth tones of the major and minor diatonic scale; the sounds are quite similar because the frequency of vibration of the higher pitch is exactly twice that of the lower

octave displacement a process used in constructing a melody whereby a simple, nearby interval is made more distant, and the melodic line more disjunct, by placing the next note up of down and octave

Ode to Joy *An die Freude* by poet Friedrich von Schiller, set to music by Beethoven as a hymn in honor of universal brotherhood and used in the finale of his Symphony No. 9

opera a dramatic work in which the actors sing some or all of their parts; it usually makes use of elaborate stage sets and costumes; the term literally means "work"

opera buffa (Italian for "comic opera") an opera on a light, often domestic subject, with tuneful melodies, comic situations, and a happy ending

opera seria a genre of opera that dominated the stage during the Baroque era, making use of serious historical or mythological subjects, da capo arias, and a lengthy overture

ophicleide a low brass instrument originating in military bands about the time of the French Revolution; the precursor of the tuba

opus Latin for "work"; the term adopted by composers to enumerate and identify their compositions

oratorio a large-scale genre of sacred music involving an overture, arias, recitatives, and choruses, but sung, whether in a theater or a church, without costumes or scenery

orchestra in Western classical music, an ensemble of musicians, organized around a core of strings, with added woodwinds and brasses, playing under a leader

orchestral score a composite of musical lines of all of the instruments of the orchestra and from which a conductor conducts

orchestration the art of assigning to the various instruments of the orchestra, or of a chamber ensemble, the diverse melodies, accompaniments, and counterpoints of a musical composition

Ordinary of the Mass the five sung portions of the Mass for which the texts are invariable. It includes the Kyrie, Gloria, Credo, Sanctus, and Agnus Dei

ostinato Italian for "obstinate;" a musical figure, motive, melody, harmony, or rhythm that is repeated again and again

overture an introductory movement usually for orchestra, that precedes an opera, oratorio, or dance suite

"Pathétique" Sonata one of his most famous compositions, Beethoven titled this piano sonata in order to suggest the passion and pathos he felt within it

pavane slow, gliding Renaissance dance in duple meter performed by couples holding hands

pedal point a note, usually in the bass, sustained or continually repeated for a period of time while the harmonies change around it

pentatonic scale a five-note scale found often in folk music and non-Western music

pianissimo term indicating a dynamic level of "very soft"

piano in musical notation, a dynamic mark indicating "soft"

pianoforte the original name of the piano

piccolo a small flute; the smallest and highest-pitched woodwind instrument

pipe organ large, complex instrument comprised of keyboards and ranks of carefully tuned pipes; when a key is depressed, air is forced through a pipe, thereby generating pitch

pitch the relative position, high or low, of a musical sound

pizzicato the process whereby a performer plucks the strings of an instrument rather than bowing them

plainsong another term for Gregorian chant

polychord the stacking of one triad or seventh chord on another so they sound simultaneously

polymeter two or more meters sounding simultaneously

polyphony a musical texture involving two or more simultaneously sounding lines; the lines are often independent and create counterpoint

polyrhythm two or more rhythms sounding simultaneously

popular music a broad category of music designed to please a large section of the general public; sometimes used in contradistinction to more "serious" or more "learned" classical music

prepared piano a piano outfitted with screws, bolts, washers, erasers, and bits of felt and plastic to transform the instrument from a melodic one to a percussive one

prima donna the leading female singer in an opera

program music a piece of instrumental music, usually for symphony orchestra, that seeks to recreate in sound the events and emotions portrayed in some extra-musical source: a story, a play, an historical event, an encounter with nature, or even a painting

program symphony a symphony with the usual three, four, or five movements in which the individual movements together tell a tale or depict a succession of specific events or scenes

ragtime an early type of jazz emerging in the 1890s and characterized by a steady bass and a syncopated, jazzy melody

realistic opera opera that treats issues of everyday life in a realistic way; afflictions of the lower classes in particular are presented on stage for all to see

recapitulation in sonata–allegro form, the return to the first theme and the tonic key following the development

recital a concert of chamber music, usually for a solo performer

recitative musically heightened speech, often used in an opera, oratorio, or cantata to report dramatic action and advance the plot; often made up of rapidly repeating notes followed by one or two long notes at the ends of phrases

recitativo accompagnato recitative accompanied by the orchestra instead of merely the harpsichord; the opposite of simple recitative

repetition process employed by a composer to validate the importance of a section of music by repeating it

rest the absence of sound in music, signaled in the score by a special sign; also, the sign or symbol that indicates a rest

retransition the end of the development section where the tonality often becomes stabilized on the dominant in preparation for the return of the tonic (and first theme) at the beginning of the recapitulation

rhythm the organization of time in music, dividing up long spans of time into smaller, more easily comprehended units; gives shape to the profile of the melody

Ring **cycle** a cycle of four interconnected music dramas by Richard Wagner that collectively tell the tale of a Germanic legend

ritornello form a musical form in which all or part of the main theme (the ritornello) is played repeatedly by the tutti, with each statement separated by a virtuosic solo section played by the concertino

rondo form classical form with at least three statements of the refrain (**A**) and at least two contrasting sections (at least **B** and **C**); placement of the refrain creates symmetrical patterns such as **ABACA**, **ABACABA**, or even **ABACADA**

rubato (Italian for "robbed") in musical notation, an expression mark indicating that the performer may take, or steal, great liberties with the tempo

Russian Five a group of young composers (Borodin, Cui, Balakirev, Rimsky-Korsakov, and Musorgsky) centered in St. Petersburg, whose aim it was to write purely Russian music free of European influence

Salzburg mountain town in Austria, birthplace of Mozart

sampling extracting a small portion of pre-recorded music and then mechanically repeating it over and over as a musical backdrop to the text of a rap song

scale an arrangement of pitches that ascends and descends in a fixed and unvarying pattern

scherzo a rapid, jovial work in triple meter often used in place of the minuet as the third movement in a string quartet or symphony

Schubertiad a social gathering for music and poetry that featured the songs and piano music of Franz Schubert

scratching manipulating the needles of one or more turntables, scratching on the vinyl of the record while other prerecorded sounds loop continually in the background

Second Viennese School three composers—Schoenberg, Berg, and Webern—who decided to take high-art music into a new atonal and, ultimately, twelve-tone style

serenade an instrumental work for a small ensemble originally intended as a light entertainment in the evening

serial music music in which some important component—pitch, dynamics, rhythm—comes in a continually repeating series

seventh chord a chord spanning seven letter names and constructed by superimposing three thirds

sharp musical symbol that raises a pitch by a half step

shawm a double-reed woodwind instrument of the late Middle Ages and Renaissance; the precursor of the oboe

simple recitative recitative that is accompanied only by the *basso continuo*

sinfonia a one-movement orchestral work in three sections (fast-slow-fast) that originated in Italy as an overture to seventeenth century operas

Singspiel (German for "singing play") a musical comedy originating in Germany with spoken dialogue, tuneful songs, and topical humor

Sistine Chapel the pope's private chapel within his Vatican apartments

snare drum a small drum consisting of a metal cylinder covered with a skin or sheet of plastic that, when played with sticks, produces the "rat-ta-tat" sound familiar from marching bands

soft pedal the left pedal on the piano that, when depressed, shifts the position of the hammers relative to the strings, reducing the dynamic level

solo concerto a concerto in which an orchestra and a single performer in turn present and develop the musical material in the spirit of harmonious competition

sonata originally "something sounded" on an instrument as opposed to "something sung" (a "cantata"); later a multi-movement work for solo instrument, or instrument with keyboard accompaniment

sonata–allegro form a dramatic musical form of the Classical and Romantic periods involving an exposition, development, and recapitulation, with optional introduction and coda

song cycle a collection of several songs united by a common textual theme or literary idea

soprano the highest female vocal part

sound waves differences in air pressure propelled from a source (instrument) and proceeding in a regular pattern to the ear and brain, where they are perceived as pitch

Sprechstimme (German for "speech-voice") a singer declaims, rather than sings, a text at only approximate pitch levels

staff a horizontal grid onto which are put the symbols of musical notation: notes, rests, accidentals, dynamic marks, etc.

statement presentation of an important musical idea

stop the knob on a pipe organ that, when pulled, allows the air to enter a specific set of pipes

string instruments instruments that produce sound when strings are bowed or plucked; the harp, the guitar, and members of the violin family are all string instruments

string quartet a standard instrumental ensemble for chamber music consisting of a first and second violin, a viola, and cello; also a genre of music, usually in three of four movements, composed for this ensemble

strophic form a musical form often used in setting a strophic, or stanzaic, text, such as a hymn or carol; the music is repeated anew for each successive strophe

style the general surface sound produced by the interaction of the elements of music: melody, rhythm, harmony, color, texture, and form

subject a term for the principal theme in a fugue

sustaining pedal the right-most pedal on the piano; when it is depressed, all dampers are removed from the strings, allowing them to vibrate freely

swing a mellow, bouncy, flowing style of jazz that originated in the 1930s

syllabic singing a vocal style that uses only one or two notes per syllable of text

symphonic jazz music (mostly of the 1920s and 1930s) that incorporates idioms of jazz into the genres and forms traditionally performed by the classical symphony orchestra

symphonic poem (see tone poem)

symphony a genre of instrumental music for orchestra consisting of several movements; also the orchestral ensemble that plays this genre

symphony orchestra the large instrumental ensemble that plays symphonies, overtures, concertos, and the like

syncopation a rhythmic device in which the natural accent falling on a strong beat is displaced to a weak beat or between the beats

synthesizer a machine that has the capacity to produce, transform, and combine electronic sounds

tempo the speed at which the beats occur in music

tenor the highest male vocal range

ternary form a three-part musical form in which the third section is a repeat of the first, hence **ABA**

terraced dynamics a term used to describe the sharp, abrupt dynamic contrasts found in the music of the Baroque era

texture the density and disposition of the musical lines that make up a musical composition

theme and variations a musical form in which a theme continually returns but is varied by changing the notes of the melody, the harmony, the rhythm, or some other feature of the music

through-composed a term used to describe music that exhibits no obvious repetitions or overt musical form from beginning to end

timbre (see color)

time signature (see meter signature)

timpani (kettle drums) a percussion instrument consisting usually of two, but sometimes four, large drums that can produce a specific pitch when struck with mallets

tonality the organization of music around a central tone (the tonic) and the scale built on that tone

tone cluster a dissonant sounding of several pitches, each only a half step away from the other, in a densely packed chord

tone (symphonic) poem a one-movement work for orchestra of the Romantic era that gives musical expression to the emotions and events associated with a story, play, political occurrence, personal experience, or encounter with nature

tonic the central pitch around which the melody and harmony gravitate; a chord built on the first degree of the scale; it is the most stable chord and the one toward which the other chords move

transition (bridge) in sonata–allegro form the unstable section in which the tonality changes from tonic to dominant (or relative major) in preparation for the appearance of the second theme

treble clef the sign placed on a staff to indicate the notes above middle C

tremolo a musical tremor produced on a string instrument by repeating the same pitch with quick up and down strokes of the bow

triad a chord consisting of three pitches and two intervals of a third

trill a rapid alternation of two neighboring pitches

trio an ensemble, vocal or instrumental, with three performers; also, a brief, self-contained composition contrasting with a previous piece, such as a minuet or a polonaise; originally the trio was performed by only three instruments

triple meter gathering of beats into three beats per measure, with every third beat stressed

trombone a brass instrument of medium to low range that is supplied with a slide, allowing a variety of pitches to sound

troubadour poet-musician of secular songs who appeared in southern France during the twelfth and thirteenth centuries and the first to appear in Western aristocratic courts

trouvère poet-musician who appeared in northern France and influenced the development of the chanson

trumpet a brass instrument of the soprano range

tuba a brass instrument of the bass range

tutti (Italian for "all") the full orchestra or full performing force

twelve-tone composition a method of composing music devised by Arnold Schoenberg that has each of the twelve notes of the chromatic scale sound in a fixed, regularly recurring order

unison two or more voices or instrumental parts singing or playing the same pitch

variation process employed by a composer to alter melody or harmony in some way

verismo **opera** the Italian word for realistic opera

vibrato a slight and continual wobbling of the pitch produced on a string instrument or by the human voice that adds richness to the tone

vielle medieval fiddle

Viennese School group of Classical composers, including Haydn, Mozart, Beethoven, and Schubert, whose careers all unfolded in Vienna

viola a string instrument, the alto member of the violin family

violin a string instrument, the soprano member of the violin family

violoncello (see cello)

virtuoso an instrumental performer or singer possessing extraordinary technical facility

vocal ensemble in opera, a group of four or more solo singers, usually the principals

walking bass a bass line that moves at a moderate pace, mostly in equal note values, and often stepwise up or down the scale

woodwind family a group of instruments initially constructed of wood; most make their sound with the aid of a single or double reed; includes the flute, piccolo, clarinet, oboe, English horn, and bassoon

word painting the process of depicting the text in music, be it subtly, overtly, or even jokingly, by means of expressive musical devices

Index

1. Beethoven: Symphony No. 5, I (exposition). Cleveland Orchestra; George Szell, conductor. Originally released 1964. All rights reserved by Sony Music Entertainment

2. R. Strauss: *Also sprach Zarathustra* (opening). Chicago Symphony; Fritz Reiner, conductor. Originally released 1954. All rights reserved by Sony Music Entertainment

3. The Basics of Rhythm. Craig Wright, piano. ℗ 2010 Cengage Learning

4. Listening Exercise 2, Hearing Meters. ℗ 2010 Cengage Learning

5. Beethoven: *Ode to Joy* from Symphony No. 9, IV (excerpt). New York Philharmonic; Leonard Bernstein, conductor. Originally released 1968. All rights reserved by Sony Music Entertainment

6. Listening Exercise 4, Hearing Major and Minor. ℗ 2010 Cengage Learning

7. Consonance and Dissonance: Cadences. ℗ 2010 Cengage Learning

8. Harmony (Chord Changes). Richards/Williams/Dixon: Chandler, "Duke of Earl." Courtesy of Vee-Jay Records

9. Listening Exercise 5. Hearing the Bass Line and Harmony. Pachelbel: Canon in D major. Baroque Chamber Orchestra; Ettore Stratta, conductor. ℗ 1973 Sony Music Entertainment

10. Puccini: *La bohème,* "Che gelida manina." Montserrat Caballe, soprano; Placido Domingo, tenor; London Philharmonic; Sir Georg Solti, conductor. ℗ 1974 Sony Music Entertainment

11–12. Mozart: *Don Giovanni,* Act I, Scene 1, "Notte e giorno faticar." Rugierro Raimondi; Kiri Te Kanawa; Paris Opera Orchestra; Lorin Maazel, conductor. ℗ 1979 Sony Music Entertainment

13–14. Mozart: *Don Giovanni,* Act I, Scene 7, "Alfin siam liberati," "Là ci darem la mano." Rugierro Raimondi; Kiri Te Kanawa; Paris Opera Orchestra; Lorin Maazel, conductor. ℗ 1979 Sony Music Entertainment

15. Strings. ℗ 2004 Wadsworth/Thomson/Cengage Learning

16. Woodwinds. ℗ 2004 Wadsworth/Thomson/Cengage Learning

17. Brasses. ℗ 2004 Wadsworth/Thomson/Cengage Learning

18. Percussion. ℗ 2004 Wadsworth/Thomson/Cengage Learning

19. Handel: "Hallelujah" chorus from *Messiah.* Musica Sacra; Richard Westenburg, conductor. ℗ 1983 Sony Music Entertainment

20. Listening Exercise 9, Hearing Musical Textures. ℗ 2010 Cengage Learning

21. Brahms: *Wiegenlied (Lullaby).* Angelika Kirchschlager, mezzo-soprano; Helmut Deutsch. ℗ 1999 Sony Music Entertainment

22. Clara Schumann: "Liebst du um Schönheit." Barbara Bonney. ℗ 1997 The Decca Music Group. Courtesy of The Decca Music Group, under license from Universal Music Enterprises

23. Mozart: Variations on "Twinkle, Twinkle, Little Star." Philippe Entremont, piano. ℗ 1986 Sony Music Entertainment

24. Haydn: Symphony No. 94, II. Cleveland Orchestra; George Szell, conductor. Originally released 1968. All rights reserved by Sony Music Entertainment

25. Tchaikovsky: "Dance of the Reed Pipes" from *Nutcracker.* Philadelphia Orchestra; Eugene Ormandy, conductor. Originally released 1965. All rights reserved by Sony Music Entertainment

26. Mouret: Rondeau from *Suite de Symphonies.* Crispian Steele-Perkins, trumpet; English Chamber Orchestra; Donald Fraser, conductor. ℗ 1992 Sony Music Entertainment